Working with Children and Adolescents in Groups

A Multimethod Approach

Sheldon D. Rose
Jeffrey L. Edleson

Working with Children and Adolescents in Groups

 J o s s e y - B a s s P u b l i s h e r s

San Francisco • London • 1987

WORKING WITH CHILDREN AND ADOLESCENTS IN GROUPS
A Multimethod Approach
   by Sheldon D. Rose and Jeffrey L. Edleson

Copyright © 1987 by: Jossey-Bass Inc., Publishers
                     433 California Street
                     San Francisco, California 94104
                              &
                     Jossey-Bass Limited
                     28 Banner Street
                     London EC1Y 8QE

Library of Congress Cataloging-in-Publication Data

Rose, Sheldon D.
   Working with children and adolescents in groups.

   (The Jossey-Bass social and behavioral science series)
   Bibliography: p. 351
   Includes index.
   1. Social work with children—United States.
2. Social work with youth—United States. 3. Social
group work. I. Edleson, Jeffrey L. II. Title.
III. Series.
HV741.R65   1987   362.7'1   86-20181
ISBN 1-55542-009-5 (alk. paper)

Manufactured in the United States of America

The paper in this book meets the guidelines for
permanence and durability of the Committee on
Production Guidelines for Book Longevity of the
Council on Library Resources.

JACKET DESIGN BY WILLI BAUM

FIRST EDITION

Code 8701

The Jossey-Bass
Social and Behavioral Science Series

Contents

Preface

Since 1972, when *Treating Children in Groups* was first published, we have witnessed an explosion of techniques for working with children, accompanied by a wave of literature describing the new approaches. Problem solving, social-skill training, cognitive restructuring, sociorecreational procedures, and small-group procedures are just a few of the techniques advanced in recent years. One result of these developments has been that available knowledge has moved well beyond some of the tenets proposed in the earlier book. Indeed, the changes have been so dramatic that an entirely new book was called for. We felt that the most useful effort we could make would be to integrate the new developments into a unified approach that links procedures to a general problem-solving paradigm for treating children and adolescents. To our knowledge, no other book has attempted this approach.

Working with Children and Adolescents in Groups is the result of our effort to achieve this integration and to produce a multimethod, empirically based group approach. In this book we have emphasized not only group interventions but the use of the group in applying all interventions discussed here. We have drawn on the most recent research on small groups, specifically on small-group treatment, to make generalizations about a multimethod approach. However, this book is not a research summary. It is a clinical book that is designed to demonstrate the myriad principles that impinge on practice and to propose solutions to the numerous problems that arise when one attempts to lead a group. Examples cover children in all age groups from kindergarten through the last years of high school, but preadolescence and early adolescence predominate. The examples describe mixed-gender as well as single-sex groups and

xi

illustrate applications of the multimethod approach with groups of children who have similar as well as diverse problems.

We have directed this book primarily toward the group leader, the group therapist, and the group counselor—toward any practitioner who works with children and adolescents in school settings, residential treatment homes, mental health and child guidance clinics, family service agencies, halfway houses, health clinics, recreation and community centers, occupational therapy workshops, and juvenile correction centers. We have used the term *group leader* to refer to anyone in such a role. Although not especially aimed at the researcher, this book emphasizes how data collection can be incorporated into practice as a means of making more effective clinical decisions as well as evaluating the progress of treatment and outcome. In formulating the principles that underlie the multimethod approach and in culling examples to illustrate applications, we have benefited from the reported experiences of hundreds of professionals and students, in courses and workshops throughout the United States and Europe, who have used the group as the context for treatment.

The multimethod approach can be described as a set of principles to be applied differentially in each phase of treatment. Although many of the components that can be used in a multimethod approach have been tested with individuals and with groups, only a few studies exist wherein most of the components have been incorporated into one package that has then been compared with other approaches or a no-treatment control group. Recent studies by Hepler and Rose (1986), LeCroy and Rose (1986), Edleson and Rose (1981), and an earlier study by La Greca and Santogrossi (1980) contain many but not all of the methods discussed in this book. Their findings suggest the greater efficacy of a multimethod group approach over waitlist controls or other kinds of control groups. However, the evidence is at best modest and further research is necessary.

Overview of the Contents

In Chapter One we present an overview of the multimethod approach. This approach is basically a problem-solving approach that draws not only on problem-solving techniques but also on the modeling sequence and on operant, cognitive change, relaxation, sociorecreational, small-group, relational, and extra-group methods of intervention. These methods are differentially applied during each of the following overlapping phases: planning for treatment, orientation to treatment, assessment, intervention, and generalization.

In Chapter Two we describe the issues involved in planning for and orienting both children and parents to group treatment. The issues to be considered during the planning phase include the type of group that is needed; the group's themes; the manner in which potential members are recruited and eventually selected into the group; the composition of the group; the settings in which group sessions are to take place; the frequency, length, and duration of each session; and the number of leaders. In orienting group members and parents, group leaders need to make extensive use of treatment contracts and formal session agendas. In addition, all procedures need to be demonstrated and discussed with the group members in advance.

Chapter Three outlines the general purposes of assessment and discusses its place in the treatment process, with particular attention being paid to the unique role of the group in that process. More specifically we describe how one carries out a situational analysis, and we define the specific concepts that are essential to this analysis, such as situation overt behavior, cognitions, affective responses, critical moments, consequences, and the situational context. This chapter also deals with the specific techniques of identifying problematic situations and of using the training strategies to familiarize the children with the above concepts. A section of this chapter is devoted to identifying such resources as potential reinforcers, health and physical attributes, and significant individuals and to examining the impact each can have on the progress of treatment. A discussion of motivational factors follows, and the chapter concludes with a discussion of the role of diagnosis in this type of assessment.

In Chapter Four the role of measurement and evaluation in the treatment process is analyzed. Criteria for selecting instruments, such as reliability and validity, relevance to the presenting problem, practical restraints, and intrusiveness of the instrument, are considered. This chapter also illustrates the application of observation methods, analogue procedures, self-observation and rating procedures, and sociometric devices to the assessment of children in small-group treatment and focuses on the more common strategies of evaluation used in group treatment and the most commonly used group and single-subject research designs.

Chapter Five examines the function of goal setting in the treatment process. Several goals are defined and the procedures used in training the children to formulate appropriate goals are discussed. Once goals have been formulated, the planning process can be initiated. In this chapter, the procedures for incorporating the ideas of the group members into the planning process are demonstrated, including the use of brainstorming and systematic evaluation. A number of different treatment plans are described—individual, group, session, and generalization—and examples of these from actual treatment groups are provided.

Chapter Six discusses the modeling sequence and outlines the prerequisites for effective modeling, such as the presence of skills in observation, incentives for observing, and appropriate characteristics on the part of the model. Principles of effective behavioral rehearsal are outlined and illustrated. Variations of behavioral rehearsal for various age groups of children are also evaluated. The advantages and disadvantages of using feedback in the group are dealt with. Guidelines for using feedback are described and training procedures are illustrated. A number of checklists offering criteria for effective feedback are also presented and discussed.

Chapter Seven illustrates operant and stimulus control procedures commonly used in the group. Specifically, operant procedures for increasing the frequency of desired behavior that have special significance for group treatment, such as social reinforcement, activities as reinforcers, and group contingencies, are examined. Examples are given of methods for expanding the reinforcement repertoires of children. We also introduce the more commonly used schedules of reinforcement and illustrate their application in groups. Also discussed are procedures for reducing the frequency of undesirable behaviors, including extinc-

tion, time-out from reinforcement, response cost, and reinforcement of other behavior. We then identify those stimuli commonly seen in group treatment, including stressful situations
that trigger excessive anger or withdrawal, commands or criticism given to adolescents that stimulate rebellious or noncom-
pliant behavior, daily hassles that may evoke depressive or passive responses and self-put-downs in some. The use of such
stimulus control procedures as physical proximity, instructions,
and commands are evaluated in terms of their effectiveness in
various situations, and the side effects of such procedures are
also discussed.

In Chapter Eight those cognitive and relaxation procedures that appear to be uniquely suited to group application are
discussed. First, we examine self-instructional training and its
variations. Then we turn to cognitive restructuring as it applies
to children in groups. The focus in this section is on the steps
used to identify self-defeating statements and replace them with
self-enhancing ones. Finally we explore the role of relaxation
and relaxation training in groups in helping the children achieve
treatment goals. A number of different relaxation training procedures appropriate to different age groups are considered. We
examine the role of the group in the teaching process and discuss how the group leader can help the children generalize to
stressful situations what they have learned about relaxation.
The chapter concludes with a discussion of meditation as an
alternative to relaxation for adolescents.

Chapter Nine deals with the role of sociorecreational activities in the group treatment process. Concepts such as physical field, constituent performance, informal behavior, and dimensions of the activity setting are defined and illustrated in
the context of the group. The heart of the chapter involves the
examination of various activities in terms of these and other
concepts. Games are carefully scrutinized for ways in which they
can facilitate the treatment process and increase group cohesion. Similarly, handicrafts and drawing, dramatics, simulated
school activities, photography, and field trips are evaluated in
terms of their place in the treatment process. Finally, we deal
with the potential of a multicomponent programming approach.

In Chapter Ten the group's structure and problems are

discussed in terms of their impact on the treatment process. First, we focus on the concrete methods used to collect information about structure and problems. In the following section, we explore ways of identifying the group's problems and of intervening. We then define and consider strategies for modifying various group attributes and close with a discussion of whether and how to prevent group problems.

Chapter Eleven considers the function of extra-group assignments. We provide examples of such different types of assignments as behavioral, cognitive, simulated, noninteractive, and self-observational tasks. Since compliance with assignments is a major problem in treatment, we examine the basic principles involved in facilitating the completion of those assignments.

Chapter Twelve covers the remaining procedures for maintaining and learning to generalize the changes that have occurred in the group. We discuss how members are gradually given responsibility for their own treatment. We show how training involves the use of varied and multiple examples, how significant others are involved in treatment, how important it is to move the treatment program into the natural environment, and how we prepare the children for potential setbacks and a hostile environment. Techniques for overtraining the children in the target behaviors are discussed, and we look at different ways of helping the children to conceptualize the learning experiences and to use general instructions to mediate changes in the natural environment. In this chapter we also look at ways of working with parents and teachers, classroom peers, and others in the child's environment who may help in the generalization process.

In Chapter Thirteen a detailed excerpt from one group is examined in order to illustrate the principles discussed in the preceding chapters.

Acknowledgments

We are grateful to a number of people for their contributions to this book. In particular we would like to recognize the help given by Cynthia Rose, of the Madison Public Schools, who provided us with many of the examples used throughout the text. Marcie Stein, of the Minnesota Children's Museum, also offered extensive advice and support throughout the long process of writing this book. We are indebted to Eileen Gambrill, who carefully read the manuscript of this book in an earlier phase of its development and made many useful suggestions. We would like also to express our thanks to the students who shared in and contributed to the development of this book through their ideas, examples, and criticism. Other colleagues too numerous to name pointed out literature we had failed to find, provided examples, and encouraged us to continue when we were ready to quit; we wish to thank them for their support and assistance. Though many contributed to the development of this book, we alone are ultimately responsible for the final content.

December 1986   Sheldon D. Rose
                                        Madison, Wisconsin

                                        Jeffrey L. Edleson
                                        Minneapolis, Minnesota

To Cindy, Leah, Wendy, and Alisa,
and to Marcie and Daniel

The Authors

Sheldon D. Rose is professor of social work at the University of Wisconsin at Madison where he is also director of the Interpersonal Skill Training and Research Project. He received his A.B. degree (1950) from the University of Missouri, his M.S.W. degree (1952) from Washington University in St. Louis, and his Ph.D. degree (1960) from the University of Amsterdam in the Netherlands with a major in social psychology. He has carried out extensive research on the effectiveness of various group approaches for the treatment of children and of adults. In addition to numerous articles, he has written three books on this topic: *Treating Children in Groups: A Behavioral Approach* (1972), *Group Therapy: A Behavioral Approach* (1977), and an edited book of case studies on groups, *A Casebook in Group Therapy* (1980). He is a coauthor of several manuals for group leaders on topics that include stress management, pain management, and assertiveness training. In addition, he serves as editor of the newsletter *Behavior Group Therapy* and as a member of the editorial boards of many psychology and social work journals.

Jeffrey L. Edleson is associate professor of social work at the University of Minnesota in Minneapolis. He is a Phi Beta Kappa graduate of the University of California at Berkeley in social welfare (1974) and received both his M.S.W. degree (1975) and his Ph.D. degree in social welfare (1979) from the University of Wisconsin at Madison. He has published widely in psychology and social work journals on the subject of group treatment for children and couples. Edleson is also the director of evaluation and research for the Domestic Abuse Project, a nonprofit social service agency. As a result of his work in the area of domestic violence, he has recently published a variety of articles on group therapy for men who batter their wives and is currently engaged in research on this topic both in Minnesota and in Israel.

Working with Children and Adolescents in Groups

A Multimethod Approach

Chapter One

The Multimethod Approach to Treating Children and Adolescents in Groups

Gwen: The situation I would like to talk about today has to do with my getting in a terrible fight with Luellen. I really lost my cool and I got kicked out of school. I guess I still need more practice in talking to myself—like we talked about last week.

Carine: My situation wasn't a problem, for a change. I had that talk with my Mom that I practiced in the group last week and I wanted to let you know that it went great. We talked for almost two hours and I didn't think she would listen at all. Maybe she does like me after all.

Willy: My situation didn't happen yet. I need some help from the rest of you to talk to those people down at the employment office, Friday. I haven't been able to sleep, I'm so scared. I just know they won't like me. I'll never get that job.

Denny: As you guys all know I have been having a lot of trouble studying. That chart I've been using really helps a lot. My mom asks me questions about the homework and gives me points if I'm right. And like you suggested, I study only at my desk.

The above are examples of the types of problems that may be addressed by the multimethod approach to group treatment. This approach is characterized by, first, the use of many

1

different methods of change that are either integrated or selectively used in the assessment, intervention, and continuing generalization of change. These methods include the overt modeling sequence (modeling-rehearsal-coaching-feedback); operant and stimulus control; cognitive restructuring; small-group intervention; sociorecreational procedures; and relational, extra-group, or environmental-modification procedures.

Second, the approach uses these intervention methods to teach those cognitive and overt behaviors required to cope with identified stressful or problematic situations. Thus the emphasis in assessment is on behavior in a situational context, and situational analysis is a crucial step in the assessment process. In learning to cope with problematic situations, the children are taught to improve their systematic problem-solving skills and their ability to manage their own behavior and cognitions. These extremely important cognitive-behavioral skills also mediate changes in overt behaviors or coping skills in concrete situations.

Third, the goal is not only change of behavior at the end of treatment but stable behavior change in appropriate situations external to the treatment context. In other words, the goal is generalization, and treatment strategies are specifically employed to achieve generalized change.

Fourth, the multimethod group approach may be regarded as a systematic problem-solving approach because it goes through the following systematic steps. The targets of behavior are arrived at through systematic assessment and goal setting. Specific treatment plans are often developed through brainstorming for potential techniques or strategies to resolve the problematic situations. The strategies are evaluated in the group. Implementation of the best combination of strategies is usually carried out in the form of homework. Finally, the results of the strategies employed are reported back to the group and, if necessary, the cycle is repeated.

Fifth, multimethod group treatment can be identified as a data-based approach. Data are collected throughout treatment for determining what the specific focuses of treatment should be, for making ongoing clinical decisions, for determining group problems, and for evaluating the effectiveness of treatment.

Sixth, multimethod group treatment is initially a highly structured approach. Later, the structure is gradually lessened and the clients' responsibility for their own treatment is gradually increased.

Seventh, a central feature of this approach that distinguishes it from all dyadic multimethod approaches is the use of the small group as both the context of treatment and a major source of potential intervention strategies. This characteristic is sufficiently central to the approach to warrant a description of its apparent advantages and limitations.

The Group

Many practitioners have avoided the use of the group because of its apparent complexity and the perception that the interaction of members will somehow interfere with the achievement of individual goals. We shall attempt to demonstrate the opportunities as well as the difficulties created by a multimethod approach within the context of the small group.

Improved assessment is an important contribution of treatment in groups. The group provides the child with a major source of feedback about those behaviors that are annoying or pleasing to others, and about those cognitions that appear to others to be self-defeating or self-enhancing. Further advantages for assessment in groups are discussed in Chapter Three.

Another reason for using groups is the frequent and varied opportunity for peer reinforcement, which for children is often far more powerful than adult reinforcement. Children are given the chance to learn or to improve their ability to mediate rewards for others in socially interactive situations (with acquaintances, friends, family members, group, teachers, or employer). The group leader can construct a situation in which each child has frequent opportunity, instructions, and rewards for reinforcing others in the group. Offering positive feedback is a highly valued skill in our society; there is good reason to believe that as children learn to reinforce others, they are reciprocally reinforced by others, and mutual liking also increases (see Lott and Lott, 1961).

In groups, a child must learn to deal with the idiosyncrasies of other individuals—to tolerate and, in some cases, to deal with minor or even major differences. Group members must learn to offer other children feedback and advice. By helping others, members practice strategies for helping themselves. Moreover, they are afforded the opportunity to learn the skills involved in giving and receiving critical feedback and advice.

The small group is a natural and highly attractive setting for most children and adolescents. Some major sources of learning for children are the small playgroup and other informal groups on the playground, in yards, and on the streets. What children learn, however, is dependent on the norms of the group. Guidance and protection by the adult is added to the small group with the presence of a group leader.

Because of its kinship with the natural peer group, the treatment group more nearly simulates the real world of most clients than does the treatment dyad of a high-status adult and a low-status child. As such, the group provides an intermediate step between performing a newly learned behavior in a therapeutic setting and transferring that performance to the community.

The group also creates the opportunity for the group leader to use many therapeutic procedures that are unavailable or less efficient in the therapeutic dyad. Among these procedures is group reinforcement, which for many children is more powerful than individual reinforcement (see Wodarski, Hamblin, Buckholdt, and Ferritor, 1973). The group also provides models of behavior, roleplayers for behavioral rehearsal, manpower for monitoring, and partners for use in a "buddy system." In addition, the group provides a natural laboratory for learning discussion and leadership skills that are important to good social relationships.

In the process of interaction in treatment groups, norms often arise that serve to control the behavior of individual members. If these norms (informal agreements among members concerning preferred modes of action and interaction in the group) are introduced and effectively maintained by the group leader, they serve as powerful therapeutic tools. The group pressures deviant members to conform to such norms as attending regularly, reinforcing peers who do well, analyzing problems systematically and specifically, and assisting peers with their problems. Of course, if the group leader is not careful, antitherapeutic norms can also be generated, for example, wild acting-out behavior by all or most of the children whenever any demand is placed on them.

To guard against such problems, a group leader can call on a body of experimentally derived knowledge about norms and other group phenomena in which individual behavior both influences and is influenced by the various attributes of the group. (See Cartwright and Zander, 1968; Shaw, 1976; and Nixon, 1979, for a review of these relationships.) In addition to modifying group norms, the group leader can facilitate the attainment of both individual and group treatment goals by modifying the group's cohesiveness, the status pattern, or the communication structure. Much of the power to achieve treatment goals is lost if negative group attributes remain unbridled.

Finally, the group appears to be at least as effective and more efficient in terms of therapist cost than dyadic treatment methods. Although there is no research comparing the treatment of children individually and in groups, research on adult groups seems to indicate far lower costs for similar results to individual cognitive-behavioral treatment of assertion and stress disorders, phobias, and depression (Linehan and others, 1979; Teri and Lewinsohn, 1985; Toseland and Siporin, 1986).

Of course, the group is not without major disadvantages: antitherapeutic norms might arise if the group leader is not vigilant and might be maintained if the leader does not deal with such norms with the group members. Moreover, group contagion and aggression can sometimes get out of hand more readily in groups than in the dyad. Strategies for dealing with such problems are available and are detailed in Chapter Ten. It is also more difficult, though not impossible, to individualize each child in the group, since, for efficiency, the group leader is continually looking for common goals to pursue. Confidentiality is more difficult to maintain in groups than in the dyad, although in our experience breeches of confidentiality among group members are rare, especially when dealt with in early sessions. Finally, even minimal effectiveness with groups requires leader training in a unique and extensive repertoire of skills.

If the group leader is aware of all of the above potential problems, they can be dealt with. But even the positive characteristics of the group become advantages only if they are opportunistically seized on by the group leader. Throughout this book we shall point out how group leaders have dealt with the difficulties encountered in group interaction and how they have taken advantage of its unique, manifold assets.

For the opportunities it affords, the group is a vital element in the approach proposed in this book. Before we discuss the various elements of a multimethod approach, let us first examine the general and specific goals of these methods.

Targets of Intervention

One can identify at least four general categories of coping skills commonly pursued in multimethod groups: interpersonal, problem-solving, cognitive and affective coping, and self-management. All of these are aimed, either directly or indirectly, toward specific problematic situations. Achievement of these skills mediates the attainment of specific treatment goals designed for each individual in the group. We will examine each of these general coping skill categories in terms of its relevance to the multimethod group-treatment approach, although these skills generally overlap and are separated in this chapter solely for analysis.

Interpersonal Skills. Interpersonal skills are critical for healthy development in children. Recognition of the importance of peer relations has been increasingly documented in research studies (Asher, Oden, and Gottman, 1976; Hartup, 1980; Swetnam, Peterson, and Clark, 1983). An emphasis on teaching social skills to children has grown in recent years because of the importance of socially effective behavior on subsequent development. Lack of social skills has been linked with a wide range of future adjustment problems (Conger and Keane, 1981; Hartup, 1979).

Hartup (1979), in his article on peer relations and the growth of social competence, suggests several reasons why peer relations are important: (1) lack of sociability in both boys and girls is associated with discomfort, anxiety, and a general unwillingness to engage the environment; (2) children master their aggressive impulses within the context of peer relations; (3) sexual socialization probably cannot take place without peer interaction; (4) peer relations are related to a child's ability for role-taking, which in turn is related to social competence; (5) children rejected by their peers have higher delinquency rates (Roff, 1961), are more likely to drop out of school (Ullman, 1957), and are at risk for emotional and behavioral difficulties (Cowen and others, 1973; Kohn and Clausen, 1955; Roff, Sells, and Golden, 1972).

Interpersonal (social) skills have been defined as "those responses which, within a given situation, prove effective or, in other words, maximize the probability of producing, maintaining or enhancing positive effects for the interactor" (Foster and Ritchey, 1979, p. 626). This definition, though not without problems (see Conger and Keane, 1981), provides a situational and interactional emphasis. Interaction is the basis of group process and, as such, a peer-group approach, not individual treatment, should be the most appropriate context for teaching and learning interpersonal skills.

As a result of increased interpersonal skills development, a child's social status may change. The group leader can structure opportunities for group members to play roles quite different from those assigned to them by their peers. For example, the group leader may assist children in assuming leadership roles, allowing them to demonstrate a wider range of skills than those previously observed by their age-mates. These kinds of experiences may produce increased feelings of mastery that strengthen the child's sense of self-efficacy (Bandura, 1977a).

Problem-Solving Skills. Interventions aimed at developing problem-solving skills have been increasingly applied to child and adolescent problems. This application has been spearheaded by Spivack and Shure's work on the assessment and teaching of interpersonal cognitive problem-solving skills (ICPS) to children

(Spivack, Platt, and Shure, 1976; Spivack and Shure, 1974). Their research consistently revealed that subjects with ICPS abilities were better adjusted. This led to their attempting to teach ICPS abilities to young children. Several studies found that young children learned the cognitive abilities, that these gains were related to adjustment, and that the results had been maintained over time (Spivack, Platt, and Shure, 1976).

Problem-solving skills can maximize a child's adjustment and interpersonal effectiveness. The components identified by Spivack and Shure (1974) as primary skills include: (1) alternative thinking, which is the ability to generate multiple solutions to interpersonal problem situations, (2) consequential thinking, which involves the ability to anticipate short- and long-term consequences of an alternative and to utilize this in decision making, (3) means-end thinking, which is the ability to plan a series of specific actions necessary to carry out the solution to an interpersonal problem. This last category includes the recognition of obstacles that need to be overcome and implies that a realistic time framework is important in achieving a goal. Problem solving is an important cognitive coping skill. But other more specific cognitive skills are equally important.

Cognitive Coping Skills. Cognitions refer to thoughts, images, thinking patterns, self-statements, or private or covert events that may be inferred from verbal or other overt behavior. Cognitive coping skills are those cognitions that facilitate coping with internal and social phenomena. Examples are the ability to analyze one's own cognitions, to label appropriately one's self-defeating statements, to observe and rehearse new, more appropriate self-statements, and to reinforce oneself covertly. Though important skills in their own right, they also mediate the attainment of the more observable social skills defined above. Thus, increasing cognitive coping skills is important for correcting anxiety-inducing and behavior-inhibiting cognitions and in improving social behavior (Meichenbaum, 1977). Self-statements such as "everyone thinks I'm weird" not only produce anxiety, they promote inaction. Changing such a statement to one like "Sure, I'm different than other kids in many ways; some things I like and some I'll change" may reflect a more accurate appraisal, may suggest avenues of change, is more self-respecting, may reduce anxiety, and ultimately should improve social behavior.

Cognitive coping skills are not, however, the only coping techniques available for dealing with stressful situations. In the next subsection we discuss targets that are not exclusively cognitive but may also require overt behavior from the child to cope with problematic or stressful events.

Active Coping Skills. Problem-solving, social, and cognitive skills can all be regarded as coping skills. Others are of equal importance. One of the most useful is the ability to relax in stressful situations. If children can respond to stressful stimuli by relaxing, they will be better able to access other coping skills. Furthermore, once relaxation is mastered, it may enhance a child's or adolescent's general quality of life.

Another coping skill is the ability to ascertain when escape from or avoidance of a highly stressful situation is appropriate. Such a skill may include cognitive and interpersonal skills in carrying out escape or avoidance.

Recreational and leisure-time skills may be regarded as coping skills as well. Although some are social in nature, they may be regarded as a separate category for coping with general life stress. In groups, children and adolescents may be taught both individual and group leisure-time activities that may enhance the quality of their day-to-day experiences. Such social skills as sharing and cooperation, handling competition, good winning and losing behaviors, getting involved and involving others, and so forth may be taught. The process of teaching social and recreational skills is discussed in detail in Chapter Nine.

Self-Management Skills. Self-management refers to those procedures through which children control their own environment as a means of controlling their own behavior by using environmental cues, self-monitoring, self-instruction, self-evaluation, and self-reinforcement. Although the data supporting the use of any one of these procedures are limited in scope, there is clinical evidence that these procedures may be effective following the use of more direct environmental strategies (Stuart, 1977). In any case, the child will still be struggling with various problems long after the group has terminated and can utilize these learned skills when only limited external support is available. Most of these skills are cognitive and are described in Chapter Eight or are operant and described in Chapter Seven.

Specific Targets of Change

The above categories suggest general areas within which the group leader formulates more specific targets of change. The specific targets are concrete behaviors or identifiable cognitions in response to a given client's problem. Some treatment areas have been: controlling violent behavior when peers criticize the child; increasing participation in social situations with peers; asking adults for help with difficulties; reducing anxiety in response to fear-inducing situations; handling impulsive behavior in a variety of social contexts; establishing relationships with the opposite sex; coping with recurring depressive responses, especially when alone; learning to help and share with others; and being the leader in group situations. Strategies for identifying these and other change goals and their situational context are elaborated upon in Chapters Three and Four.

A set of other specific targets does not involve changes in the child's behaviors, cognitions, or affective responses but rather of the child's external environment. Such targets might be the absence of food in the home, insufficient money to get to school on the bus, and abuse or neglect of the child in the home. Such situations require extra-group or environmental intervention on the part of the group leader. These situations may also require behavioral and cognitive coping skills as well as the previously described social and recreational skills. The group leader can teach all these skills in the group context. Such targets may require intervention in the community, the school, the family, or at the very least, referral to those who can better (by virtue of resources or community sanction) deal with these problems. But environmental problems cannot be ignored. Though such problems are often identified within the group, intervention to ameliorate them may fall outside its scope. In many cases the group may be the ideal setting for training children or adolescents to deal more effectively with their environment; for example, the group leader may provide the members with necessary information about job employment opportunities or obtaining food stamps. Or the group leader might encourage the entire group to accompany a person in particular need to a given agency.

We have described the major target behavior and problems the multimethod group approach is designed to deal with. Let us now examine the methods used to achieve those targets or resolve those problems.

The Various Methods

There has been extensive research on methods of teaching children various coping skills. In most of these studies the major means of intervention were limited to one or two of the following methods: problem-solving, cognitive-affective, modeling-rehearsal, operant and stimulus control, sociorecreational, relational, small-group, and extra-group. Even when carried out in the group, most of these studies ignored both the group's potential as well as the problems it could create. In the multimethod approach we have attempted to combine all or most of these methods into one integrated approach. A method was selected for inclusion if it had some independent empirical foundation and if some relationship to the above-mentioned targets could be demonstrated. In the following sections we shall review each of these in terms of its contribution to the total approach. In subsequent chapters each of these methods will be elaborated upon.

Problem-Solving Method

The problem-solving method involves learning and carrying out a systematic set of steps for solving a problem (Heppner, 1978). These steps include defining the problem, generating alternative solutions and consequences, selecting and implementing the best solution, and evaluating the outcome. Although not commonly found in others' paradigms (for example, Spivack and Shure, 1974), we have added an intermediate step, preparation for implementation, since identification of the problem and suggestions for its solution have often been insufficient to prepare the child for implementing the solution. As children identify either cognitive problems or social-skill deficiencies that prevent them from coping effectively with a given problematic situation, the problem-solving method is invoked. In using it repeatedly the children learn the skills and general problem-solving paradigm required to successfully resolve their problems.

It should also be noted that problem solving is inherent in all of the other methods used. In order to determine and plan for dealing with a social-skill deficiency, the problematic situation is analyzed, goals for learning specific social skills are established, and specific content for employing those skills is generated through group brainstorming. Children then evaluate and select the best of the procedures and prepare for implementation by having it modeled and rehearsing it in the group with feedback from peers. Finally the program is implemented via homework or a behavioral assignment to be performed in the real world. Afterwards, the children report their experiences back to the group and, if necessary, the cycle is repeated. The same steps are used to learn cognitive responses to problematic or stressful situations. Thus, one could assert that the multimethod approach is also a problem-solving approach.

Since problem solving is discussed in many other chapters as well as in the introduction, no separate chapter has been devoted to it. Because of the centrality of problem solving in the multimethod approach, we have separated it in the introduction from other cognitive strategies, several of which are discussed in the section on cognitive change methods. First, we shall discuss the modeling sequence that is used in preparation for overt social- and cognitive-skill implementation.

Modeling Sequence

The modeling sequence is designed to teach specific positive interactive behaviors and includes such techniques as overt modeling, behavior rehearsal, coaching, and group feedback. Modeling refers to learning through the observation of a model who might be an adult, a peer, or even a puppet. It is often used to demonstrate how a situation problematic to one or more children in the group might be handled effectively. Behavioral rehearsal is also a roleplay technique in which a child practices new, more effective ways of handling a problem situation. Coaching refers to instructions or verbal cues given to the child when the child is modeling or rehearsing a set of behaviors in a given situation. Group feedback is the verbal evaluation from others as to how effectively the child roleplayed or modeled. All of the procedures in the modeling sequence are demonstrated in Chapter Six. Following the modeling sequence, the child prepares for and carries out a homework assignment to practice the social skill in the real world. Such assignments are discussed in detail in Chapter Eleven.

Modifying Consequences and Antecedents

The method that modifies consequences and antecedents is derived from operant theory. It involves procedures in which the immediate consequences of a given behavior are systematically followed by a reinforcing event. It may also involve procedures in which the conditions that lead to or are parallel with a given behavior are changed to create conditions more amenable to the performance of a desired behavior. The latter is often referred to as stimulus control.

In groups children receive many kinds of reinforcement for the performance of prosocial group behavior and the completion of extra-group assignments or homework. This reinforcement takes the form of praise, tokens, points, favored activities, and whatever small, manipulable objects may be valued by and appropriate to the given age and developmental category. In all cases these reinforcers are delivered according to a systematic plan, called a schedule of reinforcement. Reinforcers are withheld in response to undesirable behaviors. This is referred to as extinction and is a common response in groups. Occasionally, reinforcement is removed (usually in the form of tokens) following undesirable behaviors—a process known as response cost.

Modifying the antecedent conditions, or stimulus control,

is exemplified within the group by games that permit and encourage cooperation rather than competition. Other examples of stimulus control are: a child who was working on nail biting who wore thin gloves to prevent him from chewing on his nails, and a child in a weight-loss group who permitted herself to eat only at a table set with food that had been cooked. Both reinforcement and stimulus control are discussed in more detail in Chapter Seven.

Cognitive Change Methods

With cognitive change methods, children are trained in more effective ways of evaluating themselves or problematic situations. Many cognitive procedures are used in groups, often in combination with each other and with other types of procedures, such as the modeling sequence. Most commonly used are cognitive restructuring, self-instructional training, and self-reinforcement.

Cognitive restructuring is used to change self-defeating or illogical patterns of thinking that interfere with social functioning to self-enhancing or logical ones. It is the first step in increasing cognitive coping skills. In a given set of circumstances, cognitions partially mediate overt behavioral responses. These cognitions include how one values oneself and one's action and how one specifically thinks or covertly responds in a given situation. Children are trained to identify self-enhancing and self-defeating thoughts in case examples or exercises. Later they learn to identify their own self-defeating thoughts and that of their peers and to change them to self-enhancing thoughts.

In self-instructional training the children are taught first to identify, then to replace self-defeating statements uttered to themselves in the face of a problematic or stress-inducing situation with new, more functional self-statements. This process consists of step-by-step verbalizations concerning the problem definition ("What's wrong with the way I'm thinking about this?"), problem focus ("What can I do about it?"), focusing of attention ("I should think about how that will get me in trouble."), coping statements ("If I keep relaxing I won't blow it!"), and self-reinforcement ("Wow! I did it! See, I can do it!"). To prepare for implementation of these strategies, the group leader or another child demonstrates (covert modeling) what might be said to oneself. This is followed by practice (covert rehearsal) by the child with the problem—first aloud, then whispered, and eventually silently. These are described in detail in the first half of Chapter Eight.

Relaxation Methods

Relaxation methods are taught to children who need help in coping with stress, pain, anger, or external environmental events in which no external coping behavior is possible. Children are taught a modified version of the alternate tension and relaxation technique (developed by Jacobsen, 1978) and then later taught to fade the tension phases. Various alternatives uniquely suited to younger children are also taught. Modest research support for the use of relaxation procedures in reducing anxiety and stress is to be found in studies by Stovya (1977) and Lyles, Burish, Korzely, and Oldham (1982). However, Heide and Borkovec (1983) have shown that, for a few persons, relaxation may increase anxiety. Relaxation training is seldom used as an isolated procedure. Details on various forms of relaxation training used in groups of children and adolescents are described in the second half of Chapter Eight.

Sociorecreational Method

The sociorecreational method involves the use of active games, board games, arts, crafts, storytelling, and dramatics to facilitate the achievement of therapeutic goals and to increase group cohesion. Whittaker (1976) notes that "despite the popularity of group treatment as a mode of helping troubled children, many clinicians underestimate the potential of program activities as a medium for growth and change in groups" (p. 459). Ross and Bernstein (1976, p. 127) state that "games and activities offer children and adolescents a workshop for discovering and developing new ways to manage obstacles."

Sociorecreational activities provide children with a highly satisfying set of stimulus conditions in which concrete skills can be informally practiced and reinforced. Such activities also form the basis for broad participation and increased group attraction. Furthermore, they provide the context for practicing social skills in a way that is more realistic and more entertaining than roleplaying. Chapter Nine describes the philosophy and specific activities of this method. Interactive sociorecreational activities are often selected to influence the group process and, as such, are classified within the general category of small-group methods.

Small-Group Method

Adjunctive to the particular strategies mentioned above are some concrete group procedures that facilitate the process of change. The effective use of these procedures may be more important than the particular strategy being utilized. These procedures include group discussion, roleplaying, the buddy system, subgrouping, leadership delegation, and group exercises—all of which are described below. The small-group method is the process of using one or more of these procedures in order to attain group goals or resolve group interactive problems.

Group Discussion. Verbal interaction between children as well as between a child and the leader is called "group discussion." It is the essential stuff by which problems are laid out and considered, solutions are shared and evaluated, decisions are formulated and affirmed, values are deliberated, and friendships are made. Implicit in group discussion is the assumption that maximum involvement of all group members is essential for high cohesion and effective treatment.

Roleplaying. In its most elementary form, roleplaying can be defined as the practice of roles in simulated conditions. The group leader, by acting as a guide and structuring the roleplaying, controls the outcome of the roleplaying process. If the group leader is clear about the purposes of roleplaying, even through focused use, this technique can prove highly beneficial in promoting change. In the modeling sequence, roleplaying is used to demonstrate specific skills and to practice them. Role-playing is also used for assessment, for teaching specific treatment skills, in role reversal, and in generalization training.

Subgrouping. A simple procedure of working in pairs, triads, or other-sized subgroups, subgrouping can serve as a means of increasing interaction among the members and providing them an opportunity to work without being overseen by the adult. It creates an opportunity to practice leadership skills. The *buddy system* (see O'Donnell, Lydgate, and Fo, 1979) is a special subgrouping procedure for children to work together outside of the group. In addition to the advantages mentioned above, it contributes to the transfer of learning within the group to situations outside of the group.

Group Exercises. Structured interactive activities or group exercises teach children skills that mediate the achievement of treatment goals. For example, an introduction exercise is used in which children interview at least two children in the group and introduce them to the others. In another exercise, the children study a case and discuss how each of them is different from the person in that case. Other exercises involve teaching children how to give and receive both praise and criticism. Usually at least one such exercise is carried out in every session.

Relational Methods

A number of skills have been identified as crucial to any helping relationship, whether or not this relationship is dyadic or within the structure of a small group. We have noted in our work with students that, in spite of a high level of technological skill in the other methods, failure to possess these relational or clinical skills results in high drop-out rates, disinterest on the part of the children, and a high frequency of group problems. In a sense it is the solution into which all the other methods are dissolved.

Many of these skills are to be found in the methods described above. For example, group leaders who can comfortably and frequently provide their members with high levels of reinforcement tend to establish sound relationships with their members. Similarly, group leaders who model self-disclosure and all of the other skills that the members are expected to carry out discover that the indicators of group problems (high levels of conflict, low cohesion, low satisfaction, and pairing) seldom arise. Those group leaders who create stimulating sociorecreational activities together with the children also enhance their relationship to the children and the children's relationship to each other. Because of their specificity, these are highly trainable skills.

Some skills are unique to relationship building. For example, the use of humor with children is not addressed elsewhere in the above methods. Yet to work with children one must be able to find joy in playing with children, in joking with them, and in permitting oneself to be teased.

Involving children in their own treatment is essential to achieving generalization of change. Although we focus on this skill in Chapter Twelve, in each of the intervening chapters, we demonstrate how members can gradually assume responsibility for their own treatment. The process by which children are involved is a vital relationship-building skill.

Listening to children is a skill not covered above, yet the absence of careful listening often results in wrong targets of change being pursued. Listening does not necessarily require seeing the underlying implications of their words but rather grasping the obvious meanings, sometimes a far more difficult task. Often, when group leaders hasten to carry out the items on the given agenda, they ponder the next step or interrupt while a child is still speaking.

Attending skills refer to such nonverbal skills as eye contact, body posture, and voice tone, all of which indicate acceptance, warmth, and trust. Although these are nonspecific characteristics, in that they are difficult to define, observations of group leaders in action tend to indicate to observers whether such skills are being used.

Identifying and dealing with a child's affective response to crisis occurring prior to the meeting but falling outside the specific purpose of the meeting requires following a difficult but necessary line of action. Ignoring such crises inevitably re-

sults in passive or chaotic meetings and failure to achieve pre-
planned objectives.

Setting limits on disruptive or off-task behavior is another
relational skill that must be considered often if the goals of
change are to be sought in a congenial milieu. This is a more difficult skill and yet one of the most frequently required. The
boundaries regarding when to set limits and when to ignore behavior are not always clear. Skill in reinforcement and program
development often protects the group leader from frequently
setting limits on disruptive behavior.

The technology for dealing with these (often called) nonspecific treatment skills is not well worked out, although much
of the work of Carkhuff (1972) for dyadic interviewing and
Toseland and Rivas (1984) in group treatment point the way to
training procedures. We suggest that modeling these basic skills
may be the most fundamental way of teaching them to incipi-
ent group leaders. Although no one chapter is devoted to the
application of relationship skills, their presence permeates most
of the chapters in this book.

Extra-Group Intervention Method

Vinter and his associates (1967) point to extra-group intervention strategies as being as important as those that occur
within the group. Similarly, Pincus and Minahan (1973), in their
classic social-work text, stress the importance of going beyond
the individual and small-group "systems" to maximize the effectiveness of treatment. These strategies involve the group leader
in working with the family, the classroom, the school administration, and other social units whose activities and policies impinge upon the outcome of specific treatment. The strategies
may involve reevaluating policies and rules, simply communicat-
ing with representatives of these social units, and training them
in reinforcement or other techniques being used in the group.
Failure to address these issues often results in the failure to
maintain treatment goals even if they can be achieved in the
group.

One interesting example of dealing with the larger social

system was demonstrated in a recently integrated school (Rose, Hepler, and Vinton, 1986). In this project social-skill groups were established for all five classes of the fifth grade. The primary target children were the rejected and isolated children, but the interest was not only in improving their social skills and social status. Since the groups included children at various levels of popularity, it was possible to train the popular children to accept and involve others in their activities. As a result, eleven of the thirteen rejected children improved their social status—in some cases, dramatically.

A completely different set of extra-group skills was demonstrated by a group leader who referred a child he believed to be neglected to the county social services department. This required extensive communication with the family, the social service worker, and the school before the referral was complete. The behavioral problems that were being worked on in the group were incidental to the problem of neglect to which the child had been subjected.

In still another example, the group leader organized a meeting for parents of group members to let them know what she was working on with the children. The parents' interest led to an ongoing group in which the parents tried out new parenting skills and directly supported the activities of the group leader.

Because such issues are extensively handled elsewhere (see, for example, Sundel, Glasser, Sarri, and Vinter, 1985), we shall not devote a chapter to these skills. However, Chapter Twelve contains several examples of applications of these principles. Extra-group interventions contribute heavily to the achievement of this generalization. Elements of most of the methods discussed in this multimethod section are used in every session. Reasons for this integration are discussed in the following section.

The Integration of Methods

Because of the inconsistent results generated by experiments using either the modeling sequence or problem-solving, cognitive strategies of intervention, a third model incorporating aspects of both approaches should prove more effective in effecting stable changes in interpersonal skills. Several studies indicate the effectiveness of a combined approach (Kendall and Finch, 1976, 1978; Kendall and Wilcox, 1979; De Lange, Lanham, and Barton, 1981; LeCroy and Rose, 1986). We suggest that by adding operant and stimulus control strategies to the problem-solving, cognitive and social-skill training combination, the approach would be still more powerful since a broader range of behaviors associated with any one problem could be taught (see LeCroy and Rose, 1986). Furthermore, the children can be taught to reinforce each other and themselves, as an additional tool in the treatment process and as an important skill in its own right.

Another deficiency is that training programs may be dull and uninteresting to children. Activities and games should teach children the skills necessary to handle problematic situations in an enjoyable and challenging manner. Though lacking empirical support as an isolated program tool, sociorecreational activities clearly enhance the attractiveness of the group in a multimethod approach. In addition, new sociorecreational skills have the potential of enhancing the self-esteem of the child and the way in which he or she is valued in the classroom group.

Finally, while several of the above-mentioned studies have involved the treatment of children in small groups, few have focused on group processes and the use of group procedures as a means to improve social skills. Using these group procedures as a means and a context for the achievement of goals can offer the advantages mentioned earlier.

In general the children's problems are not restricted to learning one clearly isolated behavior or cognition or handling one kind of problem situation. Impulsive children, for example, often have to learn more systematic problem-solving skills. They must often learn new ways of evaluating themselves. The same children may need to interact more effectively with their peers. Often simple operant behaviors (such as smiling) also need to be learned through reinforcement, and other behaviors (such as nail biting) can be reduced in frequency through stimulus control. As in the case of the child referred for impulsive behavior, the child and the referring adult often complain of many current problem situations, each of which requires a range of new or modified skills in order to be dealt with adequately. For this reason, broad-based treatment appears to provide the greatest benefit. The findings from at least one study provide modest support for this notion (LeCroy and Rose, 1986).

In spite of its variety of methods, this approach is neither haphazard nor unsystematic. We shall attempt to show how these various methods can be integrated and systematically applied in the assessment and achievement of treatment goals. We begin this task by describing the major steps in a multimethod group approach.

Phases in the Multimethod Group Approach

The major phases in this approach are (1) planning for group treatment, (2) orientation of the client and significant others to the possibilities and limitations of group treatment, (3) assessment of the presenting problems and client resources, (4) intervention to effect change, and (5) generalization of that change to the real world. These phases are guided by the group leader rather than evolving naturally out of the group. They are somewhat overlapping in time and in content. Each phase implies a different emphasis for the group leader. Let us examine briefly the techniques involved in each of these steps.

Planning for Treatment. In planning for treatment, the group leader must establish the group's purposes, assess potential membership, recruit members, decide on the group's social environment or structure, and create its physical environment. In determining the group's purposes the leader can draw on several sources. Based on experience with clients in the agency or community, the agency may identify a need for a certain type of program. Parents in the community or school may request help for certain types of children's problems for which help is not generally or readily available. Newspapers may publicize public figures and others who deplore the unavailability of certain types of programs. Teachers may seek help in areas where little help exists. To the degree that these needs can be translated into interactive or anxiety-related behavior of children in response to identifiable problematic situations, a multimethod group approach can be considered.

Once it is determined that a multimethod group can meet the given client need, the group leader must determine whether a population of children exists that can be reached and served by such a group. As the population responds to the group, the best possible structure for such a group to achieve its general purposes must be established. What should its central theme be, should it be open or closed, and should it have a given duration? If so, how long? What is the appropriate number of clients? How similar should the members be in terms of types of problems and demographic characteristics—age, gender, socio-economic, and cultural factors? How many leaders should there be?

Once these issues are settled, the group members need to be recruited. Recruitment serves to screen members for needs that match the goals set for the group as well as the potential ability to work in a group setting. As part of the planning process, the physical environment of the group is usually a concern. What are the minimal physical requirements to carry out such a group in terms of equipment, physical space, and accessibility of that space to the clientele? If there are any costs, such as for recreational items or trips, these and the person or agency who will bear them should be determined.

Orientation to Group Treatment. As part of recruitment and later, during the group process, members and their parents and/or teachers need to be oriented to the purposes of the group, the methods to be used, and the potential goals that can be achieved. Inadequate orientation often leads to high dropout rates. As part of orientation, group contracts are developed. These group contracts establish what the children's and their parents' responsibilities are and what they can expect from the group leader and the agency. This contract is usually in writing and is signed by members, their parents, and the group leader. All of the above issues about organization and orientation are discussed in detail in Chapter Two.

Assessment of Presenting Problems. Assessment is a concept central to all empirical approaches. The purpose of assessment is to determine the specific targets of intervention in order to make them amenable to intervention. It also determines whether the given group or another type of treatment might be the most appropriate setting for each potential client. It is designed to determine the clients' personal resources for working toward the achievement of goals. Assessment must also examine any potential barriers to participation in treatment or to achieving treatment goals. The assessor must determine the nature of group goals and group problems, whether goals are being achieved, and whether problems are being resolved in the group. Finally, assessment is used as the first step in determining to what degree and for whom treatment is effective.

To answer all of these questions, data must be systematically collected before treatment, during treatment, immediately following treatment, and at some time after treatment. Some of the methods of collecting data include personality inventories and checklists, roleplay tests, sociometric tests, diaries, self-observation, direct observations of the group or of individuals when not in the group, postsession questionnaires, and interviews. In Chapter Three the basic principles of how assessment is applied in groups are presented. Chapter Four provides details of the specific techniques and evaluates them in terms of their applicability to a multimethod group approach. In Chapter Ten the group data-collection procedures are described.

Interventions to Achieve Change. In this phase the appropriate intervention strategies are selected, the children are oriented to these procedures, and with their concurrence the strategies are applied. Let us examine how the various intervention strategies described in the section on multimethods might be integrated. To begin with, problem situations are analyzed and solutions are generated, decided on, and a plan is developed to learn the necessary skills to achieve the solution. Thus, all situations are first dealt with through problem solving. To prepare a person for carrying out the decided-upon solutions, either the modeling-sequence or one of the several cognitive procedures, and often both, are used. Often a plan is established in which the child receives reinforcement for carrying out steps in the plan. And reinforcement is distributed lavishly throughout the session for achievements within the group and for completion of behavioral homework outside of the group.

At first, common problem situations are worked on. Later, individual problem situations, which the children have recorded in their diaries, are the focus of treatment. Homework to try out solutions to problem situations in the real world is designed, carried out between sessions, and subsequently monitored.

Sociorecreational activities, especially games, are included in every session, usually at the end as a means of keeping the attraction to the group high; however, they are usually diminished in frequency towards the end of treatment. Group procedures, too, are used throughout treatment. Group feedback is requested after every cognitive or behavioral rehearsal. The buddy system is used between every session to monitor and lend support to the carrying out of homework assignments. At least one group exercise is used at every session to facilitate the teaching of such skills as reinforcing others, giving and receiving criticism, and identifying self-defeating statements. Many of these exercises are carried out in subgroups of two or three. The integration of these many procedures is made possible because of the highly structured nature of the group. However, as the group progresses this structure gradually diminishes. This and other generalization practices are discussed below.

Generalization of Change. Generalization refers to the process of transferring what the child has learned in the group to the outside world and maintaining what he or she has learned beyond the end of treatment. One of the major strategies for transferring learning from the group to outside situations is homework.

At the end of every meeting the children design assignments to be carried out at home, at school, on the playground, or at any other extra-group location. These assignments are characterized by their specificity as to what, when, where, or with whom certain behaviors and/or cognitions are to be manifested within a given time period. The purpose of homework is to create an opportunity for the children to try out in the real world what they have learned in the group. Since they are rarely monitored, it provides the children with an opportunity to try out behaviors on their own and in so doing, lessen their dependency on the group leader.

A portion of every meeting is devoted to the designing of new assignments and the monitoring of the results of the previous meeting's assignments. If one views the treatment process as analogous to a problem-solving process, homework may be viewed as the implementation phase of treatment, and reporting back to the group as the validation phase. In any case, homework is an essential part of the treatment process.

Clients are prepared for termination by their developing a plan to apply what they learned in the group after the group ends and by designing activities appropriate to practicing their newly learned skills. Potential self-referral sources are discussed, such as the school counselor or a local clinic. The group leader identifies with each of the children the specific behavioral and cognitive cues for seeking outside help.

In order to diminish the intensity of the members' relationship to each other and to the group leader, he or she encourages the establishment of relationships outside of the group and the involvement in extra-group activities, such as after-school interest or sport groups, boy scouts, girl scouts, or YMCA or YWCA groups. Furthermore, nongroup members whom they have befriended may be invited as guests to hear what they have achieved in the group. Assignments to carry out activities with these friends are encouraged.

In this phase, material reinforcement is ended for homework completion and conformity to group rules. Homework has become less structured but more extensive. Preparation is largely in the hands of the child. Monitoring is less strict. Social, recreational, and other group cohesion-building activities are held to a minimum. Many of the leadership functions are performed by group members. Finally, as part of this phase, a follow-up may also be included in which a "booster" session is held two or three months following treatment. In "booster" sessions children have an opportunity to discuss their achievements and any new problems that may arise. This final phase is described in detail in Chapter Twelve.

Summary

Chapter One has presented an overview of the multimethod approach to group treatment. This overview provides the reader with background for understanding the relationship of any one chapter to the entire approach. In the final chapter we present a detailed excerpt from one meeting in which many of the principles discussed throughout the book are exemplified and integrated. In the next chapter we detail the preparatory steps one must take before the group begins.

Chapter Two

Planning Treatment and Orienting Children and Parents

Because of the need expressed by parents of children in the middle school, a friendship club was developed in which the general goal was to learn how to make and keep friends. The specific social skills to be worked on were developing conversational skills, showing an interest in the ideas and activities of others, listening to others without interrupting, and asking others for help and information. The cognitive skill to be worked on was the replacement of put-downs many of the children seemed to be making about themselves. The group was to meet at lunch once a week for eight weeks with the group leader, with an option of four additional weeks if the members and the group leader thought it necessary. In organizing the group, the leader would also be going to the various classrooms to let children know about the group and to contact parents and teachers. The group would be no larger than eight children and care would be taken to include at least two children who could serve as models for the others. The group leader would meet with all children who were referred prior to the first group meeting to tell them about the group and to decide on what social skills they would like to work.

The above example describes a brief plan for setting up a new group. Planning in advance is one of the salient characteristics of the multimethod approach. Areas of planning include: putting the group together, arranging a series of meetings, deciding on the focus of each separate meeting, selecting treatment procedures, and planning for transfer or generalization. The planning is not haphazard, but rather is based on the best available information collected from parents and teachers, children in the pregroup interview, ongoing observations, and contacts with the children and significant others throughout group treatment. It also draws on data from empirical studies. The plan is not a rigid structure that can never be departed from, but rather a well-thought-out point of departure on which to base preparation and ongoing decision making. It provides a basis for explaining to the children and their parents what the group is all about and what will happen next.

The process by which members and significant others are informed about the group in general and each procedure and meeting in particular is referred to as orientation. Another characteristic of the multimethod approach is that members are informed about potential learning, advantages of the group, and possible risks involved in being in the group. As a new procedure is introduced, information about it is shared with the children. In this chapter we present a discussion of the planning and orientation processes and their implication for a multimethod group approach.

Type of Group

The first decision a group leader must make is to determine the type of group that should be worked with. There are many different types; the major ones are discussed below.

Time-Limited Group. In a time-limited group the members, for the most part, begin together and end together six to eighteen weeks later. It is the most common type of group and the one that most of this book will focus on. The advantages of such groups are that the members go through the same phases of development, which facilitates planning. However, such a model requires having a sufficient number of members who meet the requirement of good composition in order to start the group (see below). Since most of this chapter will describe the major characteristics of such a model, we will restrict our discussion here. In the following subsections, we briefly present other models of treatment, their goals, their advantages and limitations, and how their organization differs from the time-limited model.

Open-Ended Groups. Groups that admit new members throughout the year are "open-ended groups." Members come as they are referred and leave the group as goals are achieved or as they drop out for other reasons. Usually such a group is limited in size. Most institutional units, halfway houses, group homes, and transitional units are characterized by their open-endedness. Long-term therapy groups often have a fixed beginning, but their therapists will add people as the group progresses and members leave the group. Specific training groups, in such areas as social-skill training or stress-management training, rarely fall into this category unless they are part of an institutional program. However, we see no reason why they cannot be organized along open-ended principles if the usual intake process yields inadequate numbers.

The chief advantage of open-ended groups is that the problem of insufficient recruitment is dramatically reduced. If, in a hospital pain clinic, a pain group for children is organized, even with as few as three members, the initial group can be added to as new children and their parents express an interest in such a group.

Such open-ended groups also have the advantage of drawing on a large number of applicants over a long period of time, once the group has begun. Errors in the initial composition can sometimes be corrected by adding in a way that brings about a desirable set of individuals. Another potential advantage is that resistance has usually been worked through by the other members when the new members arrive. Group leaders seldom have to deal with resistance of the group as a whole, and the old group members provide models to the incoming members of how to handle their isolated concerns.

One disadvantage of the open-ended group is that incoming members are strangers in a world of friends. This is not an easy role to play, but one which each member has to learn to respond to on frequent occasions. Another problem often expressed is that the phases of treatment are different for each person. The new members are concerned with getting to know others and feeling comfortable in the group. More experienced members may be working on problems identified in previous meetings while those about to terminate are focusing on generalization plans. To deal with these problems, the group leader may provide added opportunities for leadership responsibilities to the experienced members, including leading discussion, orienting new members, and peer tutoring. If these skills have not been demonstrated in the group, they may be taught through modeling, rehearsal, and group feedback prior to the admission of new persons. New members are rapidly integrated into the group through the pregroup orientation with an experienced member as orienter. Furthermore, in order to avoid creating low-status isolates, it is usually best to admit two or three new members at a time.

Transition Groups. One particular kind of open-ended group is the transition group. Usually found in institutions, the transition group is oriented toward preparing the member to leave the institution. The groups may last anywhere from two weeks to six months. If they are of one month duration or less they usually meet daily. In behaviorally oriented transition groups the focuses are on those behaviors the members need to survive in their immediate new environment. To a large degree social-skill training deals with such issues as how to meet new friends, how to get along with a probation officer, and how to deal with peer pressure to commit delinquent acts. In addition some noninteractive skills, such as handling money and budgeting, using the telephone, and using social resources, are also taught. In most groups, members provide each other with mutual support for leaving the institution. Former institutional residents are invited to discuss their experiences. Considerable time is spent on systematic problem solving of potential problems the children identify in their own unique future environment. Extensive homework, to be performed primarily when group is not meeting regularly, is encouraged. In general, the size of the transition group varies from week to week depending on who is eligible to leave. Groups larger than nine are usually divided into subgroups in order to provide maximum individualization.

Maintenance Groups. A maintenance group is usually a time-limited group in which the members, following a series of sessions in another type of group, meet for the purpose of maintaining what they had learned in the original group. They usually meet as infrequently as once a month and are less structured than other groups described in this book. Most of the group leadership functions are delegated to the members. Sessions generally focus on successes in maintaining behaviors learned in the group and evaluating problems that arose in maintaining them. This kind of group is described in more detail in Chapter Twelve.

Cross-Age Tutoring Training Groups. Cross-age tutoring was developed by Lippitt (1969) in the early sixties as a method of having older children (with behavior and learning problems) serve as tutors for younger children. The basic assumption was that children, especially adolescents, learn far more when performing the teaching role than when acting as students in the classroom (Gartner, Kohler, and Riessman, 1971). Moreover, the child as tutor is forced to grasp not only the content of what he or she is teaching, but also extremely important communication skills. Finally, in learning to teach, children learn to learn.

In one of our projects, five sixth-graders, who themselves were finding school difficult and unstimulating, were taught as a group to each tutor one kindergardener to differentiate colors. The tutoring sessions took place for five minutes daily over a two-week period. It became a "teacher"-training program for the tutors, who were trained in specific teaching skills. At the weekly treatment sessions for the tutors only, they dealt with lesson plans, behavior problems of their "pupils," the role of a teacher, and their own feelings about their new roles. Teachers reported that the frequency of disruptive behaviors was dramatically reduced in all five boys. Four of them improved their own grades, on average, a full grade (for example, from D to C). In general, through using behavioral methods, cross-age tutoring is a form of *role* therapy. In the above example the child's role as *helpee* was changed to that of *helper*. During this process children learn to look at and identify with the role and difficulties of the teacher.

Although a promising procedure that is widely used by educators, it has been used only occasionally by group leaders because of the concern over the effect of failure on the tutees as well as the tutors. In our limited experience, if the lesson plans are simple and brief but meaningful, if the tutors are well-rehearsed, if the teaching itself is supervised by a teacher rotating around the room, the program is enthusiastically endorsed by all the participants. Moreover, behavior change in the tutors generalizes (according to anecdotal accounts) to their classroom behavior. For excellent details on the method as it is applied by teachers in the schools, as well as a summary of research, the reader is referred to Gartner, Kohler, and Reissman (1971).

Recent Life Change Groups. Many children's groups are not organized toward behavioral change. In the schools, for example, one such group consists of those children who hold in common a recent major life change. Examples of such changes are a recent divorce of the parents or a recent death of a sibling or close relative. Such children come together to deal with their reactions to the life change and to obtain help in getting through the initial phase. Group leaders have noted that discovery of others who have similar problems and who they can talk to about how they feel appears to be quite supportive. Children seem to feel understanding from those who have undergone the same kind of experience. The structure of such groups is often amorphous. Group leaders tend to be supportive but nondirective (Titkin and Cobb, 1983; Wilkinson and Bleck, 1977; Cantor, 1977).

Often such support is sufficient, but for many, further treatment is required. In our experience many of the children also have persistent social-skill deficits and/or cognitive distortions that tend to interfere with their adaptation to their new situations. Moreover, many kinds of situations arise in which such children have no idea what they must do or say, for example, when a distant relative starts pitying them or when the parents are fighting about them, attempting to induce them to take sides.

In such situations both the modeling sequence and cognitive restructuring strategies might facilitate the adjustment. Systematic problem solving may also be helpful—to get a set of ideas about possible reactions in these difficult situations. In our experience it has been helpful for the group leader to begin by involving all of the children in (unstructured) discussion to develop in them a sense of commonality about their predicament. As problem situations arise that the members commonly view as problematic, these are handled with the appropriate behavioral or cognitive-behavioral strategy. In groups that deal with traumatic life changes, group leaders seem to go back and forth between the less directive and the more structured behavioral strategies.

Unfortunately, there is very little research to guide us in such groups. Self-reports from children and parents (where such have been noted) seem to support the efficacy of this approach as well as of the totally nondirective discussions (Bednar and Kaul, 1978).

Structurally, these groups are similar to most short-term groups. Although usually time-limited, such groups may also be open-ended. It appears that grouping is based solely on having a common problem and being within two or three years of each other in age. All the groups we have observed or participated in were composed of both boys and girls. Also, children of all ages seem to respond favorably to these groups. Although groups as small as two children have been conducted, the average size tends to be about eight to ten. This is usually determined by practical considerations. A group of six or seven would, in our opinion, be preferable for better individualization. Occasionally such issues as recently divorced parents, the death of a relative, and a permanent injury or impairment are dealt with in the whole class, especially where the given problem is a common one. This has often led to the establishment of small groups for children with one recent common traumatic experience. Recent life change is one of many general models that lend themselves to the multimethod group approach with children. Within each model, the specific theme of that group is usually identified by the group leader prior to the initiation of the group.

Group Themes

A group leader does not merely put a group together. He or she must consider the major theme of such a group and compose that group around that theme. The group theme provides the rationale for further decisions about the composition of the group, for planning a program, and for orienting prospective members and their significant others. The theme is determined on the basis of a common need established in the population served (see Chapter Three for a description of how such needs are determined).

Some of the major themes around which groups have been organized are: social-skill training for excessive shyness or aggressiveness, anger control, social-skill training for entire classes, stress management for anxious and often overly demanding children, pain management in a hospital, classroom self-management skill training, weight loss for overweight adolescents, smoke ending, alcohol and drug abuse, anorexia and bulimia, depressed adolescents, agoraphobia, pregnant teenagers, and adolescent job interviewing and preparation. These themes can be extended to many categories defined in the *Diagnostic and Statistical Manual* (1980; see Rapoport and Ismond, 1984). It should be noted (1) that the first principle of putting a group together is some degree of similarity within the range of the group theme and (2) that themes may fall into several of the general models mentioned earlier. For example, social-skill training groups, though usually short-term and time-limited, may also be open-ended, may be conducted indirectly within a cross-age tutoring program, or may be the major focus for some of the transitional groups.

Once a decision has been made about the general model and specific theme, the group leader must then decide, based on pregroup interviews and assessment strategies, whether a given individual should be in a group; what kinds of persons with what kinds of problems fit best together; the length, frequency, duration, and size of the group; and the number of group leaders in relation to the size. Once these decisions are made, they are discussed with potential members and their parents and teachers. Once a set of children select or are selected for the group, these decisions form the basis of a treatment contract. Each of these decisions are discussed below. But the question must first be answered—how do the children or their parents or teachers hear about the group?

Recruitment of Potential Group Members

One group leader, who had just entered a new school and observed in the classroom and on the playground and briefly interviewed a number of individuals, decided that it would be important to organize social-skill groups. After gaining the support of the principal and several of the teachers from whose classrooms children might be taken, she wrote letters to the parents of all the children in the fourth and fifth grades, asking which of them would be interested in having their children participate in social-skill training groups. She described the group and some of the goals that had been worked on in the school where she had previously worked. The response to the letter was overwhelming and yielded more children than the group leader could incorporate into her groups. Parents generally felt the existence of social problems that they could be quite explicit about and that the teachers were often unaware of. The children had to be interested in the group before they were admitted. The group leader also recruited a number of children referred by the teachers, once

they understood the program. Both the children
and their parents had to agree before they were admitted to the group.

The first prerequisite of a group program is obtaining an
adequate number of potential members. In order to identify
this population, a large number of people must become familiar
with the group program and consider it useful for themselves,
their children, their students, or their clients. A recruitment
campaign is an essential part of any group program, in spite of
the many advantages obvious to the group leader. In the above
example, the group leader demonstrated a number of recruitment procedures. Having determined there was a need, she discussed how a group program might meet this need with the
teaching staff and the principal in order to ensure their support. She then wrote the parents directly, describing the program and the potential benefits to the children. The enlistment
of the teachers' aid resulted in their better understanding of the
group, its purposes and methods; consequently, they became a
source of referrals as well.

In a child guidance clinic, the group leader learned
from the staff that there was no effective service
available for anxious young adolescents. Following lengthy discussions with the director and colleagues, he developed a small brochure that described the kinds of groups that might be useful to
that age group. He was allotted thirty minutes at
a staff meeting to explain the program and to answer questions about it. At that time he distributed
the brochure to clinic staff to give to appropriate
clients. He also advertised the group in the local advertising weekly as a service to be offered by the
clinic. He was able to obtain spots on the public
service and commercial radio stations. The director
also organized an interview with a feature writer in
the local paper. When this article appeared, it
seemed to draw the largest number of referrals.

Within several weeks, he had a sufficiently large number of candidates to begin the selection process.

This example demonstrates the following additional recruitment procedures: radio and newspaper advertising, a feature article in the newspaper, and the distribution of brochures to agency members. However, it was important once again to inform the staff and director and enlist their support, without which the recruitment program would not have gotten started.

A few additional recruitment strategies might also be considered. When the agency has a waiting list, groups become especially interesting to the potential clientele, who have already committed themselves to wanting help. Posters in the school and at the agency have attracted a number of applicants. One group leader arranged to be interviewed on a radio talk show in which she told about her program and its research foundations in great detail.

One group that is particularly difficult to recruit is adolescents. Referrals by adults, whether parents or teachers, are often ignored. One creative method by which adolescents have been recruited has been the "drop-in" group, which is a large, informal group of fifteen to forty children, usually adolescents, who come together in an open room whenever the agency or center is open. The drop-in group program is characterized by various informal activities scattered throughout the room. Usually there are several group leaders, each of whom stay with a given activity and attempt to learn names of the children, their interests, and eventually their concerns. Activities may consist of such programs as dancing in one corner, a set of pinball machines in another, an informal discussion session in another, a bike repair center, and a reading corner. Special events, such as dances or sports demonstrations, may be used to attract and maintain potential members.

The purpose of such an informal group is to bring in those adolescents who need help but who find it difficult to approach a person or an agency for individual or group counseling. The drop-in center provides a first step for the adolescent to meet with adults who have demonstrated that they accept and understand the problems of young people. Gradually discussion, problem-solving, sex education, study-skill improvement, dating, and job-finding groups can evolve out of the informal activities. These will occur publicly so that new members can observe or sit in whenever they choose. As the group develops, the adolescents may choose to become more focused in order to further their own learning.

In shifting from drop-in to treatment, a number of difficulties have been noted. Too-rapid transitions, highly-deviant group leadership, too-little cooperation, and inadequate resources may combine to prevent the adolescents' participation in the program. Nevertheless, the transition from drop-in to treatment or training groups has been achieved in numerous ways. Interest groups can be set up around the special problems unique to this group, such as dating, sexual information, job hunting, and school survival skills. Interested volunteers can be involved in publicizing and organizing these time-limited groups.

As common problems are noted, long-term treatment can be organized to which those adolescents with identifiable problems can be invited. During and following the transition phase, large-group activities are maintained to keep adolescents coming to the center or agency.

The community center is not the only agency in which drop-in programs have been organized. Both the school, through its social work or educational psychology program, and family service agencies have organized variations of the drop-in program with some success. Although there is some clinical experience with such groups, there are no data-based experiments or even data-based case studies. However, the need of something dramatic to attract the resistant adolescent recommends this alternative, especially when other more direct methods may have failed.

Once a successful recruitment program has been established, it needs to be screened and evaluated for its appropriateness and effectiveness in obtaining members. If the machinery is kept in place and modified to meet the changing needs of the community, it will serve the group leader well for a long period of time—as long as the programs meet the expectations of the children and their parents.

Once the potential members begin to refer themselves or be referred, a new set of decisions has to be made. Should the applicants be placed in a group, and if the answer is yes, what is the nature of that group?

Selection of Group Members

Prior to treatment, the group leader usually interviews the child and—depending on the resources of the agency and on the referral source—the parent, teacher, supervisor, parole officer, or other significant persons in the child's life. The purpose of these interviews is to make several basic decisions: Is treatment necessary? Is group treatment appropriate? What kind of group would work best for the potential member? And how should the group be composed? (These interviews also play a major role in orientation and assessment. The orientation function is discussed in a later section of this chapter. The assessment function is discussed further in the next two chapters.) In this section we shall focus on the interview's function in putting the group together. These three functions, however, often overlap. The group leader attempts to ferret out from each individual involved with the child at least some of the child's behavioral attributes and to focus on specific incidents in which they are manifested. Those interviews are usually brief, focused on precipitating events, and geared toward the interactive pattern of the child and adult, and of the child with other children.

To determine whether individuals should be treated at all, one should consider the ultimate consequences of their present pattern of behavior. In a third-grade class, for example, the ultimate consequence would have been suspension from or failure in school for several boys involved in aggressive behavior. One also should explore the concerns expressed by the teachers and parents during their interviews. In addition, there are certain practical considerations in recommendation for treatment. In the case of a teacher referral, do the parents agree? Are adequate alternate resources available? Is there a danger that treatment will only create an additional handicap if the child, as a result, is labeled "a troublemaker" or "sick"? Is there an appropriate group available to which the child can be assigned, or must the child be wait-listed. Is waiting on a list possible or would individual treatment be better? These questions can only be fully answered with knowledge of community agency resources.

A general guideline for placing a child in a group as opposed to individual treatment is "the absence of behavior so bizarre as to frighten others, and no wide differences that are personally or culturally beyond acceptance" (Klein, 1972, p. 60). Although it may be possible to have an entire group of children who occasionally hallucinate, one child who hallucinates may be far too threatening to the other children. Similarly, a group of passive children with a limited repertoire of assertive skills may be startled and frightened by a highly aggressive child, who might be better placed in another group. In the next section we deal with the procedures involved in appropriate composition.

Group Composition

Once each potential group member's problems have been described in a preliminary statement based on data from interviews and any pregroup testing and a decision has been made that group treatment is appropriate, the group leader must decide how the group should be composed. Though limited research exists in this area, we have attempted to develop several composition models from this research as well as from recent theory and clinical experience. Before determining the characteristics of its members, the first issue to be resolved is the size of the group.

Group Size. The size of a group depends on its purpose. Since individualization within a group context is highly valued, groups usually range in size from three to eight members. When smaller than three members, groups seem to lose many of the beneficial attributes discussed in Chapter One. Groups larger than eight make it difficult to permit every member to bring in a problematic situation at every meeting. We have also noted that members' satisfaction tends to increase until a total of six members has been reached, and to decline slightly after that. Most other authors dealing with treatment groups also recommend a similar range (Garvin, 1981; Yalom, 1985). In spite of agreement, there is little empirical research to support this or any other range.

There are clinical reasons to modify this range. In the initial phases, upwards of twelve adolescents have been put into one group to permit the adolescent to "look and see" and escape the intimacy of the small group. Occasionally, still larger drop-in groups of fifteen to thirty adolescents have been organized to permit experimenting in subgroups with a variety of programs, without putting too much pressure on the adolescent. Even in these cases the goal is to eventually establish a number of small-group and individual-treatment possibilities. Larger groups of younger children can also be treated successfully, provided that all the children share a common problem, or that there are two therapists who enable the group activities to frequently be conducted in subgroups.

In some cases, where there have been too few referrals, group leaders have started with a pair of children and added children as they were referred. The earlier-recruited children serve to orient the newer children, which affords the original children practice in their newly acquired skills and a chance to try out leadership skills.

The size of groups tends to change over time. Illness, dropouts, and referrals to other services often reduce group size. If the change in number is too dramatic, group cohesion and satisfaction tends to decrease. In some cases, the group leader may add new members to compensate for attrition. The possibility of modifying the existing composition is discussed below.

Behavioral Attribute Composition. Festinger (1954) points out that, when motivated to evaluate their opinions and abilities and when no objective standard exists, people tend to compare themselves to those who are similar rather than different. The implication for grouping is that each individual may differ from the others in some characteristics but that one needs to find someone in the group from whom there is not too much

distance in terms of social skills, social background, or presenting problem. On the basis of the above implication, one might
assume that it would be ideal to have a group composed entirely
of children with exactly the same presenting problem, for example, aggression towards other children. Our clinical experience
shows that groups of this nature become quite cohesive. However,
since the cohesiveness is based on similarities in the targeted
problem areas, considerable resistance, mutually reinforced, is
generated towards the group leader and against acceptance of
the treatment contract. Treatment of a group of adolescents
with unipolar depression resulted primarily in mutual support
of the belief in the importance of their problem and its underlying philosophy. Clinical experience and social-psychological
theory suggest, then, a somewhat more complex basis for grouping than similar or dissimilar behavioral manifestations.

　　It is useful to compose groups according to members' behavioral attributes and skills. The group leader ranks the behavioral deficits or assets of each member on a scale from one to
ten ("ten" representing a high level of the given characteristic).
Some of the possible categories are academic, problem-solving,
athletic, social, and handicraft skills. Some of these may be
broken down into smaller subcategories, the specific nature of
which depends on the assessed attributes of potential members.
Table 1 shows the analysis of behavioral attributes and recreational skills of one potential set of members. Based on pregroup
data, the group leader rated six children on each of the five
characteristics shown in the table. The number eight is equivalent to a high frequency of the given behavior. One is an extremely low frequency.

　　As one sees in this example, no one is left out. Storytelling was added as a means of finding a source of skills for which
Dennis could acquire some status in the group. It turns out that
Ron and Harry are quite aggressive and were referred to the
group for this behavior. If there had been only one it might
have been advisable to put him in the group. Everyone except
Ron was low in assertiveness, which is not surprising since this
is an assertiveness group. It is helpful to have at least one person
who might serve as a model in the problem area—Ron might

Table 1. Rated Characteristics of Assertiveness Group.

	Assert-iveness	Athletic Skills	Study Skills	Fight-ing	Story-telling
Ron	5	8	1	6	2
Harry	2	2	4	5	3
Ken	1	1	5	2	3
Leon	2	1	4	2	2
Tammi	2	3	2	1	1
Dennis	2	1	1	1	5

serve that role. The one danger is that Ron's prowess in athletic skills may isolate him from the others. If at least one other member (not always the same person) is near a child on most of the continua, it is possible to consider somewhat more heterogeneous groups. However, the more heterogeneous the target behaviors, the more time required to deal with everyone's target behaviors or situations.

Age and Socioemotional Development. In the above example all of the children were about the same age or socioemotional development. In most groups this similarity is preferred because a few markedly older children tend to dominate the younger children in decision making and other group processes, and a few markedly younger children find it difficult to participate at all. Occasionally a highly aggressive child is placed in a group of older or at least bigger children to protect the group. Occasionally, where there is an insufficient number of children at a given physical or developmental age, children with somewhat diverse problems are placed together. Though difficult, this is possible as long as the group leader is sensitive to the potentially disruptive effect, the disparate participation, and the differences in concerns. Usually such a group requires more time. A slightly older child is occasionally added as a model for the other children. Models are an essential component of any group for reasons discussed below.

Including a Model. Modeling is one of the major tools of intervention. Although the group leader may serve as model, group members are far more effective in this capacity. In heterogeneous groups, if requirements of the continua can be met, children with target behaviors in one area can often serve as models for children with target behaviors in another area. In homogeneous groups, models without major target problems may have to be placed in the group primarily for modeling rather than for their own treatment. In composing a group it is extremely helpful to include models for children with serious problems. These models should have at least some of the skills in which the target children are deficient. (This does not mean that the models do not have any behavioral or cognitive problems of their own.) The models should be as similar as possible to the target children with the exception of the target behavior. The ideal model is slightly older, slightly more intelligent, and slightly more competent in the target area, but not necessarily in all areas (Bandura, 1977b).

Some practitioners have expressed concern that the models or their parents may object to the model children being placed in the group with the fear that the model may learn undesirable behaviors from the target children. This has not been our experience. Parents and the children have, for the most part, been pleased to hear that their child seems to be getting along well socially and that they could be helpful to other children. Moreover, as parents often pointed out, there were a few situations that the best-adapted models also found difficult and could work on in the group. A discussion of how models are explicitly used in the group is presented in Chapter Six.

Gender Composition. Many of the examples in this book consist of either all boys or all girls. Nevertheless, in most cases we have attempted to put together, wherever possible, groups consisting of both sexes. As Hansen, Warner, and Smith (1980) note, situations in which mixed groups are productive far outnumber situations in which they are not. Certainly, with adolescents many of the problems concern the relationship between the sexes.

One problem we constantly have faced with mixed groups is that for latency-age children the group often divides into boy-girl subgroups immediately. Communication tends to be either among the boys or among the girls. Sometimes the norms of both genders are so in opposition that children will not go into an other-gender group. Another problem is that certain issues of central concern are not readily discussed in mixed groups.

We found that most of these problems can be addressed in the group and represent a valuable learning experience. Occasionally, we formally split the group into subgroups for the purposes of getting another point of view or broaching a topic that was not being developed. On the other hand, where the norms were strongly established, we often began with one gender and then, when the members expressed willingness, combined them with a group of the other gender.

Of course, some themes tend to attract more children of one gender than another, although this may vary from agency to agency or school to school. Moreover, we are often dependent on referrals from others who see certain problems as uniquely boy or girl problems. Furthermore, if we get only one referral in one gender and all the rest are in the other, we generally avoid, for reasons mentioned above, putting the isolate in such a group. As a result we often end up with all-male or all-female groups even though this is not always our intent. There have been many groups organized for just one sex by plan: a group for female adolescents with premenstrual syndrome; an assertiveness-training group for the second phase of a consciousness-raising group (where the members invited the group leader); a group of boys and a separate group of girls with a great deal of contact in other social contexts who requested their own "space" in separate stress-management groups.

Racial Composition. Wherever possible, groups are racially mixed. In schools where racial tensions are high or where the problems are peculiar to a given racial group, the group leader might consider the possibility of racially homogeneous groups, especially if only one referral is from a racially different group. However, at least with latency-age children, the preference is for the mixed group. In a school that had been recently integrated (through pairing of two schools), where we worked with seventeen social-skills groups—five classes of the entire fifth grade—we carefully integrated every group, both racially and sexually (Rose, Hepler, and Vinton, 1986). A pre- and postsociometric test revealed that relationships between racial groups improved significantly over time. Since there were no control groups, we cannot safely assume that the groups were the causal factor, but it remains a strong hypothesis.

Since socioeconomic factors are often closely related to racial differences, we have not discussed this issue as a separate topic. Even when the differences are not linked to racial factors, it is useful to have socioeconomic diversity for the same reasons as racial diversity. The problems of socioeconomic differences within a group are similar to those of racial differences.

Modifying Existing Groups. Unfortunately, even when the group is carefully composed we are not always able to find the correct combination. Sometimes as a means of resolving group problems it becomes necessary to add new members. In one situation, after the second meeting we discovered that our original assessment failed to take into consideration aggressive behavior in response to the unique characteristics of the group. The following pattern had become clear: all except Harvey, a rather quiet child, were at the upper end of the aggression scale (that is, they were aggressive in a wide variety of situations) and, as a result, Harvey became a scapegoat. With the addition of two others who were unassertive in most situations and, like Harvey, rarely aggressive, Harvey was provided with some support, and he was less isolated and scapegoated than before.

Of course, all of the above principles are meant to serve as guidelines to the group leader. Often practical issues impinge upon the careful composition of children's groups. Nevertheless, with some minor adjustments, the practical barriers can be overcome. For example, a third-grade teacher referred three children to the group leader: two girls who rarely interacted with others and a boy who was so aggressive none of the other children would play with him. Even though the composition of this group did not meet the standards described above, the group leader attempted to correct for this by adding as models an additional boy and girl. This reduced the isolation of the one target boy and provided all of the members with feasible models.

Complications. With all of the above principles neatly outlined, the reader may be surprised to find that some situations arise in which composition becomes a nightmare. In a mental health clinic, referrals trickled in at the rate of one every week or two. The problems were quite diverse: enuresis, depression, obesity, impulsive problem solving. The ages were also disparate, ranging from nine to fourteen. The group leader initially met individually with some of the children and in pairs and triads with others who had similar problems and who were in the same developmental phase. Gradually as these members became more numerous, with agreement of the children, he joined a dyad and triad and an individual together. All six children in this group had social-skill deficits and cognitive distortions for which they continually put themselves down. The age range was from twelve to fourteen, and the group was evenly divided between boys and girls. The reasons for the original referrals were quite different, although they shared the problems mentioned above. Since this was a clinic it was difficult to find a model. The group leader used case studies of models that the group discussed from time to time. As additional younger children were added to the potential member roster, the group leader put together a group of younger children. He used one of the better-adapted twelve-year-olds as the model for the younger children, with permission of the parent. As in this example, group leaders may be forced to use the guidelines as points of great departure along with their creative initiative.

Summary. Homogeneity in presenting problem is desirable, provided models are present in the group. Some degree of heterogeneity in behavioral attributes is possible, provided that each child has a "neighbor" in the group along each behavioral continuum. To facilitate communication, homogeneity of developmental age is recommended. Diversity in such areas as socio-economic status has not resulted in serious problems and, in fact, has proven advantageous in many instances. In most cases, homogeneity in developmental age is useful for preventing isolation and providing a reasonable distribution of communication among the members. In most instances diversity in sexual and racial composition is also desirable. At least one person in the group should be able to serve as a model in a target area for the others. Finally, it should be noted that group composition is never final. Adjustments can be made by adding new members and/or by splitting the group into several subgroups. (See Bertcher and Maple, 1971, for a training manual in group-composition principles similar to those espoused above.)

Once the group is composed it must meet somewhere. The location is strongly influenced by the auspices of the organization. Both agency auspices and setting are discussed below.

Group Settings

Though not all social agencies provide treatment facilities for children, the examples in this book are drawn from a broad sample of education, recreation, and welfare organizations as well as from private practice. The youngest children's groups were organized under the auspices of nursery-school and Head Start programs, and a large number of groups were organized in elementary, junior, and senior high schools. Group treatment has also been sponsored by community centers and settlement houses. One community center used the groups as the basis of a first offenders project with the back of a station wagon or a storefront as the meeting room (Rose and others, 1971). Typical psychiatric outpatient services, such as mental health and child guidance clinics, have also been experimenting with behaviorally focused small groups. In addition, this approach has been utilized in correctional institutions (Brierton, Rose, and Flanagan, 1975) and small treatment homes (Phillips, 1968), where groups are used to train children in behaviors needed to adapt to the institution or to negotiate the demands of the outside world. Hospitals and health clinics have sponsored pain- and stress-management, weight-loss and other eating-disorder, smoking-cessation, and alcohol and drug-abuse groups—for adolescent outpatients as well as inpatients.

In most cases, the setting for a given group is within the walls of the sponsoring agency. There are however many creative exceptions to this pattern. Groups have met not only in the schools, agencies, storefronts, and station wagons mentioned above, but also in members' homes, homemade club-

houses, restaurants, and so forth. The principles involved in
these natural settings are twofold: simulate as nearly as possible the setting in which the problems occur and find as attractive a setting as possible to increase the attractiveness of the
group. When the two principles are in conflict, we begin with
increasing attractiveness and later simulate the real world.

Although it is desirable to have adequate space, recreational equipment, audiovisual aids, movable chairs, equipment
for sports and crafts, and other facilities, most group treatment
is carried out with only a few of these amenities. In our opinion
such facilities enhance groups but are neither necessary nor sufficient for successful outcomes. In most cases group leaders take
advantage of whatever facilities are available to them (or are
struggled for). It is indeed helpful to have a regular place to
meet—at least for the first few meetings—and some protection
from interruption.

Frequency, Length, and Duration of Group Sessions

Most groups discussed in this book are time-limited, and
meet for approximately one hour a week for about eight weeks.
Regular weekly sessions are the general pattern rather than the
more variable schedule recommended below, primarily because
of the personal or work schedules of the families, of the children, and of the group leader rather than for any particular
treatment rationale. Ideally we prefer at least two and sometimes three meetings per week during the initial phase of treatment, with frequency gradually fading to once a week, later to
once every two weeks, and eventually to once a month for the
remainder of the treatment year. In practice we have not succeeded in departing from the weekly schedule until the end of
treatment, when bimonthly and monthly sessions have become
somewhat more common. The reason for a gradually decreasing
frequency of meetings is based on a principle of maintenance
of learning. In research on learning, it is suggested that when
reinforcement is reasonably continuous, newly learned behaviors will rapidly fade away if reinforcement is terminated too
abruptly (Goldstein, Heller, and Sechrest, 1966). If one assumes
that the group is a source of a great deal of reinforcement, then

in the beginning phase there should be many meetings to build the desired behaviors into the child's repertoire as quickly as possible; in later phases, there can be fewer meetings and longer time periods between meetings in order to maintain the desired behaviors after the group has terminated.

The exact number of sessions depends on the purpose of the group, its composition, and certain practical limitations. In heterogeneous groups, to deal with treatment goals of a wide range of problems, ten to sixteen sessions are usually required. The same number of sessions are required for groups with complex treatment goals that involve many diverse situations. In groups with preventative goals, such as social-skill training for the entire classroom, eight sessions have been sufficient for the majority of children (LeCroy and Rose, 1986). When a highly specific and limited goal is pursued, still fewer sessions may suffice. For example, a number of adolescents wanted to learn how to interview for a seasonal job at a local cheese factory. Two sessions were sufficient for demonstrating and practicing simple interviewing skills and providing information about appearance.

Children's groups, even in nonschool settings, are usually organized in conjunction with the school semester. It is a rare group that is carried out during the summer months, although some groups may be connected with treatment summer camps or residential treatment centers. Referrals usually begin in October when parents and teachers are frustrated with the response of the children to demands at home, to social situations, to pressures at school and in playgrounds, or in other extra-school situations. The groups organized at this time will last until the Christmas break, until April, or until the end of the school year. New groups may be started in January and meet until the end of the school year. Adolescent groups have a way of fading at the beginning of spring. We have rarely carried groups over into a second year, although individuals have been referred to other treatment groups for periods as long as three years. In general, however, assuming major goals have been achieved after one set of treatment sessions, children are referred to nontreatment groups such as at the YMCA or YWCA or Girl or Boy Scouts. Referral to individual treatment may also occur.

Some groups are organized on a completely different

time basis. For example, some adolescent groups may meet for a marathon three Saturdays in a row for six to seven hours each Saturday. Some group leaders have organized entire weekends for as long as ten hours a day for treatment groups. In institutions, transitional groups (mentioned earlier in this chapter) meet from one to three hours daily from their start until termination, which is usually about three to six weeks later. In one recent project the entire seventh and eighth grades received a one-hour treatment session daily for two weeks (LeCroy and Rose, 1986). In general, though, intensive daily programs are avoided. Marathons and daily meetings restrict the frequency and relevance of homework assignments, which are an important part of this approach. Since the only research for determining the adequate length of groups has been with adults, group leaders have felt free to experiment with many variations. In adult treatment groups for social anxiety, D'Alelio and Murray (1981) demonstrated that eight two-hour sessions were significantly more effective than four two-hour sessions.

As we mentioned earlier the open-ended groups have no set duration. When the group leader or the child provides evidence that goals have been attained and a plan for generalization has been designed, the child may terminate. Of course, in such groups termination of a given individual may also occur against the advice of the group leader as the attraction of the group fades for that individual.

Number of Group Leaders

As the number of group leaders in any one group increases, so does the cost to the parent or to the agency. There is no evidence that two group leaders are more effective than one, assuming they are both experienced. In most cases one group leader is adequate and less costly. There are, however, several situations that call for more than one group leader. (See also Middleman, 1980; and Galinski and Schopler, 1980.) A second group leader might be considered in the following cases.

1.   If the second leader is a trainee.

2. If both leaders are leading a new type of group for the first or second time.
3. If the second leader is a supervisor of the first.
4. If the second leader alternates with the first as observer (having an observer, however, is cheaper).
5. If there are clearly demonstrated skills necessary to lead the group, and these skills are split between the leaders.
6. If the group is larger than eight (although it is usually better to have two groups if the group is as large as ten).
7. If one leader is unlikely to be able to remain with the group until the end. Usually in this case, one leader is gradually faded in and the other is faded out.
8. In groups of highly active or aggressive children where control is initially a major problem.

It should also be noted that coleaders sometimes create problems for themselves and the group by competing with each other, by dominating the group interaction, and by frequent amplification and repetition of what the other says.

Orienting the Group Members

Another way of structuring the group and the members' expectations is to provide some orientation to the activities and procedures to be used. This is done in several ways. As noted above, the pregroup interviews with the child and parents are an ideal place to begin and are one of the major vehicles of orientation. Another context of orientation is the first group meeting of the children or of their parents. As group meetings begin, discussions of the group contract provide a broad orientation to the entire approach. On a weekly basis, the group-session agenda provides an orientation to that specific activity. Finally, as each new intervention procedure is introduced and discussed, a specific orientation to each procedure is provided.

Orienting the Child. In the individual pregroup interview, in addition to obtaining data for assessing the problem and planning for the group, children are given details about the group program—how it might be of help to them, the kind of children that might be in the group with them, and the sociorecreational activities. At the end of the interview, the children should have at least a global idea of what they can expect and what will be expected from them. In order to give a clear idea about the group, videotapes may be shown or former members may describe their experiences at the first group session.

Orienting the Parents. Whenever the parents' interest warrants it, a parents' meeting prior to the first children's group session is organized to tell the parents what they can expect to occur in their children's group. Occasionally the parents have asked for additional group sessions for themselves to learn the skills being used by the group leader. In the Hartwig Project (Rose and others, 1971), we learned that cooperation by either the parents or the teachers dramatically increased the likelihood of success. The parent meeting usually obtains that cooperation. When a meeting is not possible, orientation to the group occurs in individual sessions or on the phone.

These sessions or individual contacts include an explanation of the group's purpose and activities, the type of behaviors and situations to be worked on, the role of homework and the ways in which the parents might help in that area, and a brief explanation of the major intervention strategies. Videotapes of children's groups as well as brief testimonials by parents of children in previous groups are included in the parent session.

Treatment Contracts. An important procedure for orienting the children to the group and ensuring that they understand the nature and purpose of the group is the treatment contract. An example follows:

> We, the members of the Players, agree to discuss the problems we're having at home and at school and to try to help each other find better ways of dealing with them. We'll do lots of roleplaying, too. We also agree to come to all meetings and on time. In return, Ms. Johnson and the clinic will give us a room to meet in, refreshments, games, and trips, and she'll lead the group every week. We shall

spend at least as much time talking and roleplaying as doing the other fun things during the meetings. We understand that there will be eight meetings and that each meeting will last forty-five minutes.

The above agreement is an example of a treatment contract for a group of eleven- and twelve-year-old boys and girls. The treatment contract involves a statement, usually in writing, of the general responsibilities of the members on one hand and the group leader and agency on the other, over an extended period of time. It usually specifies goals and commonly used procedures as well as mutual expectations. One important condition of a group treatment contract is that the members agree to help one another. The treatment contract differs from a contingency contract in that the latter specifies a more narrow relationship between an expected member's behavior and the reinforcement that follows. The treatment contract is broader in scope and covers a longer time period.

There is evidence to support the contention that clear knowledge about treatment and agreement to participate are prerequisites for success in treatment (Hoehn-Saric and others, 1964). Ausubel (1963) provides evidence that links success in learning with advance knowledge about what one is to learn. It also appears that knowledge about the parameters of a situation reduces one's anxiety about that situation. For these reasons, a treatment contract is a major strategy in orientation for structured group treatment.

The contract, however, is not a static set of statements or agreements. As the relationships of the members to each other are established, negotiation skills are enhanced, and early expectations are clarified, the contracts begin to get greater input from the members. The contracts increasingly reflect the members' ideas of what they can learn from the group. Moreover, a growing degree of detail and structure is added to the contract. One cannot clarify every detail at a first meeting. The group leader must successively structure the contract in a step-by-step process as the members experience growing success and satisfaction with the approach (Rotter, 1966). In the initial example, after the members had interacted with each other for several meetings, the revised contract had developed as follows:

> We, the members of the Players, agree to bring to each meeting a problem situation that we encountered during the week for which each will seek the help of the group. These problem situations are usually events that occur with other people in which we are dissatisfied with what we did or said. We will then help each other through demonstrations and roleplaying to try out new ways of dealing with the problems. We agree to do homework between meetings, which will usually be to try out what we learned in the group. We understand that at the end of each meeting we will evaluate the meeting and our own behavior in the meeting. Should group problems arise, we will discuss them with each other. We still will continue to have refreshments and games at each meeting and, should we earn it, a field trip at the end of next month. We also get to meet in the music room from now on and to play the piano if we don't mess around with it. Ms. Johnson will also coach us to be the discussion leaders of the group ourselves, but only if we volunteer.

Early in the treatment of highly resistive members, the contract may be informal and extremely general, in stark contrast to the example above. Members' expectations may be minimal. Adolescents may be asked only to observe and to participate when they are willing. The only expectation is that they not be disruptive. They are made aware of the group leader's long-term expectations, but initially the members are asked to do nothing to advance those therapeutic goals. Vinter (1974a) refers to this as a preliminary treatment contract. The preliminary treatment contract in our experience is primarily useful with highly resistive members and/or juvenile offenders. The following is an example of a preliminary contract.

The eight group members, all early juvenile offenders were referred to the agency by the police. At the first session they were reluctant to discuss problems or the reasons that brought them into contact with the police. Since it was winter and they had no place to go, they agreed to meet with the group leader twice a week, use the school gym, and eat the food provided by the group leader. In exchange they agreed to spend fifteen minutes talking about the school and their families. They also said they understood that they had to follow the school rules or they would be kicked out of the meeting. It was clear that the group leader could not initially expect them to take much responsibility for their own actions. The above minimal contract was informal but it provided a preliminary contact and promised a more treatment-oriented contract at a later date.

For most groups initially, and for the above group in a later phase of development, the treatment contract is more specific and more demanding of the members. Just as the group treatment contract orients the child and significant others to the overall group approach, the use of weekly session agendas developed with the children orients the child to the expectations and structure of each meeting.

Session Agendas

Most group leaders use the session agenda to plan their weekly meetings. The agendas are either put on the blackboard or mimeographed and distributed to the members. Most children and adolescents seem impressed with having a typed agenda that they can show to friends and family. Initially the agenda is planned by the group leader. Later the children are involved in the planning. At the end of a meeting the group leader may describe his or her tentative plan for the next meeting for the group's comments. Some group leaders have had special planning sessions between meetings with representatives of the group.

Thus, the agenda is an excellent planning document as well as a tool for orientation and provides one more opportunity for children and adolescents to be involved in the planning process. Furthermore, the agenda makes it possible to set limits in a nonpersonalized way on off-task behavior, as we see in the following example.

Group leader: How many people would like to tell us what they did last week?

Larry: The last meeting was really fun. Could we play that game again?

Group leader: Gee, Larry, let's talk about that when we get to "evaluation" on the agenda. Right now we're talking about "homework"; that's item number 1.

One example of an agenda taken from the above adolescent group is the following:

1.   Review homework.
2.   Review evaluations from the previous week and homework completion-rate data.
3.   Discuss problem of irregular attendance in group; then problem solve what we can do about it.
4.   Plan for next week's meeting with guests from school.
5.   Roleplay Harry's and Annette's situation in trying to talk to the teacher.
6.   Provide feedback and discuss talking with teachers in general.
7.   Design homework for next week in pairs.
8.   Play board game for ten minutes.
9.   Evaluate.

Summary

We have described many types of groups that can use the multimethod approach. These include time-limited, open-ended, cross-age tutoring, transitional, maintenance, and recent-life-change groups. Some of these groups had central behavioral themes such as managing stress, learning new social skills, managing depression, losing weight, and dealing with alcohol and drugs. Methods of recruitment and selection were discussed. Principles of group composition in terms of size, behavioral attributes, relative age and socioeducational developmental level, inclusion of a model, and gender and racial balance were discussed. Other organizational concerns were evaluated, such as the optimal setting, frequency, and duration of group sessions, and the number of group leaders needed.

In the closing section, the function of orientation was described and illustrated. Examples of such orientation tools as treatment contracts and session agendas were presented. Throughout the chapter the need for adequate information for both planning and orientation was emphasized.

In the next chapter we look more closely at the process by which information is accrued and at assessment and its several purposes. Above all, we scrutinize assessment's central relationship to the multimethod group approach.

Chapter Three

Assessing Children's Problems and Resources

Marnie is eleven years old and in the sixth grade. She has been referred to the group by her teacher for having often physically threatened and, on several occasions, attacked other students. Marnie told the group members that she gets frustrated with others, especially when they cheat at games or call her names and then she "lets them have it." In reporting about a number of such incidents, she consistently reports the use of threats or actual violence as her major method of resolving conflicts. She says it does not matter because no one likes her anyway. She likes active sports but most children do not want to play with her.

Judd, a seven-year-old, told the other members of the family change group that every time he thinks about his recently divorced parents he becomes sad and he feels very lonely. He told other group members that he wonders what he could do to get his parents back together again. Then he told himself what an awful kid he must have been to have caused his parents to divorce. When the other members asked him what would be fun for him to do, Judd said he could not think of anything. He was too upset to play or do anything like play.

Suzanne is a fifth grader who teases the other children in the group viciously and rarely compliments or makes other positive statements to them. She says that her goal in the group is to make new friends, but because the kids in her class and in the group are so "touchy," she claims she has trouble doing so. For example, she wanted to be friends with Charlene, another group member, so she teased her about the scar on her face "just to be funny." Suzanne said she was surprised when Charlene ran out of the room crying.

Sid, a fourth grader, is a member of a weight-loss group. He says he has a lot of trouble refusing ice cream and other sweets when they are offered by family members or kids at school. Sid also puts himself down a lot. He often makes statements in the group meetings such as, "I'll never have any will power," "nobody will ever like me," and "I feel fat and ugly and I'll never get any better." In an interview the teacher told the group leader that Sid spends much of his free time using pencils, crayons, and paint in creating artwork. While the artwork is high-quality and very creative, the teacher was concerned about how isolated Sid had become.

Marnie, Judd, Suzanne, and Sid present problems that represent the concerns that children and adolescents bring to the group-treatment setting. This chapter presents guidelines for the assessment of individual behavioral, affective, and cognitive problems and the situations in which they occur. It focuses on a description of the major elements in the assessment process prior to setting treatment goals. Before examining this process, let us examine the purposes of assessment.

Purposes of Assessment

The major purposes of assessment in small-group treatment are to formulate the presenting problem to determine whether a child can utilize a small treatment group to resolve the problem(s), to ascertain what kind of group can best serve him or her, to identify individual and group plans of intervention, to evaluate whether ongoing treatment is having an impact or whether the completed treatment was effective, and, finally, to contribute to knowledge about the parameters of the treatment strategies in general.

To achieve these purposes, problems presented by the children, their parents, or teachers are formulated together with the children in terms of concrete overt and covert behavior, as it occurs in a specified situational context. In these situations, goals are mutually developed for behavioral change that can be achieved within the limits of the group's duration and maintained following group treatment. The group leader, in continued collaboration with the children, also identifies two more factors: personal and environmental resources for achieving treatment goals, and those personal and environmental attributes that might inhibit or enhance treatment. Decisions regarding the suitability of a child for a group and the composition of a group were discussed in the previous chapter. Another purpose of assessment is to determine the existence of group problems for resolution. Procedures for collecting relevant group data and strategies for identifying and resolving such problems are discussed in Chapter Eleven.

In this chapter we shall describe how situational and resource analysis contribute to treatment planning; the varied ways in which data are collected for situational analysis; and, unique to this text, how the group is used in the process of individual data collection and situational analysis. How these situations are used in evaluation and research is discussed in Chapter Four.

The multimethod and other cognitive-behavioral approaches to assessment are quite different from traditional approaches, which emphasize diagnosis of personality traits. Mash and Terdal (1981, p. 17) have stated that children who "present themselves for assessment show characteristic behavior-situation patterns or clusters, rather than specific target symptoms, and that assessment can best proceed from an understanding of such characteristic patterns." In multimethod group assessment "the focus shifts from describing situation-free people with broad trait adjectives to analyzing the specific interactions between conditions and the cognitions and behaviors of interest" (Mischel, 1973, p. 265).

It should be noted that, though the focus of the pregroup interviews and the early group sessions is on assessment, it is a process that continues throughout treatment. Initially, determining the appropriate group and individual target problems are the focuses of assessment. Later, continuing assessment is used to facilitate decision making. Finally, assessment shifts to evaluating the ongoing progress and outcomes of individuals and the group.

Each of the components is described separately for purposes of analysis. The foundation of the assessment process is the behavior in a situation. Let us look at some analyses of situational behavior.

Situational Analyses

I guess I worry a lot. For example, yesterday, when my mom was gone, and I was alone in my bedroom for a while, I worried that she might die and then I'd be alone forever.

I am lonely most of the time but I guess I don't do much about it. For instance, when I saw some kids my age playing together Saturday on the playground in the park near my house, I wanted to ask if I could play, but I didn't because I knew they'd say no.

I have a lot of trouble controlling what I eat, even though I know better. Even though I didn't feel hungry, last night while I was watching TV, and no grown-up was at home, I got something to eat every few minutes—bread, potato chips, and stuff like that. I often do that when I'm alone.

Just this morning, some older kids were teasing me in the hall at school, but they didn't hit me or anything like that. I started yelling names at them, and

I punched one of 'em out. That's when the principal caught me. That was third time something like that happened this week. I'm going to get suspended, but I can't control it. Nobody is going to push me around.

If one examines the above incidents, one can identify a situation, a response, and, in some cases, a consequence of that response. When a child complains of a problem or an adult complains that a child is presenting a problem, the locus of that problem is the behavior of the child in a given situation or set of situations. Either (1) the desired behavior is not present or infrequent (for example, a child who is not sharing toys in a play situation) or (2) an undesirable or excessive behavior (such as abusive language or a temper tantrum in response to an adult instruction or command) is present in response to the situation. Treatment would usually involve modification of the consequences of the behavior, modification of the situation itself, and/or direct demonstration and practice in the target behavior. For this reason, in assessment, the situation, the response of the child to the situation, and the consequences of the situation are carefully examined. Although it is difficult to separate the behavior from its situation and its consequences, we shall briefly examine the kind of situations most commonly occurring in group treatment.

The Situation

In the above examples, the children identified recurring situations to which they had responded with inappropriate behaviors or cognitions. Each is problematic or stress-inducing to the child who described it. The goal of treatment would be either to help the children modify their situational responses or evaluation or to help them change or even avoid the situation. None of these strategies can be determined without a careful description of the components of the situation and the child's responses to it.

The following questions should be asked in the interview

or in the group: Who was involved? When did the situation occur? What was happening? Where did it take place? What were
the characteristics of that location? Was this a recurring event?
And what was the child's response to the situation? Answers to
each of these questions often reveal the appropriate method of
intervention. Children rarely, at least in the initial phases of
treatment, describe problems in sufficiently specific terms.
When a new situation is introduced, the above questions are
asked first by the group leader and later by the children of each
other.

Two types of situations stand out because of their implication for differential treatment in groups: interactive and noninteractive. In interactive situations, the child describes an event
that involves talking to, playing with, or in other ways commu-
nicating with other people. In group treatment most situations
are interactive, since interaction can be simulated and can be
altered by modeling, cognitive restructuring, and other procedures commonly applied in the multimethod approach. In
groups, however, that focus on such behaviors as excessive eating, poor study habits, reduced alcohol and drug intake, increased exercise, and similar behaviors that require extensive
"self control," the purpose of situational analysis is to determine the conditions under which the target behaviors occur. In
noninteractive situations, the term *antecedent conditions* is
commonly used instead of *situation* (Cormier and Cormier,
1985, p. 185).

We have found it useful to group children with similar
types of problem situations. Such commonality makes the intervention process more efficient because of mutual modeling of
self-disclosure and the discovery of a wealth of potential alternative responses. The group leader can also devote more time to
a shared situation since it is relevant to almost all the members
of the group. All of the examples in the preceding section involved shared situations with some or all of the group members.

One of the advantages of the group is that problematic
and stressful situations arise within the normal interaction of
the group. For example, one child pushes another by accident
and the second child attacks him violently. In another group a

child refuses to share the scissors even though only one pair of scissors is available. Since such situations are directly observed by all the members and the group leader, a great deal of reliable information is available. Most other situations rely solely on the self-report of the child with the problem. The in-group situations provide a natural setting for reanalyzing and redoing them and finding more effective responses to them.

Thus far we have discussed situations as if they occurred as isolated events. However, situations often occur in a sequence, as in the following examples:

> Ellie told the group members that she was being taunted by Bernie (situation one). She responded by crying, to which Bernie in turn responded with still more vicious teasing (situation two). Ellie then told how she ran crying hysterically from the playground with Bernie looking on and laughing.

> Rog described a situation in which he was really tired and grouchy when the teacher asked him to clean the blackboard (situation one). He responded by telling her he was too tired and he admitted that his tone of voice might have been a little unpleasant. The teacher then changed her request to an angry demand (situation two), to which he responded by swearing at her. The result was that he was sent to the principal, who called his mother.

In these two examples, as in most other situations, the group leaders must look not only at the isolated incident but at the entire sequence of situations to obtain an accurate picture of a situation's relevance.

Overt Behavior. In most of the above examples the responses to the situations were either overt behavior or cognitions; at times they may have also been emotional. In each case the overt behavior could be specifically described and observed. In almost all instances the behavior was a response to a given situation. The behaviors were often inappropriate or maladap-

tive in that the responses failed to resolve the problem, to reduce the inherent stress, or to maximize the probability of
achieving the child's goals. For example, when Peter was asked
to do anything by his mother, he would begin to whine. In
other situations the appropriate behaviors were absent or of insufficient frequency to meet the child's goals. For example,
when asked to lend others his car or his money, Aaron (who
wanted to refuse) was unable to refuse in a decisive manner.
Much of assessment is aimed at identifying and defining behaviors that become the target of change. These behaviors are defined in highly specific terms that lend themselves to observation and monitoring.

Cognitions. Cognitions are regarded as private or covert
behaviors. These have been described as thoughts, beliefs, images, conceptual schemes, values, evaluations, and/or silent self-
instructions. A cognition is usually identified by asking the
child to describe it in writing or aloud, or it is deduced from
other behaviors or statements. We are particularly concerned
with cognitions as responses to situations or recurring thoughts
in certain types of situations. In an earlier example, one child
had the recurring thought he might die. In another, the child responded to a difficult situation by silently predicting his absolute failure to achieve his goal. In a third situation, a child evaluated himself as a "total loss." All of these are examples of
cognitions requiring the attention of the group leader. Because
of their private quality, cognitions are difficult to ascertain.
Nevertheless, since they often appear to impinge on the resolution of many problematic situations, it is important to explore
their presence as a response to problematic situations with the
children.

Affective Responses. Affective responses refer to the
emotional reaction to or in a given situation. In general they are
identified by the statement a child makes: for example, "I felt
awful when he said that; I was really angry when he pushed me
down; I was depressed sitting at home all alone yesterday; and I
was excited when our team won the ball game." The distinction
between cognitive and affective statements is not always clear,
since one often uses a cognitive statement to describe the af-

fect. Affective responses can often be identified from nonverbal cues, especially with younger children. Excitement, depression, joy, fatigue, and disgust seem often to emanate from their face, body posture, and other nonverbal cues in play and therapeutic work. Yet group leaders vary in their skill in identifying these cues. It is often helpful to check these cues with the child and the other group members to see whether the child indeed feels the affective response perceived by the group leader. "I have the feeling that Jen is really upset at losing that game. Am I right, Jen? What do some of the rest of you think? I guess losing is a little difficult for a lot of us."

As we review the potential targets of change, we view them as overt behavior or covert cognitions and affective responses to carefully described situations. For purposes of analysis, the situation and its responses have been separated. In practice they are usually inseparable.

The Critical Moment

To determine the nature of the link between an interactive situation and the response, the "critical moment" concept is proposed. The interface between the interactive situation and the response is the critical moment. It is the point at which the child determines that a response is called for. Arnold describes a recent encounter as follows: "At the moment that Jerry brushed up against me in the hall, I hit him." The critical moment is that instant in time in which Arnold had just experienced being brushed by Jerry. If further enquiry led Arnold to state, "Actually, when I heard Jerry coming down the hall, I positioned myself so that I could be bumped," the critical moment would be that instant after he heard Jerry coming down the hall. The nature of the eventual intervention would change with a change from what was originally defined as the critical moment.

The purpose of establishing a critical moment is to determine that point in time when the child could do (think and/or feel) something other than what he or she actually did (thought and/or felt). With younger children the term *tough point* has often been used instead of the more technical term *critical mo-*

ment. Older children have jokingly used the expression, "the moment of truth."

In any complicated event or set of ongoing interactions, there are often multiple critical moments. For example, when Penny, who was rushing to get out of the house on time for school, tripped over her brother's lunch box (the first critical moment), she yelled at her brother, who ran screaming to their mother. Mother, in turn, told her to leave Pierre alone (the second critical moment), so Penny screamed it was his fault, angrily slammed the door, and ran out of the house. Her mother called her back and began to admonish her once again (the third critical moment), to which Penny responded, "I'll be late forever." In the group, Penny would have been asked to identify the critical moment of most concern to her. The group would then help her to find alternative responses at the selected critical moment.

If the group leader and/or members do not agree that a given moment is the most critical, the members will discuss it. But the child whose situations are being discussed is the final arbiter of his or her own critical moment, based on the child's perception of which situation in a sequence is the most difficult for him or her to handle. In the evaluation of various alternative responses, children will often shift unquestioningly from one critical moment to another if the critical moment of concern is not momentarily, at least, pinned down. We shall discuss the implication of the critical moment for treatment throughout the intervention chapters.

Immediate and Long-Term Consequences

A child's response to a given situation has both immediate and long-term consequences. Heloise's violent responses to losing games (swearing, blaming others for their mistakes, shoving those she blames) has the immediate consequence of getting her thrown out of the game by the teachers and the long-term result of her being ostracized by her peers. Immediate consequences may appear to be negative, as in the above case, but in some cases may still be reinforcing. (Heloise's behavior may be reinforced by the teachers' and the other girls' attention.) Similarly, Anatole's worrying aloud to his peers about the slightest low grade results immediately in derision from them and in extended feelings of unhappiness.

In some cases the immediate consequences alter the nature of the child's response pattern and, as a result, may become the major source of intervention. For example, Lucky's crying response to the least provocation by other children has as an immediate consequence the teacher's running to him on the playground and consoling him. If such a consequence were withheld for an extended period of time, it is likely that the crying would diminish. Identification of immediate consequences in the assessment phase of group treatment points the way to the selection of intervention strategies in the next phase.

Identifying Problematic Situations

Having described the major elements in a situational analysis, we shall now elaborate on the procedures used to collect the information necessary for developing such an analysis. Many of the techniques make systematic use of the unique characteristics of the group.

Group Procedures. A number of strategies are used to identify problematic situations. These include individual and group interviewing, group discussion, keeping a diary, case studies, assessment roleplays, and behavioral checklists. These same strategies may be employed to train the members in identifying appropriate and inappropriate responses to those situations. In the following sections we discuss children's training in the use of these procedures as well as their function in the data-gathering process.

Group and Individual Interviewing. In the initial interviews and in the first group sessions children are asked to describe situations in which they are unhappy or dissatisfied with their responses. Often this technique alone is sufficient to provide a wide range of responses that require only further specification in the group. This request is often preceded by the group leader's providing examples from his or her own experience or from previous group members.

Often, the descriptions initially provided by the children are too general or too vague. In the following example, the group leader has given cards to a group of fourth graders with the words *who, what, where, when,* or *recent* written on them. The children were instructed to ask a question using the word on their cards when another child described a problem situation.

Sparky: My situation is that I don't like to be bossed around.

Group leader: Who has the card with the word *recent* on it?

Toni: My card says, "recent." Tell us about a recent (looks at group leader) . . . aaah?

Group leader: Experience?

Toni: Yeah, that's it . . . a recent experience. Tell us about a recent experience.

Sparky: Last week when I was playing with someone on the playground, Danielle came over and bossed us around.

Group leader: Who's got another card?

Claire: My card says "who." Who were you playing with?

Sparky: I was playing house with Emily.

Sunny: Hey that's my question, what were you doing? Oh well, what did Danielle do that was so bossy?

Sparky: When Danielle asked to play with us, we said, "Okay." But then she said she didn't want to play house; she had to play tag. We didn't want to but she got mad, so we played tag anyway. We don't like her bossing us around.

This procedure is only used as long as the children are unable to interview each other without the cards. Eventually, the cards are eliminated and replaced with verbal cues by the group leader. Ultimately, the cues are eliminated entirely. Thus, the children not only help each other to develop useful situations, they also learn how to become involved in group discussion.

Keeping a Diary. Once the children are trained (through questioning one another) in the correct formulation of problematic events, they are then asked to keep a diary of situations in which they are both satisfied and dissatisfied with their responses. The satisfied situations afford an opportunity to reinforce the children while the others provide the potential targets of change. Even if the child is satisfied, the group leader or members may disagree—which points to another potential target situation for the child. The diaries are discussed at the beginning of every session.

To train children in the use of diaries, model diaries are presented and discussed. An exercise is given in which part of a diary entry is described and the group members are asked to fill in the rest, as in the following example.

Group leader: Let me read to you from my diary: "I was about to be interviewed for the job of stockboy at Catch's department store. He asked me some questions. Then I really blew it." In order to make this a useful diary I want you to ask me some questions that will make this more complete. Write them down first, before anybody answers. (Waits a minute while everyone writes.) Okay, Tammi, you were writing furiously.

Tammi: Could you tell us just exactly what questions he asked?

Cal: Yeah, and what did you say? That would be really important if we were going to make other suggestions.

Earl: What were you thinking and feeling when all that was going on?

Group leader: Okay, those are great questions. In your diaries you'll describe your problem situation, just as I did, but it's also helpful to remember what the other people in the situation were saying. In addition, as clearly as possible, write what you did or said and what you thought and felt, as well. I guess I was just too general. I'll have to do better next time.

Members: (Laughter)

The Case Study Technique. When children, especially adolescents, are reluctant to bring in problematic situations, we commonly present them with a case study. This involves presenting a short story or videotape about another child who is experiencing difficulties similar to the child or children being assessed. The child is asked in what ways he or she is similar and in what ways he or she is different from the child in the story. The brief transcript below is an example of how the case study might be used.

Rikki (the group leader):   Today, I want to start our meeting by telling you a story about a girl who is about the same age as all of you and even has had some of the same experiences as some of you. Her name is Tracy and she's ten years old, like all of you. Tracy gets into fights a lot with her sisters and brothers. She gets really mad when they don't do what she wants them to do. When she gets mad she often hits or pinches them, sometimes she yells and sometimes she breaks their things. She considers herself a fun-loving kid and likes games and sports and to be with her friends. (pause) I'd like us to all talk about Tracy and how each of us is like her and how each of us is different from her.

Lianne: Well, I have fights with my little brothers sometimes but I usually just yell a lot and tell my mom. I like to be with my friends, too.

Bonnie: I'm just like Tracy. I like to have lot of fun, too. I guess I hit my little sister but only if she messes with my things too much. If I don't she'll just take all my stuff and break it. She doesn't know how to play with them.

Lynn: We don't yell or fight in my house. If we do Mom just cries. Sometimes I really get angry though and then I just cry myself. I don't like sports as much as Tracy; I'd rather play dolls. You don't get so dirty then.

Rikki: You guys did a great job of describing how you were unlike and like Tracy. I wonder if each of you could give a recent example of how you handled a situation in which your little sister was messing with your things, or your big brother or little brother was teasing or pestering you.

We see in the above example that the children have little

or no difficulty in talking about themselves compared to a fictional case. These very same children had been having difficulty discussing themselves or coming up with diary situations in the previous session. The case study is a valuable step in encouraging children in the early steps of treatment to self-disclose. It is possible to make the case study much more complicated by including the fictional client's thinking and feeling in a given situation as well. In this way the children get practice in looking at and comparing their own cognitions with those of the case and each other. In general this exercise is used in the first or second session. With younger children tokens may be used to reinforce all self-descriptions.

Roleplaying Assessment Procedures. Case studies, diaries, and group or individual interviews with the children or their parents or teachers may not be sufficient to discover what the children actually say or how they physically react. Less costly and less intrusive than observations, roleplaying provides a great deal of information about the responses of a child to various predetermined problematic situations. In this technique a child describes a problematic situation that has been recorded in his or her diary. The child is asked to roleplay the response as it actually occurred; the responses may be recorded and eventually coded along predetermined criteria as in the following example.

Gary: I was standing in line at McDonald's waiting to order a hamburger when an older boy and girl pushed in front of me. The man behind the counter asked me if I wasn't next. I said it didn't matter, but I was really mad.

Group leader: Listen, why don't we roleplay this situation like we did with Ernie. Remember he said exactly what he said to his mother and in the same tone of voice. Don't improve upon it—we'll do that later. I'll be the guy behind the counter and Larry will push in front of you. Here's the counter.

(Larry pushes ahead of Gary)

Group leader: Hey kid, aren't you next?

Gary: (almost in tears) Oh, I guess, it's okay, I'm only in a little hurry.

In this situation the group leader gets a better picture of the child's affect than when the child told about the situation. Moreover, the group leader can go on to question the child about his cognitive responses as well.

Some children may be reluctant to roleplay. Often as other children roleplay, with the opportunity to practice others' situations, and through the encouragement of the others, the reluctant child will try out the roleplay. If not, the child is permitted to wait until he or she feels ready.

A more systematic roleplay procedure is a behavior roleplay test. This test may be given prior to treatment and uses from six to twelve standard situations. Examples of roleplay tests, how they are used, how they might be developed, and how they are coded are presented in Chapter Four.

Paper-and-Pencil Tests. Tests given with paper and pencil may also be used to determine problematic situations. Easier to code than roleplay tests, they are often preferred by practitioners. Unfortunately, most of them focus primarily on general responses rather than on a response to a specific situation. One exception to that is the Child Assertive Behavior Scale (Wood and Michelson, 1978; Wood, Michelson, and Flynn, 1978) in which the child is confronted with a series of hypothetical events much like the roleplay test and then asked to circle one of several possible responses. An example is given in the next chapter. This test can be readily administered in the group to all the children at the same time if they have sufficient reading skills. Although the group leader obtains specific responses, no information about concurrent affect and other nonverbal characteristics are available with this test.

Such a test points to the general problem situations that each child finds it difficult to deal with. It also provides general scores that suggest the breadth of situations to which each responds with passivity, assertiveness, or aggressiveness. (This and other paper-and-pencil measures are discussed further in Chapter Four.)

Observations. Some group leaders work in collaboration with an observer in the group or in informal settings, such as on the playground. Direct observation of young children in problematic interactive settings is helpful to extend the range of difficult situations. Information gained from observation is usually more relevant and more lifelike. Furthermore, a range of situational as well as response components can be noted. For older children the presence of an observer may be too intrusive. Unfortunately observation in extra-group situations is a costly process, which limits its widespread use.

In summary, the group leader, together with children and significant others, develops and keeps track of all situations: (1) that are obtained in interviews, (2) that evolve out of the group discussion, (3) that are recorded in the diaries, and (4) that have been extrapolated from roleplay, observations, situational checklists, and other tests.

Training in Behavioral Specificity

There are many ways in which children can be trained to identify specific behavioral responses to situations. The major way is through the group interview. For example, in a family change group, Robin complained that whenever her mother was the least bit sad (a recurring situation), she (Robin) became depressed. The group leader asked the other group members what they imagined a person their age did or felt or thought when they were depressed. He also reminded them of the criteria mentioned above. When the children had provided a list of descriptions of behaviors such as eating very little, sleeping poorly, crying a lot, feeling sad, and blaming themselves for their mother's sadness, the group leader asked Robin which of these or other characteristics best described her response. The leader then asked for a description of the most recent situations in which these identified behaviors occurred. In principle, a general description is always accepted as valid for the child, but the child or referring adult is asked (and sometimes helped) to clarify the specific manifestations as they occurred in a recent situation.

Training in behavioral specificity is also carried out through group exercises. The children are presented with case studies in which the behavioral responses to problematic situations are described in general terms or character attributes, such as, "When Irwin is asked by his mother to help with the dishes, he becomes lazy" or "When Tina doesn't get to do what she wants to do, she gets mad." The children are then asked to re-formulate the responses in terms of observable behaviors. Another training opportunity occurs when the children describe situations from their diaries. Group members are encouraged to evaluate the response descriptions in terms of specificity as well as to evaluate the appropriateness of the responses.

The roleplay test, behavior checklists filled in by the children themselves, case study discussions, and the observational methods briefly described above provide additional sources of the behaviors that children are relying on most heavily. A major source of behavioral responses comes from checklists filled in by the parents, such as Walker's Problem Behavior Checklist (1970) or Miller's School Behavioral Checklist (1972). These checklists also tend to look at general patterns that the group leader can specify further in group discussion. Children will often be asked to self-monitor certain behaviors to ascertain their frequency and the situations in which they usually occur. For example, in a smoking group, the members monitored the frequency and situations in which they smoked. In a social-skill group, the children monitored the occasions during which they successfully and unsuccessfully responded to pressure from their peers by standing up for their own position.

Training in Identifying Cognitive Responses. Most children are not readily able to identify their thinking in response to a given situation. For them, training in cognition perception and expression is an important prerequisite for cognitive assessment and treatment. In training young children to look at their cognitions, the group leader may use an imagination game in which the children shut their eyes and imagine the group leader as a tiny person on the floor or a tree growing rapidly in the room. The children are then instructed to say aloud what they are imagining, and then to whisper softly what they are thinking. In the following step the members are asked to imagine the situation using their lips but making no sounds. Finally, they are asked to imagine the scene in complete silence. In the second exercise, the group leader asks the members to silently tell themselves to do something with their hands. Then she asks them to follow their silent instructions. The other members must then guess what each person was thinking while performing the hand movement. In a third exercise in the series, she has them each roleplay a situation such as one in which a neighbor is blaming them for knocking over their garbage can, although they had not been responsible. Then the members imagine what they would say to themselves and write it down. After all members of the group have done this, she has them tell the group what they have been thinking in response to the situation.

Somewhat older children may, after an initial explanation of thoughts and cognitions, be instructed to respond to a series of situations by writing down what they would think if they were the target person in that situation. Some examples commonly used in groups of adolescents follow.

> You have just been rejected by your best friend who says that he or she likes someone better.
> You are being asked to play with someone who in the past has teased you a lot.
> You are being pushed around by someone bigger and stronger than you. No adult is in the vicinity.
> The teacher is asking you a question, and you do not have the slightest idea of the answer.
> There is a thing in front of you that makes you deathly afraid. Your friend says to you, "Don't be a sissy. No one else is afraid. Pick it up."

The children then present to each other what they wrote down and give feedback to each other as to the level of effectiveness of the cognition in helping the individual to cope with the stressful situation.

A number of additional exercises have been developed to improve children's competence in identifying cognitions. Meichenbaum (1976) has suggested a range of tasks that may be used in assessing children's cognitions: imagery exercises of tasks during which internal dialogues are verbalized, and projective techniques using pictures of people interacting. Meichenbaum's suggested use of imagery focuses on the children recalling a critical incident and running it through their minds "like a movie." While imagining an incident, the children report their cognitions during the event. In the same manner, the children's cognitive strengths may be assessed by "running through" situations in which they succeeded in some way.

In a similar vein, Meichenbaum has suggested the use of behavioral tasks for assessing cognitive behavior. Much like the roleplay tests mentioned above, the children are asked to engage in problematic behavior. This can be done in a real-life setting or in a simulated one. The difference here is that the children are asked either during the event or immediately following it what they were saying to themselves as well as what physiological events (such as faster heartbeat or tight stomach) occurred.

Another procedure suggested by Meichenbaum is the use of a set of pictures involving children with problems similar to those children being assessed. Like the case study method described earlier, each child or group of children is asked to report on what is happening in a set of pictures. They are also asked to describe what the child in the picture is thinking or feeling.

Occasionally, children will identify a given cognition as occurring all the time or across so many situations that its relationship to specific situational cues is unclear. For example, one child stated that "in all situations in which I find it difficult to do what is asked of me, I think to myself 'I'll never get it done.' " When this happens, the child is usually asked to discuss the most recent occurrence of the response and the situation that provoked it. Repetition of this analysis often yields identifiable components that precede or coincide with the response. Thus, patterns of cognitions may be discovered that interfere with or enhance the child's functioning in many diverse situations.

Training in Identifying Critical Moments. In training children to use the concept of critical moment, they are first presented with a number of examples of critical moments. Then they are asked to identify the critical moment from a list of responses to situations. An excerpt from a commonly used list is the following.

When Jerry was teased by his brother, Jerry ignored him.

When Susan was being hassled at school by Sara and EmmyLou, she ran crying to the teacher.

Just as Alexander came running down the steps, his mother told him to walk slowly or he'd fall. Alexander yelled at her not to nag him all the time. His mother slapped him and he slapped her back.

When Beatrice was looking at all her assignments in the library last week, she began to think, "I'll never get all my homework done. I'll fail for sure. I'm just an idiot."

In the discussion that follows the presentation of such a list, it is often noted that more than one critical moment can be identified in several of these situations. The group leader points out that the child is ultimately responsible for determining what was most important for him or her. It is also possible to work on each situation immediately preceding each critical moment, one at a time. Once the children can identify, with reasonable accuracy, the critical moments and the responses in a wide variety of situations, they begin to look at and evaluate the potential immediate and long-term consequences of the responses.

Training in Identifying Consequences. Having identified a series of problematic situations, the critical moment, and the responses to those situations, the group can be introduced to another exercise. The children are asked to identify and evaluate the short- and long-term consequences of the given response in similar lists of situations. Once the children become proficient in identifying the potential consequences, they can learn to identify environmental resources that might reinforce consequences or help them to achieve their goals. (See Chapter Seven for a further discussion of reinforcement.)

Identifying Resources and Impediments to Treatment. In assessment it is essential to determine both resources and impediments to treatment. These include personal characteristics, persons in the child's environment, physical attributes, and potential reinforcers. One determines these characteristics through testing, interviewing, and observing as the group progresses. Let us examine in more detail how we discover reinforcers together with the client and the group.

Discovering Potential Reinforcers

One of the major intervention strategies is reinforcement. As a result, some of the most important resources at a child's disposal are events that can serve as reinforcers for behaviors. Other reinforcing events (or objects) might include the attention of parents, teachers, friends, or the group leader; physical goods or toys; and participation in certain events with others. In order to obtain a list of these reinforcers for each child, at the pregroup interview or the first meeting, a reinforcement survey schedule is administered. Although a number of these are available (see Keats, 1974, and Chapter Four for additional examples), the reinforcement survey we most commonly use includes such questions as the following:

> If you could be with whomever you wanted, name three persons you would most like to be with.
> If you could eat anything you wanted, name three foods you would most like to eat.
> If you could play any game you wanted, name three games you would play.
> If you could have a dollar to buy whatever you wanted, what three things might you buy?
> If you could go wherever you wanted, what three places would you go to?
> If you could do at school whatever you wanted, what three things would you do?
> If you could do whatever you wanted in the group, what three things would you do?

The children fill in the survey, and then individually present a summary of the events, persons, foods, and so forth that they like best in order to find common reinforcers. Many of the children we work with have access to a very limited variety of reinforcers. If this limitation is a barrier to treatment, then some treatment might initially be devoted to expanding the list. For very young or developmentally delayed children, a picture survey may be used (Daley, 1976). In this survey, pictograms of children in various activities are presented and the group members must choose those activities they like best.

Personal Attributes. Every child comes to treatment with a number of social and other skills, interests, personal characteristics, and unique sets of knowledge or information that may enhance or interfere with the achievement of treatment goals. Many of the behavioral and cognitive attributes that are not direct targets of change may be used as resources in treatment. For example, Wilbur is skilled at roleplaying, Henrietta makes extremely good suggestions when asked, Annalee listens attentively to the other children when they are despondent, and Guy can effectively relate to the feelings of other children. These skills may facilitate group interaction as well as enhance treatment. They also may function as a source of recognition and reinforcement even though such skills are not the targets of intervention.

Health and Physical Attributes. The children may come to the group with major physical health impairments, athletic skills, unique physical attributes, required medications, or limits on particular activities. Any of these attributes may facilitate relationships, separate the child from others, focus attention on the child, or in other ways affect the progress of treatment. The group leader usually requests information about such attributes from the person referring the child. The children in the group are also asked for their perceptions of their own characteristics. Physical limitations in particular may be closely linked to self-defeating cognitions. When invited to play in the group games, Eddie usually responds with something like, "Because I'm bow-legged, I'll just trip over my own feet and fall down. Then my team will lose and everyone will blame me." Such self-defeating cognitions often become embedded into the problem situations and determine the kind of response that is emitted.

It is helpful to have a medical clearance and knowledge of physical restraints to activities, if any exist. If the child is receiving any medication, the group leader should be aware of it. Some medications may interact with even such innocent-appearing activities as relaxation training to create surprising side effects (see Everly and Rosenfeld, 1981, pp. 112-113, for more detail). Other medications may cause fatigue or hyperactivity. Obviously, treatment goals may be affected by such medications.

Persons as Resources. The child's environment may contain certain characteristics or persons that can enhance the achievement of treatment goals. For example, cooperative parents, interested teachers, a good friend, adequate material support, and ready access to the treatment group would all enhance treatment. Where such resources are missing, they may need to be developed before effective treatment can begin. For example, the group leader or a colleague might meet with parents on an occasional basis to discuss plans and progress.

Parents, siblings, or other significant others may also interfere with the achievement of change. Some parents may be unwilling to reinforce the behavior being reinforced in the group. Siblings may attempt to maintain the very behaviors we have been working to eliminate. Some significant others remain passive and leave everything up to the group. In assessment, such family situations must at least be ascertained and, where possible, significant others included in goal setting and treatment. In our experience, the greater the involvement of family members, the greater the likelihood of success.

Information About Resources. There are several sources of information about resources and barriers to effective treatment. In the initial interviews, especially with parents or teachers, a discussion of what a child does well often produces an extended list. It also provides information about the persons being interviewed and their attitudes toward the child. A similar question addressed to the child will provide many resources and barriers to add to the list. In addition, at least one question must be asked regarding the goals the children perceive their parents and others must have for them. A major source of information comes from the group discussion of familial and school events, favorite activities, or what they did the previous week. Many ideas are generated as the members exchange and evaluate suggestions with each other. Finally, the observations of group interaction also contribute to this information.

In one group the leader asked the members to list all the aspects of their lives that might help them to solve a problem that they had identified. He then asked for those aspects that might prevent them from solving the problem. Although an entire session was devoted to discussing the results of this exercise, the group leader and the children had a much clearer picture of what resources they could draw on and what barriers they must deal with, not only in relation to the immediate problem but also to future problems.

Resource or Impediment? No one characteristic is always an advantage or disadvantage in facilitating change. For example, a high level of intelligence may result in greater ease in understanding the concepts required to analyze situations or to use sophisticated cognitive strategies. This same level of intelligence may also cause children to become excessively critical and unaccepting of the treatment process. Enthusiasm, though a desirable characteristic, in excess may result in a child's closing out more taciturn children in the group discussion. Each attribute must be considered within the context of specific situations as to its contribution to achieving treatment goals and whether it should be encouraged or ignored.

Motivation

To determine children's level of motivation, one must examine their perception of the long-term consequences of behavior. If the child is clear about long-term consequences and is concerned about them, this can be considered one index of motivation. Motivation is also weighed by asking children to indicate how dissatisfied they are with their responses to each identified situation on a five-point scale. Ratings are then discussed in the group. If a child is not very dissatisfied with a given response, it is unlikely that he or she will work very hard to change it. Moreover, if the children are not dissatisfied with responses to any situation, it may be assumed that motivation is generally low for this form of treatment at this point in time.

A third indicator of motivation is the willingness of the

child to take a risk. As we discussed above, each child examines the risk in any set of alternative responses. If the child is not well-motivated, one could expect that he or she would persistently choose the lowest-risk strategies. A fourth indicator of low motivation is the persistent blaming of others for one's problems. Although initially most children fail to assume responsibility for their part in interactive problems, the poorly motivated child continues to blame others over time.

Fortunately, the level of motivation is not static. With most children it tends to increase over time. As other group members clearly identify problematic situations, as the program becomes more attractive, as the interest in reinforcers increases, and as the relationships to peers and the group leader are enhanced, motivation will often increase. However, in those instances where motivation remains low, each of the above indices can be worked on separately. For example, Arnie, a poorly motivated adolescent, rarely admitted dissatisfaction with his responses, was unwilling to risk trying out any new strategy for dealing with what he perceived to be the central problem, and blamed others for all his problems. He was paired for many group activities with a high-status member who was better motivated. The group leader also occasionally encouraged the group to play soccer, a game in which Arnie excelled and received positive recognition. Gradually Arnie was willing to disclose an event he found difficult to manage. On these rare occasions, Arnie received praise from his partner and the group leader. As a result the behaviors associated with apparent motivation clearly increased over time.

In summary, motivation is continually included in the assessment of each child so that, if necessary, it can be dealt with as part of the treatment. This discussion of motivation concludes the analysis of a situationally focused multimethod assessment strategy. One question remains. Is there room for a more general diagnostic approach within this strategy? This issue is discussed next.

Diagnostic Approach

Although our emphasis has been on a thorough analysis of concrete situations and behaviors that define a given problem, problems can be organized into diagnostic classifications. Currently, one of the most commonly used systems is the third edition of the *Diagnostic and Statistical Manual of Mental Disorders* (DSM-III) (1980). This consists, for the most part, of a variety of mental and psychological disorders that are divided into sixteen major classes and numerous subclasses. An analysis of reliability for children has been done (Cantwell, Russell, Mattison, and Will, 1979a, 1979b). Although the DSM-III is considerably more reliable than the DSM-II, except in the area of mental retardation, the interjudge correlations are not very impressive. Typical was an average agreement among judges of 55 percent for psychotic disorders.

In spite of the low interjudge reliability and the fact that the DSM-III retains its bias toward the medical model, the practitioner can use the diagnostic system in the assessment process in several ways. First, diagnostic categories help refer the practitioner to a wealth of clinical and research information. Some, but by no means all, of the diagnostic categories provide us with help in determining the specific treatment modalities (Nelson and Barlow, 1981). For example, a diagnosis of phobic disorders suggests that clients would profit from both modeling and fear-reduction approaches. Often no one behavior provides us with sufficient information to describe a problem. The diagnostic category will at least suggest other specific behaviors to look at (Taylor, 1983). These behaviors often covary with the initially appearing or more apparent behavior within a given diagnostic category. Because of the limited resources often available to group leaders, there may be insufficient information to reach a supportable diagnosis. However, as treatment progresses and more information is collected—especially from direct observation of interaction between children and adults— more substantial diagnoses can be developed. For the above reasons, familiarity with the DSM-III is certainly an advantage to the group leader and ultimately should aid in the treatment of clients. A valuable text for the further study of the DSM-III is Spitzer, Skodol, Gibbon, and Williams (1981).

Summary

In this chapter we have defined and exemplified the essential components of a situational analysis, and the way in which group members and significant others are trained to help each other in the situational analysis. The major components are the situation, the critical moment, the responses (behavioral, cognitive, and affective), the consequences, and the resources for and impediments to treatment. As a backdrop for evaluating and determining appropriate treatment goals, the physical attributes and limitations of the child and his or her motivation must also be considered. On the basis of this assessment, goals are established and intervention strategies are planned. Before we address the subjects of goal setting and intervention planning, we shall expand on the procedures for data collection and ways in which these data are used to evaluate progress and outcomes of group treatment.

Chapter Four

Procedures for Measuring Progress

The assessment principles and procedures outlined in the previous chapter depend on the systematic collection of data about each child's problem(s). In Chapter Three we described a number of interviewing procedures that were used to identify relevant information about problem situations and client responses. Many of these procedures, such as pregroup and in-group interviews, case study evaluations, and the use of diaries provide abundant information but may not offer systematic data to be used in evaluation. Other procedures were touched on that lend themselves not only to assessment of target behaviors but also to the systematic collection of data for evaluating treatment effectiveness. Data-collection procedures included roleplay, observation, problem-solving tests, behavioral checklists, rating scales, and postsession questionnaires. In this chapter we will describe these and other data-collection instruments in detail, in addition to exploring a number of alternatives in each category and some of the advantages and disadvantages of each. We will also point out how data-collection instruments are employed to evaluate outcome and ongoing changes of individuals in groups. Finally, a few of the less complex research designs commonly used in group treatment will be examined. All of these issues will be seen primarily from the viewpoint of the practitioner who uses data to make clinical decisions and to evaluate his or her own practice. The general criteria for selecting these instruments are discussed first.

Selection of Instruments

A number of factors must be considered in the selection of measurement instruments to be used in the assessment process. These include the relevance of the instruments to the presenting problem, practical constraints in the use of the instrument, intrusiveness in the treatment process, and reliability and validity of the instruments.

Relevance to the Treatment Process. The most important factor to consider in the selection of information-gathering procedures is the degree to which a procedure helps to identify appropriate targets of change. For example, if a child is referred for excessive fighting, such measurement instruments as observations of frequency, reports by others, self-reports, and monitoring of the fighting are all directly related to the target behavior. Behavioral checklists or self-rating scales might be used to determine the child's adaptive social skills and other behavioral attributes that might facilitate the treatment process.

Many procedures are linked far too indirectly to the children's problem situations or presenting problems to be useful to the group leader in planning for treatment. For example, a general measure of depression, such as Beck's Depression Inventory (Beck, Mendelson, Mock, and Erbaugh, 1961), would provide us little information on situations that might be stressful to a client referred for hyperactivity. However, the instrument might be useful in evaluating changes over time in self-reported depressive behaviors for a child specifically complaining of mood swings or other depressive behaviors.

Theory may establish the relevance of measurement instruments. If theory suggests that aggressive children have relatively poor prosocial skills, a behavior roleplay test designed to provide the stimulus for performing interactive behaviors may be called for. Finally, relevance of a given instrument may be determined by nondirective procedures such as interviews, group discussions of cases, or nonstructured observations in the pregroup or early sessions.

Practical Restraints. Once relevance of a problem behavior is established, the group leader examines practical constraints to a procedure imposed by the skill of the leader, time required to administer it, and cost of administering and analyzing it. In most practice settings the group leader's resources are very limited. In most agencies or institutions it is often far too costly in staff time and other resources, for example, to observe the group members in their home or class, on the playground, or in their neighborhood on a continuous basis. For this reason, we usually limit data-gathering procedures to behavioral checklists, rating scales, self-monitoring, simulation procedures, information reported by group members and others, and to limited observation in the natural environment.

Intrusiveness. In selecting an instrument, the group leader must weigh its intrusiveness or how much the measurement interferes or reacts with the treatment process. Observing group members in their natural environments by following them around a playground may alter the way in which they and others around them behave. By just being in the same situation as the child, the group leader has altered the natural environment. For older children it may also be a source of great embarrassment. Intrusiveness is also relevant when asking the children, their parents, teachers, or others to collect information, although some styles of questioning and certain questions are far less intrusive than others. Too many tests may also be intrusive. After a half hour most children grow restless and the responses to testing procedures grow increasingly unreliable. It is either necessary to test at intervals or to limit the tests to those that can be completed in a half hour. In the use of some procedures, such as self-monitoring, the measurement may intrude positively on the treatment; that is, it may increase the desired behavior or decrease the undesired one. Although confounding the interpretation of what is causing change, such procedures are highly desirable from a clinical point of view.

Reliability and Validity. Issues of reliability and validity of instruments are also of major concern. *Reliability* refers to the consistency of an instrument from one administration to another, or the consistency of one part of a measure with another. If an instrument is stable over time (assuming no intervention has taken place) it is said to be reliable. *Intercoder reliability* refers to the degree of similarity between two or more coders of a given test. *Interobserver reliability* refers to the degree of similarity among two or more observers in coding observational categories.

Validity refers to the accuracy or soundness of the measurement instrument. Does it measure what it says it measures? There are many different types of validity. Most commonly used is *predictive validity,* which refers to the extent to which a measure permits prediction of a given outcome. *Concurrent validity* refers to the extent to which a given instrument correlates with other previously validated instruments utilized at the same time. *Content validity* refers to the degree to which a given instrument adequately samples the universe of behaviors. For example, does the frequency with which a child talks with other children provide an adequate indicator of the level of the child's social skills? Most texts on behavioral assessment report the reliability and validity of the tests being used (see, for example, Barlow and Hersen, 1982). Since it is usually not possible for group leaders to carry out their own reliability and validity testing, they can usually draw on the work of others to obtain this information.

In summary, in selecting measurement instruments, consideration is given to direct relevance of an instrument to the purposes of treatment and to instruments that point to the potential treatment procedures. A major emphasis must also be placed on instruments that are not too costly in time and resources. Further consideration is given to a procedure's intrusiveness, reliability, and validity.

Most of the remainder of this chapter is devoted to those procedures we have found most useful and practical to employ before, during, and/or after group treatment. Additional techniques that require greater resources than are commonly used at present will also be mentioned. Most procedures will be evaluated in terms of the above considerations. Should still greater technical information be required, the reader will be referred to other sources for more information. Specifically, the procedures to be discussed have been grouped under the following categories: observational methods, analogue methods, self-monitoring and self-reporting techniques, peer evaluation procedures, and adult significant-other evaluation techniques.

Observational Methods

In the early stages of assessment it is often desirable to obtain a systematic sampling of the most salient of the children's behaviors, either in the group or in various natural settings. These behaviors are either problematic or indicate potential or actual skills of the child. Direct observation is one method of clarifying the relationships between behaviors and various settings or events. Depending on the type of observation, the complexity of the observational categories, and the number of potential observations to be made, it can be a very costly and often an intrusive procedure to use. For this reason our use of direct observation is most often limited to in-group observation or to institutional settings, where sufficient adults are present at all times and one more does not disrupt the interactive process. However, under the conditions specified below we may also observe behavior in the classroom or the home. Several of the more commonly used observational methods will be discussed below. Strictly in-group observational methods will be discussed in Chapter Ten, where group assessment and intervention methods will be dealt with in greater detail.

Continuous Recording. When observing a child in the classroom, on the playground, or in a home setting, it is possible to record most behavior as it occurs. This form of continuous recording is used primarily for research purposes or in intensive clinical situations when ample resources are available. Such recording can yield a great deal of information on the types of behavior in which a particular child engages and events that elicit and follow these behaviors. An example of continuous observation is shown in Table 2. Obviously such a system would require a great deal of time to develop and to train observers to a reasonable level of reliability. In using most other methods, many subtle behavioral problems may be readily overlooked. Elaborate coding systems with reasonable levels of reliability and validity are available; however, each requires a great deal of time to learn and often yields more data than is needed (see Pat-

Table 2. Example of Coding Categories.

What Is Observed	Coding Categories
Johnny walks over to Pete.	J — P
Johnny shoves Pete.	J sh P
Pete begins to yell.	P y
Rest of group, yelling, approaches Pete and Johnny.	Gp y — P + J
Pete socks Johnny, who hits Pete twice.	P x J xx P
Group leader steps in between Pete and Johnny.	L —/ P + J

terson, Ray, Shaw, and Cobb, 1969; Hops, Wills, Weiss, and Patterson, 1976; Cobb and Ray, 1975). For this reason, when observation is used, most group leaders count only a limited number of specific behaviors in specific situations.

Frequency Counting. A somewhat simpler procedure, if observers are available, is to count each occurrence of a specific behavior related to preidentified problem situations or problem patterns. For example, for children in one social-skills group, an observer (a student volunteer) counted the number of positive-approach responses of several group members to other children on the playground. For one child in a stress-management group, the observer (an older sister) noted the number of crying episodes in the home. A student teacher kept track of the number of times the members of a disruptive-behavior group raised their hands in class. When compared to more comprehensive observational methods, frequency counts require less training and are somewhat less intrusive when introduced into a school, neighborhood, or family routine. They also focus more directly on target behaviors.

Teachers or parents are occasionally asked to take frequency counts and report these back to the group leader. Such recording can be done on an index card using a tally system or some type of counter. The task of designing careful observation systems is demanding and time-consuming. Unless the behavior is extremely apparent, well-defined, and sufficiently low-frequency (several times a day), even a request for frequency counts may understandably be unacceptable to the teacher or parents. Under these circumstances, interval or time-sampling recording would be employed.

Interval and Time-Sampling Recording. Interval recording, like frequency counting, focuses on a specific behavior or group of behaviors. It may also focus on the antecedent conditions and consequences of a given behavior. Using this type of recording system, an observer indicates whether a behavior occurred under specified conditions during a specified period of time. Although for research purposes intervals as short as ten seconds may be used, in practice, when volunteer observers are used, intervals ranging from ten minutes to as long as the entire morning may be used.

For example, the teacher recorded at noon and immediately after school (with a + or 0) whether the targeted child had interacted with other children during free time, or recorded every hour whether a child disrupted the classroom. This resulted in a total of ten observations per week for each child. (If five children from the group were in a teacher's class, the teacher would have a total of fifty observations per week to record, which is indeed an added burden.) The length of the interval depends on the frequency and complexity of the behavior, and the training and time available to the observer.

One time-sampling technique used to slow down interaction so that the group leader or teacher could record several children's behaviors at the same time is the "freeze" technique. A kitchen timer is set at random intervals (five to twenty minutes), long enough to permit the ongoing activity to continue. When the timer goes off the children are requested to "freeze" or remain perfectly still. The group leader or teacher records the behavior of each of the children and then "unfreezes" them. This counting procedure is often combined with reinforcement.

Who Are the Observers? Because of other classroom or group responsibilities, teachers and group leaders are not always the best observers. We have used student teachers, student counselors, social workers, parent visitors, volunteers from a college, and family members as observers. In general, using volunteers as observers permits only a fairly simple observation system, since volunteers can usually commit themselves to a minimal amount of time and training.

Direct observation procedures generally offer the group leader a set of repeated measurements of target behaviors and

situations for evaluating ongoing changes, as well as final outcome. The use of these data can help clarify the contexts in
which presenting problems occur as well as the situations where
the child functions well. Observational methods usually provide
frequencies or rates of behaviors that can be compared before,
during, and after treatment. In spite of their advantages, observational procedures are considered to be overly intrusive by
some adolescents and in some situations. Sometimes, even the
interval recording may be too costly in terms of available resources. Reliability of the observers, especially without adequate training, may also be low. Cooperation of significant
others in the home is not always forthcoming. Nevertheless,
wherever possible, we have encouraged some form of extra-
group observation. Where observation is not possible in the real-
life situation, analogous situations within the group or in other
prestructured locations have been used.

Analogue Procedures

Some important situations occur with such a low frequency that the observer would rarely, if ever, be able to observe a response to them during a one-week or even a one-month
period. For example, a group of adolescents wanted to keep
track of the number of times they asked for a job. The total for
the entire group over a two-month period was twice. In order to
provide children and adolescents with more frequent opportunities to demonstrate behavioral responses to crucial but low-
frequency situations, a number of analogue procedures have
been used by group leaders. These include: (1) creating semistructured situations in the group, family, school, playground,
or other social context and observing the children's responses,
(2) setting up roleplay or simulated real-world situations that
are important to group members and then observing responses
to these situations, and (3) providing standardized roleplay
tests for all the group members.

Semistructured Tasks and Activities. Several group leaders use observational assessment techniques in which children
engage in a specified task or activity for a specific time period,

during which an observer records the child's behavior. It is practically impossible to daily spend time continuously observing or waiting to count low-frequency behaviors or to depend on others in the child's natural environment to be observers.

A number of authors have explicitly described their use of such observational assessment devices. Robin (1981), in his work with problem families, asked each family to engage in two ten-minute discussions during which they were to attempt to resolve two previously identified problems. Each family's discussions were audiotaped and later coded using the Parent-Adolescent Interaction Coding System (PAIC). The PAIC classifies each verbalization by a family member according to fifteen predetermined codes.

Similar to Robin's assessment procedure is one developed by Oden and Asher (1977) in which pairs of children played together during a series of short twelve-minute play periods. Each pair consisted of a child who had been selected for treatment based on low peer ratings on a roster-rating scale (described in a later section of this chapter) and a child who was rated as being moderately liked by peers. During observed play periods the two children would be given a game and asked to try to play it.

An observer then rated the target child's degree of social interaction. Social interaction was coded as one of four mutually exclusive categories: (a) peer oriented/support, (b) task oriented, (c) uncooperative/rejecting, or (d) other. The target child's behavior was coded at ten-second intervals during each twelve-minute play period.

This type of play-period assessment is readily adapted for use in groups. In one group, the leader instructed the children to develop a play. No roles were assigned and no additional instructions were given. This gave the group leader an opportunity to systematically observe the social behavior of targeted children without having to spend a great deal of time in a classroom or on a playground or developing a more structured roleplay test. In this situation he primarily observed who initiated acts of planning, of disagreement, of cooperation, and of giving help and suggestions.

Although these coding systems resolve some of the problems of observational systems, they are still quite complex and require a great deal of time to learn reliably. Only a few group leaders report having used them regularly. Alternative indirect methods of assessment that involve roleplaying take advantage of the benefits of direct observation but require somewhat less staff time and observer training. This analogue method is described below.

Individualized Roleplay Procedures. Roleplay procedures usually require that the group member interact with others under prescribed conditions so that the observer may record the response in a variety of potentially problematic situations. The ways in which roleplays have been used for assessment vary a great deal. We discussed a relatively unstructured approach to roleplay assessment in Chapter Three, where the children described and roleplayed a recent situation and their responses to it. To convert the observations into data that can be used in evaluation of outcome, observers usually record their judgments on a set of five-point scales. These scales include, among other things, the appropriateness of the content to the situation, the appropriateness of nonverbal responses, or other predetermined skills. Since observation takes place in the group, the observer may be a coleader or, in the case of adolescents, a group member. The situation can also be taped and coded later. Usually problematic situations are selected from the early diary entries that the child has rated as very important. For example, in the first session of one group for socially withdrawn children, two girls described situations in which they sat down next to someone and did not know what to do or say. Each was asked to roleplay the situation as it actually happened. Another child was instructed on how to act as the person next to the girl. The girl was then instructed to act as she did when this really happened in school. The reactions of each of the children was videotaped and coded for verbal, nonverbal, and physical components of social skills (see Exhibit 1). Goals were then determined for each of the children on several different attributes. The same situations were recreated at the end of treatment to compare any changes in response. For other children in the

Exhibit 1. Criteria for Judging Roleplay Response.

	No	Yes
Did the girl introduce herself to the significant other?	1-------------5	
Did the girl ask the significant other about herself?	1-------------5	
Did the girl speak in an appropriately loud and clear voice?	1------3------5	
Did the girl use appropriate eye contact?	1------3------5	
Did the girl use appropriate affect (e.g., smile)?	1------3------5	
Did the girl physically turn toward the person when talking?	1------3------5	

group, situations taken from their diaries were similarly handled.

The results of the simulation yielded important assessment information on what each of these girls was and was not able to do in the given situation. It also provided social-skill scores on several attributes that could be compared with a similar test given at the last session. This informally designed roleplay test, however, has a number of weaknesses. The children may learn the correct responses from each other as the group meetings progress. The presentations of the group leader may not always be standardized. The posttests may, as a result, differ somewhat from the pretests. The coding system may not be well designed. Though rich in information, the informally designed roleplays may provide only weak data for purposes of evaluation unless the above problems are corrected. For this reason, more systematically developed roleplay tests have been more commonly used. Such tests have been developed by Freedman (1974); Rosenthal (1978); Gottman, Gonso, and Rasmussen, (1975); and Edleson, Ordman, and Rose (1983).

Standardized Behavioral Roleplay Tests. Since the Behavior Role Play Test (BRT) is one of the most frequently used procedures to evaluate change in behavior, we have elaborated on its construction and use in somewhat more detail than other procedures. BRTs usually require that a child engage in several highly structured roleplays with others acting the role of significant other. The child's response to each hypothetical situation is then recorded on audio- or videotape, and later scored according to predetermined criteria, such as those used in Exhibit 1. Because the roleplay tests supply a great deal of performance information and systematic and somewhat reliable data, we have relied on them a great deal in our assessments and evaluations of group members.

Several authors have reported using roleplay tests when evaluating interventions with children and adolescents (Bornstein, Bellack, and Hersen, 1977; Gottman, Gonso, and Rasmussen, 1975) and when assessing a child's skill levels (Freedman and others, 1978; Cox, Gunn, and Cox, 1976). The development of roleplay tests usually follows a five-step approach, as originally outlined by Goldfried and D'Zurilla (1969), in order to maximize content validity. Briefly, these steps help to structure a wide variety of potentially difficult situations and many responses to them. Once responses have been generated (enumerated), situations that distinguish highly skilled and less-skilled children are incorporated into a roleplay test of six to fifty situations and a scoring system is developed for each item. Our tests used from six to twelve items to lessen the problem of satiation and fatigue.

While the reader is referred to the literature cited above for greater technical detail, an example from our research might help make this process and the nature of the test easier to understand (Edleson, Ordman, and Rose, 1983). In developing a roleplay test to measure children's social skills we generated a large assortment of situations that involved interaction with peers. An example is: "Pretend that your friend treats you nicer when you are alone together than when the two of you are with a group of other friends. You have been thinking a lot about this lately and do not like it. You are alone together right now."

Twelve situations that we found to differentiate skilled from unskilled children were then formed into a roleplay test. These situations involved interaction with peers at school, siblings at home, other children in the neighborhood, teachers, parents, or other adults.

It would be desirable to have a larger number of situations in order to generate more information on each child's skill level. Our experience is, however, that twelve roleplays are probably the most that preadolescent children could perform without becoming distracted.

Roleplay tests are usually administered to an individual by the group leader in a pregroup assessment interview. First, general instructions such as the following are read:

> Hi. My name is _____. We are going to play an acting game for about the next fifteen minutes. I am doing this to find out how kids your age play with other kids and talk to adults.
>
> To play this game, I am going to tell you where you are and what you are doing. I want you to make sure you picture it and then just act like you really *would* if this were actually happening to you, and *not* like you think you *should* act. I'm going to record what you say. Okay?

In order to clarify whether or not the child has clearly understood the above instructions we have used the following practice situation:

> Let's try a practice one first. Pretend you are at the ice cream store and you want to buy an ice cream cone. Okay? Do you want me to repeat the situation? (If yes, do so.)
>
> Okay, just think about it for a minute.
>
> Are you ready? Okay, pretend you are at the ice cream store and you want to buy an ice cream cone. I'll play like I'm the person who works at the ice cream store. What would you say to me?

If the child does act as if he or she were actually in the situation, then the roleplaying continues with problematic sit-

uations developed earlier. If the child does not appear to understand the mechanics of roleplaying, the group leader will usually
model how one roleplays and practice with the child in several
nonthreatening situations.

When eliciting a roleplayed response, the group leader
acts as the significant other in the selected situations and audiotapes the child's response. For greater standardization in creating the situation, some researchers, such as Freedman (1974)
and Rosenthal (1978), have used pretaped significant others.
This allows children to play the role of significant other children on the tape.

Each child's response to each situation is then video- or
audiotaped and later scored according to a predetermined set of
criteria. An example of one scoring system is described for one
item on a twelve-item roleplay test in Exhibit 2.

Exhibit 2. Coding System.

Situation Ten

Pretend it's lunch time at school and you are out on the playground. Let's
pretend that all of your friends are on a field trip. You see two kids about
your age playing a game on the playground. You don't know these kids
but the game looks like fun and you would like to play.

Score	*Criteria*
5	Must include: *greeting* the other children (e.g., "Hello."), *intro-ducing self* (e.g., "My name is _____."), a *statement of inter-est by child* (e.g., "That game looks like fun."), and *asking to enter* the game (e.g., "Can I play?").
4	Includes three of four above.
3	Includes two of four above.
2	Includes one of four above.
1	Includes none of the above. Example: "I'm going to play with you two."
0	No response.

Source: Edleson, 1979, p. 278.

Those without access to video- or audiotapes or without
the time to score them may use an evaluation system that can
be completed during or immediately following each roleplayed
response. For example, one group leader coded every roleplay

test item on a scale of one (low) to five (high) on the following criteria: assertive content, eye contact, voice volume, appropriate affect, and response latency (similar to criteria developed by Bornstein, Bellack, and Hersen, 1977).

The roleplay format offers practical advantages that direct observations do not. In many cases it is not practical to place observers in a school or neighborhood to await the occurrence of a target problem and situation. To do so would, in certain cases, require a large expenditure of resources and an intrusion into the natural environment. The roleplay format is also more advantageous than a written format. Roleplays do not require reading and writing skills. Another advantage is that a roleplay more nearly approximates the natural environment than does a written response, which loses nonverbal components of a response.

As part of our research we were able to develop our own roleplay test. However, the practitioner must rely on the tests of others if he or she is going to have time to carry out the treatment. A number of precoded tests exist. For example, Hazel, Schumaker, Sherman, and Sheldon-Wildon (1981) have developed a test primarily for adolescents in order to evaluate the effects of their skill-training package. Many if not all of the items would be relevant to most practitioners working with the same population. Freedman (1974) developed a roleplay test for male delinquents and Rosenthal (1978) developed a similar one for female delinquents. For younger children, Bornstein, Bellack, and Hersen (1977) developed a roleplay test to measure the progress of children receiving treatment over a period of several weeks. We (Edleson, Ordman, and Rose, 1983) have developed a roleplay test for preadolescents that can be used to compare children's individual skills at the beginning of group treatment to their skill level at the end of treatment and several months later.

One of the problems of a roleplay test is that most of them require only a single response to a given situation. In real life a series of responses may be required to an everchanging set of stimulus conditions. To deal with this problem, LeCroy (1983) developed a roleplay test with multiple responses. The antagonist in the roleplay was given additional potential responses to whatever the child might say. For example:

> *Group leader:*   Imagine you are in a situation in which other kids are playing a game and you are standing on the sidelines. You would say . . .
>
> (Regardless of child's response)
>
> *Group leader:*   Hey, kid, we got enough!
>
> (Regardless of next response)
>
> *Group leader:*   Well, I don't know.

The reader should note that the standardized responses of the group leader are appropriate to almost any response of the child. Although difficult to develop, such a roleplay test is more lifelike than the single-answer response described earlier.

In this section we have elaborated on the use of various types of roleplayed testing procedures that group leaders could develop for themselves or could get from predeveloped tests. Such roleplays have been commonly used as part of the assessment process. Although there are some disadvantages, the simulation provides the group leader with the opportunity to observe a large number of behaviors in a short period of time. Not all simulations involve roleplaying. The simulations described below use storytelling as the main ingredient and are designed to ascertain the child's problem-solving skills.

Problem-Solving Simulations. One particular form of simulation is used to evaluate the problem-solving skills of group members. This involves the presentation of problems in various phases of being solved and requesting the members to demonstrate their problem-solving skills. This is particularly important since one set of goals taught by the multimethod approach is problem-solving skills.

The major type of problem-solving assessment procedure used by group leaders and others is called the Means-End Problem-Solving (MEPS) procedure for elementary-school-aged children. The MEPS for children was developed by Shure and Spivack (1972) and consists of a series of stories with beginnings and endings. Children are evaluated on the means by which they indicate the character reaches the outcome of the story. Spivack and Shure (1974) have developed similar assessment devices for preschoolers—the Preschool Interpersonal Problem-Solving (PIPS) Test and the "What Happens Next?" game. The "What Happens Next?" game tests consequential thinking of preschoolers. This assessment device introduces a series of stories and each child is asked what might happen next in the story. It also uses pictures to illustrate each story. The number of consequences generated are summed, with this total being the child's score on the "What Happens Next?" game. Spivack and Shure provide evidence of a reasonable level of reliability and validity of the instrument.

In cases where observation of the natural environment or simulated interactions are not feasible, the judgments of children about themselves may provide much-needed information. These judgments or self-observations are also used in addition to the observational and simulation methods and the judgments or observations of significant others. The next section describes various instruments designed to help a child gather self-observations.

Self-Observation and Rating Procedures

Some of the most important and easily accessible sources of assessment information may come directly from the child or adolescent. Several approaches allow even fairly young children to contribute information to the assessment process. These include the case-study method, diaries, self-monitoring, and self-report questionnaires. Since several of these have already been discussed in the previous chapter, we shall elaborate first on self-monitoring and later on the use of self-report questionnaires. The advantages and limitations of each of these assessment techniques are elaborated on below.

Self-Monitoring. Self-monitoring encompasses a wide variety of procedures that focus on the observation and recording of thoughts, affective states, and behavior by a child. Most commonly, a thought, affective state, or overt behavior is specified and the group member is in some way required to record the occurrence of the specified behavior. This can be facilitated in a wide variety of ways.

The most common procedure for counting one's own behavior has been a standard-size index card with the desired behaviors written on it. The child merely tallies each time the specified behavior or cognition occurs. To make counting more interesting and often easier, wrist golf counters or plastic hand-held grocery counters may be used. Each time the specified thought, overt behavior, or physiological reaction occurs the child or adolescent simply clicks the counter and at the end of the day records the frequency of behavior.

Frequency counts have also been achieved by using Greek "worry" beads on a leather string. By placing a knot on the string a simple abacus is formed, with one side having beads added as the frequency of the targeted behavior increases. Similar bead-type counting systems have been used on handmade belts and wristbands, where the bead counter is built into the design of the belt or band. For behaviors related to academic work, a tally device used for counting knitting stitches, which fits readily on the end of a pencil or pen, has been suggested by Thoresen and Mahoney (1974).

If the behavior is related to a specific period or if it is a high-frequency behavior, a time-sampling procedure might be developed whereby children self-observe fixed or random samples of their day. For example, a child might be asked to record after-school activities from the time school ends until dinner time. This period of time might be simplified still further for younger children by dividing the observation period into three or four one-hour intervals that require the child to check the type of activity engaged in during the previous hour. A kitchen timer may be set at random and when it goes off, the children are required to record whether they are performing a prosocial behavior. This was labeled the "freeze technique" earlier and was used by the teacher or parent to record the behavior of multiple persons at the same time.

Since self-monitoring is a new behavior for most children, it must be taught as any other new behavior. Group leaders will often design in-group exercises to practice self-monitoring be-

fore it is requested. For example, members of the Jays, a group
of adolescents on probation, counted the number of times they
interrupted each other in the group session as an exercise in
counting. Later the members practiced counting the particular
behavior in the group that they were going to count at school or
at home. By encouraging group participation in the design of
monitoring forms or in the selection of counting devices, the
group leader is more likely to develop monitoring procedures
within the capability of the members. In addition, by establishing a "buddy system" (see O'Donnell, Lydgate, and Fo, 1979)
the group leader encourages members to help each other with
self-observation tasks. Also, going public in the group with the
results of each child's counting increases its reliability. Some
group leaders have reinforced children in the first phase of treatment merely for successful self-monitoring, as a means of training them in the self-monitoring behavior. The reliability of self-
monitoring is not readily determined unless compared with the
monitoring of significant others. Occasionally random checks
by peers have been organized into the monitoring plan as a
means of both checking reliability and of improving it.

While the above devices offer easily accessible and relatively unobtrusive means of measurement, it is often important
to collect data that supply more information than simple frequency counts of one behavior. Children's own descriptions of
their thoughts, affect, and behavior are also data in that they
point directly to targets of change. For example, in a weight-
loss group, adolescents recorded urges to eat and their overt responses to those urges. In a stress-management group, children
monitored the situations they experienced as stressful throughout the day and wrote down their cognitive responses to those
situations. In all groups, at the end of each session, older children are asked to describe their affective responses during the
meeting. Though readily responded to, such covert descriptions
are not necessarily reliable. It should be noted that even self-
monitoring of overt behavior is not always reliable. However,
accurate self-monitoring can be enhanced by adequate training,
reinforcement of success, and intermittent external monitoring
by an observer (see Ollendick and Hersen, 1984, pp. 155-158).
Exhibit 3 shows an example of a self-monitored assignment

Exhibit 3. Weekly Tabulation Sheet.

Name **Jamie J.** _____ Date **6/23** To **6/29**

Behavior Observed **Arguments where I yelled and kept calm**

Time Sample **at 12:00, 5:00 and at 9:00 — record for last 4 hours**

	SUN 23rd	MON 24th	TUES 25th	WED 26th	THURS 27th	FRI 28th	SAT 29th
YELL A.M. / CALM	/// /	/ 0	0 //	/ /	0 0	0 0	₥ // //
YELL P.M. / CALM	// /	0 //	// //	/ /	0 /	0 0	// ///
YELL EVE. / CALM	₥ //	/// /	₥ / ///	// /	/ //	0 /	/// //

from a member of the Steelers, an anger control group for adolescents.

Self-monitoring is not the only means for group members to define their problems. Questionnaires that amplify the narrow descriptions of self-monitored behavior are also useful.

Self-Report Questionnaires. A wide variety of self-report questionnaires have been developed for use with children. Some utilize a checklist format; others are rating scales. Some measure behaviors and others measure types of thinking and feelings about oneself and one's environment. Still others are activity inventories.

One innovative behavior checklist, the Child Assertive Behavior Scale (Wood, Michelson, and Flynn, 1978), has been developed to measure an individual child's assertive responses in a series of hypothetical situations. An example of one item on the checklist follows:

> Item: Someone else makes a mistake and *someone* blames it on you.

> You would usually:
>   a. Say, "You're crazy."
>   b. Say, "That wasn't my fault; someone else made the mistake."
>   c. Say, "I don't think it was my fault."
>   d. Say, "Wasn't me, you don't know what you're talking about!"
>   e. Take the blame or say nothing.

Children completing the inventory read the hypothetical situation and then circle the letter of the response that they would most likely use in the given situation. The choice of answers is structured so that in each item there is the possibility of selecting aggressive, assertive, or unassertive responses.

The checklist yields a variety of scores. For the overall score, the higher a positive score, the more aggressive the child's responses; the lower a negative score, the more unassertive a child's responses; and scores near zero indicate the most assertive responding. Other possible scores include raw unassertive and aggressive response totals, and response totals for five content areas (positives, negatives, requests, empathy, and conversations).

A different type of self-report questionnaire has been termed a Rapid Assessment Instrument (RAI) by Levitt and Reid (1981). RAIs are short standardized questionnaires that can be easily used repeatedly to assess client problems and evaluate the progress of treatment.

Two excellent RAIs have been published by Hudson (1982) and Giuli and Hudson (1977). The two measures are the Child's Attitude Towards Mother (CAM) and the Child's Attitude Towards Father (CAF) scales. Part of a larger package of clinical measurement devices for the family, these two scales require that children rate twenty-five questions about their relationship with their mother or father. Ratings use a 5-point Likert-type scale with "1" being "Rarely or none of the time" and "5" being "Most or all of the time." The CAM and CAF scales are both scored in the same way, with any score over 30 indicating severe enough dysfunction to warrant clinical intervention. (Readers are referred to Hudson, 1982, for detailed instructions on scoring and use, and information about reliability and validity.) Such tests primarily provide a general attitudinal score, but also provide some specific information about parental situations in which the child is having difficulty.

Self-report instruments are all forms of measurement in which the data is derived from the responses of the children themselves. A great deal of data is also derived from the perceptions and judgments of significant others in the children's lives. Samples of these judgments are discussed next.

Judgments by Others

Several methods for collecting judgments of a child's behavior include sociometric measures that elicit ratings of a child by peers and a wide variety of standardized measures in which teachers, parents, or other adults make judgments about a child's behavior. In the following sections we will discuss methods for eliciting both peer and adult judgments of a child's behavior.

Peer Sociometric Measures. Many group leaders use sociometric measures to analyze group process (see Toseland and Rivas, 1984). Of more interest in the multimethod approach are the sociometric ratings by peers in a child's natural environment. Sociometric data that assess a child's acceptance by peers are increasingly utilized in the assessment of a child's problems. This is based on empirical evidence that links peer acceptance with adjustment in later life (Cowen and others, 1973; Roff, Sells, and Golden, 1972; Ullmann, 1957).

Sociometric assessment of peer acceptance most commonly involves a nomination method of measurement (Charlesworth and Hartup, 1967; Gottman, Gonso, and Schuler, 1976). Using this method, children are asked to name a specified number of peers who meet certain criteria, for example, "Name your three best friends." The major disadvantage of such a method is the probability that being selected by one's peers will decrease when a child is not present.

An alternative method of gathering sociometric data utilizes class rosters and Likert-type rating scales (Roistacher, 1974). This method requires that each child in a participating class rate all other classmates in response to a question such as "How much do you like to play with this person?" Permitted choices most often range from "1," "don't like to at all," to "5," "like to a lot." In Exhibit 4 we have reproduced such a roster-rating scale for a small class of ten children.

There are two obvious advantages to using a roster-rating scale measure rather than a nomination system. First, the roster-rating scale decreases the likelihood of a child not being chosen by others due to absence and, second, it provides an indication of the individual child's overall acceptance by all classmates.

Exhibit 4. Roster-Rating Scale.

How much do you like to play with this person at school?

1.	Scott A.	1.	1 2 3 4 5
2.	Tommy B.	2.	1 2 3 4 5
3.	Kevin C.	3.	1 2 3 4 5
4.	Darren E.	4.	1 2 3 4 5
5.	Todd F.	5.	1 2 3 4 5
6.	David F.	6.	1 2 3 4 5
7.	Lisa G.	7.	1 2 3 4 5
8.	Bonnie H.	8.	1 2 3 4 5
9.	Shary H.	9.	1 2 3 4 5
10.	Brian H.	10.	1 2 3 4 5

Roster-rating scale instruments have been used by several investigators for both assessment and evaluation purposes (Carter, DeTine, Spero, and Benson, 1975; Gottman, Gonso, and Rasmussen, 1975; Gottman, Gonso, and Schuler, 1976; Singleton and Asher, 1977; Oden and Asher, 1977). We have used roster-rating scales as one way of assessing a child's level of acceptance by peers and as a measure of the effects of our group interventions upon such acceptance (Edleson and Rose, 1981; Hepler and Rose, 1986; LeCroy and Rose, 1986).

There are many ways to look at the data generated in a five-point roster-rating scale such as the one in Exhibit 4. One way is to look at the average rating given to a child by all classmates. In determining which classmates offer the possibility of improved friendships, we look at those classmates rating a child at "4" or above. We can then, in our group sessions, target those classmates as ones with whom there is a likelihood of success in developing closer friendships. We can also pinpoint those classmates that gave a child ratings of "1" or "2" and attempt to look more closely for problems between a child and those classmates.

Sociometric measures such as the nomination system or the roster-rating scale can also be used to select members of a group. Selections can be made to include various levels of peer acceptance, with highly rated children being used as models. In fact, Gronlund (1955) and Spector (1953) have both used sociometric measures for just such reasons. Chennault (1967) and Lilly (1971) have both paired low- and high-status children in activities such as skit production or filmmaking in order to raise the acceptance level of the low-status children.

As an important caution, sociometric data may be affected by many factors other than the child's own social behavior. It may be affected by athletic or academic ability, race, sex, and physical attributes (Buchanan, Blankenbaker, and Cotten, 1976; Asher, Oden, and Gottman, 1976; Foster and Ritchey, 1979; Edleson, 1980). Furthermore, the data are often skewed by those children whose friends are primarily outside of the classroom.

A more advanced but more complex method for eliciting peer judgments, called the Pupil Evaluation Inventory (PEI), was developed by Pekarik and his colleagues (1976). The PEI is a thirty-five-item behavior checklist on which all classmates score each other on various behavioral categories. Items include "Those who give dirty looks," "Those who always seem to understand things," "Those who act like a baby," "Those who make fun of people," and "Those who are liked by everyone." Because such a procedure requires a great deal of class time, we have not used it in our projects, in spite of the vast amount of information it provides about others' perceptions of each of the children in the group.

Judgments by Teachers and Parents. In every group we use at least one behavioral checklist or rating scale completed by either teachers, parents, or both, since their perception will remain important long after the group has ended. Furthermore, in most cases parents and teachers spend the most time with the children in the largest variety of situations. These checklists permit a broad look at the behavior and more general characteristics of the child. They may point to areas that should be observed in more detail or more directly. They may suggest general diagnostic categories or descriptions.

There are hundreds of such checklists (cataloged by Walls, Werner, Bacon, and Zane, 1977). The majority describe primarily maladaptive behaviors or characteristics. Many describe both maladaptive and adaptive behaviors, while a few describe primarily positive attributes or competencies. Several investigators have developed checklists that utilize teachers' judgments. These include the Pittsburg Adjustment Survey Scales (PASS) (Ross, Lacey, and Parton, 1965), the Devereux Child Behavior Rating Scale (Spivack and Spotts, 1966), the School Behavior Checklist (SBCL) (Miller, 1972), the Walker Problem Behavior Identification Checklist (Walker, 1970), and the Self-Control Rating Scale (Kendall and Wilcox, 1979).

One of the more widely used is the Walker Problem Behavior Identification Checklist, which lists fifty different problem behaviors. For example, two items are "Disturbs other children: teases, provokes fights, interrupts others," and "Is hypercritical of self." Each of the fifty items that have been observed to occur in the last two months are checked by the child's teacher. The teacher's responses yield scores on five subscales: (1) acting-out, (2) withdrawal, (3) distractibility, (4) disturbed peer relations, and (5) immaturity. The Walker Checklist has been standardized using a sample of 534 children, and each subscale score of the checklist can be assigned a standardized score based on this sample.

Miller's SBCL modified the preceding PASS. The SBCL contains six subscales: (1) low need achievement—an inverted prosocial scale, (2) aggression—the combined PASS aggressive and passive-aggressive scales, (3) anxiety—includes the PASS withdrawal scale plus several anxiety items, (4) academic disability, (5) hostile isolation, and (6) extroversion—a prosocial scale. Such a prosocial scale is missing on the Walker Checklist.

The SBCL consists of ninety-six statements that the teacher is asked to declare either true or false. Examples of SBCL items are: "Acts up when adults not watching," "Is sure of self," and "Sulks when things go wrong." This checklist has been standardized using ratings by teachers on both male ($N = 2,627$) and female ($N = 2,746$) elementary school children between the ages of seven and thirteen. It has also been used to evaluate several different types of interventions (Camp, 1977; Camp, Bloom, Herbert, and Van Doorninck, 1977; Edleson and Rose, 1981).

A newer teacher-completed scale is the SCRS, which was developed to gather information on children's ability to control themselves in school settings. A child may score anywhere on the continuum from high self-control to low self-control (impulsive). The SCRS consists of thirty-three items that are rated by the teacher on a seven-point scale with "1" indicating maximum self-control and "7" maximum impulsivity. Other checklists are available for children with more specific problems, such as Conner's hyperkinesis index for the measurement of hyperactivity (1973).

At thirty-three items, the SCRS is somewhat shorter than some of the checklists mentioned above. In working with groups of children from the same institution, classroom, or family, it may be difficult for teachers to find time to fill in a large number of items. In this case selected items from longer checklists are given to the teachers (usually not more than fifteen items). Though they sacrifice breadth and some degree of content validity, such shortened checklists engender greater cooperation from the teacher. When there is only one child from a given treatment group in a given classroom, the longer forms are usually not a problem.

In many practice settings and with certain types of problems, the judgments of teachers or other school personnel will not be as valuable as that of the child's parents or guardians. For this reason it may be desirable to obtain parents' views of their child's behavior with measures similar to those developed for teachers. Especially suited to parents is the Eyberg Child Behavior Inventory (Eyberg, 1980), which uses two formats: one in which the parent indicates the intensity of a given behavior and another in which the parent indicates whether the behavior is a problem. Two other checklists are useful with parents: the Behavior Problem Checklist (Quay and Peterson, 1979) and the Child Behavior Checklist (Achenbach, 1978). All three tests have established reasonable levels of reliability and validity and demonstrated sensitivity to change over time. Because of the large number of checklists to choose from, readers are advised to consult an extensive review of such checklists (such as "Behavior Checklists" by Walls, Werner, Bacon, and Zane, 1977) before selecting or developing their own. The reliability and validity of each of the tests is briefly described in "Behavior Checklists" to facilitate the selection of the test.

Evaluation

The tools described so far in this chapter may not only help in the preliminary assessment process but may also generate useful data for evaluating the progress and outcome of treatment. The purpose of evaluation is to determine whether we achieve the goals we have established with and for children. The clinician who uses data is in the best position to evaluate them. Controls, as determined by research design, are necessary in order to rule out the major alternative explanations to treatment effect. Although no group or series of groups can completely answer the question of effectiveness, the establishment of controls increases our confidence in the clinical significance of the results. However, even if group leaders merely make explicit what they have done, the first step towards evaluation of outcome has been taken.

Research Design. "Research design is the plan, structure, and strategy of investigation conceived so as to obtain answers to research questions and the control variance. The *plan* is the overall scheme or program of the research. It includes an outline of what the investigator will do, from writing the hypotheses and their operational implications to the final analysis of data" (Kerlinger, 1964, p. 300). The simplest and most common design used in evaluation is the before- and after-research design without a control group. Such a design is readily available to the group leader who uses the instruments described in this chapter prior to and following treatment. In this way, the group leader can determine whether changes occurred in the predicted direction. The leader can examine which children improved and on that basis can further develop a theory of grouping as well as hypotheses about treatment effects and the children who best profit from a given approach. No statistical analysis is necessary or even possible, since the number of subjects is small.

Most group leaders, however, lead more than one group, and in most agencies, more than one leader is leading groups. If data is collected for several groups with similar characteristics over a period of time, a replicated before- and after-design may be used. Again the changes may be examined to see who seemed to make the best use of the program and in what dimensions. The sample is now sufficiently large to test whether the changes are statistically significant. If the differences from pre- to post-tests are found to be significant, this does not necessarily point to the programs being the cause. To test assumptions of causality, control groups are required.

There are many kinds of control groups. The one most readily available to the group leader would be a waitlisted control. If there are more children referred for treatment than there is staff available to treat at a given period of time, it is then possible to randomly assign children either to treatment or to the waitlist. Both groups are tested prior to and following the treatment given to the treatment group. In some cases it is easier to compare two kinds of treatment for groups of children with similar problems: children are randomly assigned to one of two (or more) kinds of treatment. For example, in one agency, children were assigned to either a play-therapy group or a social-skills training group. Pre- and posttesting are carried out in the same way as with the treatment and waitlist control groups.

Sometimes, when random assignment to groups is not feasible, it is possible to randomly assign treatments. For example, in one school we randomly assigned two fifth-grade class-rooms to either a multimethod group treatment or to a waitlist (Hepler and Rose, 1986). In the treatment classroom there were three groups.

In many agencies it is difficult to randomly assign clients: there may be insufficient clients or staff may object to random assignment. It is sometimes possible, however, to assign children to the waitlist who sign up after the treatment group is filled. Although not randomly assigned, the treatment group and control waitlist groups can be checked for equivalency on the pretest measures and on major population characteristics, such as level of education, sex, socioeconomic status, and age. If found to be equivalent, these two groups may be compared on shifts from pretest to posttest.

In the above designs we have only looked at changes from pre- to posttests. Each of the above designs may be modified to examine the results of tests given after the completion of treatment—for example, six months following the posttests—to ascertain whether gains occurring following treatment are maintained during the follow-up period. Since we are obligated to provide treatment to the waitlisted group as soon as possible, in such designs the use of a follow-up test may not be possible unless the waitlist treatment does not begin until after the follow-up period. In this design, the waitlist period following treatment is usually quite short (one to three months).

We have only introduced the topic of research design to place the interpretation of evaluation results in its proper perspective. Those wishing to conduct rigorous evaluations should look to the expansive literature on experimental designs for more detail (see Campbell and Stanley, 1963; Selltiz, Wrightsman, and Cook, 1976; Hersen and Bellack, 1981; Kazdin, 1982).

Single-System Designs. Use of a single pretest and posttest measurement may demonstrate that change has taken place from beginning to end of treatment. As we have seen above, the use of replicated before-after designs provides a great deal of information on whether goals are being achieved but provides little information about the progress of treatment. In view of this limitation, it is often preferable to use repeated-measure or single-system designs (Barlow and Hersen, 1982). These evaluation designs can be used with one group or even a single group member.

The fundamental requirement of all time-series designs is that the target behavior be clearly defined and that repeated measures be taken during the multiple-phase course of treatment. In addition, a stable baseline of observations made before treatment begins is desirable. Bloom and Fischer (1982) recommend from seven to ten measurements in each phase. With weekly observations, we can usually obtain only three to four observations before treatment begins. For example, a simple repeated measure across a baseline and a treatment phase might be conducted using peer relation scores (as measured on a 100-point scale at pretest, at the beginning of every session, and at posttest). This is shown in Figure 1. In the initial baseline phase, which included the pretest and the first three sessions, only orientation and assessment took place. Intervention did not begin until the fourth session.

Sometimes a fortuitous experiment can be carried out. In Figure 2 we note that satisfaction with the group, rated on a five-point scale, drops dramatically at the sixth session. The group leader, on seeing this, discussed the drop in satisfaction and, during the seventh session, brainstormed what could be done about it. This intervention appeared to result in the group members once again viewing the group as satisfying. In such a case, one does not wait for a stable baseline before intervening, but uses the dramatic drop as clinical indication that intervention should take place.

Other commonly used measures that can be repeated at

Figure 1. John's Weekly Scores on Index of Peer Relations (IPR).

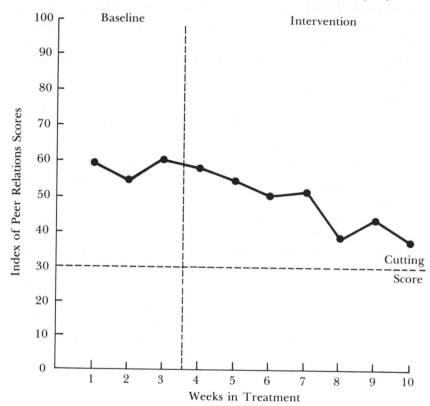

every session are the Rapid Assessment Instruments, classroom and home observations, assignment completion rates, group cohesion scores, and participation rates during each session. The postsession weekly questionnaire provides a great deal of repeated-measures data.

In the above figures, we found a shift in the average score following intervention. It is also possible to explore for shifts in the slope or trend of the data or in the variability of the data following interventions. See Figures 3 and 4 for illustrations of such shifts. These shifts are not always clear without graphing the data. For this reason, wherever possible, all ongoing data

Figure 2. Satisfaction with Group over Ten Sessions.

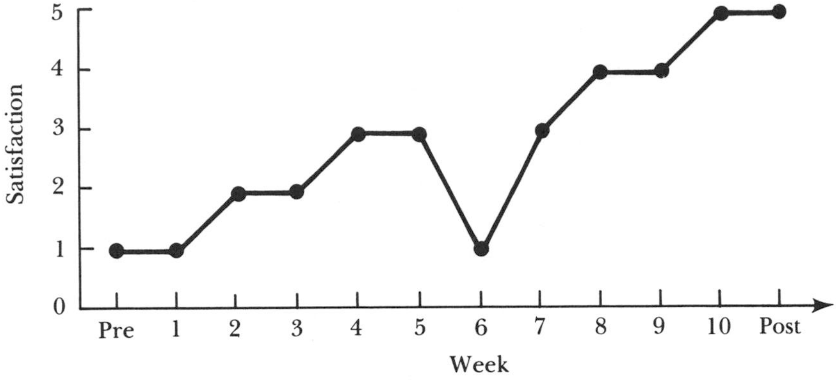

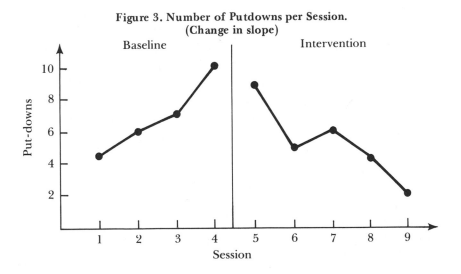

collected in groups is graphed weekly and reviewed to note possible shifts.

Of course, there are many threats to the validity of any conclusion that the intervention caused the shift. Unless the design is replicated, one cannot rule out the possibility that any results were peculiar to the one case.

Group leaders who collect ongoing data for group members automatically have at their disposal a replicated time-series

Figure 3. Number of Putdowns per Session.
(Change in slope)

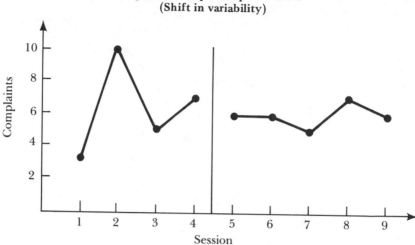

Figure 4. Complaints per Session.
(Shift in variability)

design that is more powerful than a single case. Such data provide comparisons of both progress of treatment and the outcome, although statistical analysis is rarely possible because of the small number of observations. If patterns are noted across several groups, the group leader can begin to contribute to the common pool of knowledge about the treatment methods used and the types of children and problems effectively treated. In our opinion, this replicated design is uniquely suited to ongoing clinical practice with few resources. The mere use of such ongoing data contributes to our awareness of ongoing problems that need to be dealt with; as such, the measurement itself contributes to outcome. Such uses of measurement may confound the interpretation of causative factors. For this reason, more powerful and complex designs may be required to point out potential causative factors. These complex designs may lie more in the domain of the researcher than of the practitioner who uses data.

Even in the area of time series, several sophisticated designs have been developed to gain greater experimental control over the effects of other possible causative factors. These designs include multiple-baseline, multiple-criterion, withdrawal, and reversal designs. Since these are rarely employed in group work, we will not cover them here. Instead, we suggest books by Bloom and Fischer (1982), Barlow and Hersen (1982), and Kratochwill (1978) to understand these designs and their applicability in both individual and group-treatment programs.

Summary

In summary, the role of data in working with groups is refining the assessment, improving the quality of treatment decisions, and evaluating progress and outcome of treatment. In order to evaluate progress, continuous measurement is required, with tests or observations taken prior to, during, and following treatment. Both replicated and before-after research designs are readily available to the group leader who uses tests and observations. More powerful designs can be employed to eliminate factors other than treatment that may be causing any shifts in behavior. However, these designs may require more resources than are readily available to the practitioner.

Assessment and evaluation are ongoing processes and occur throughout treatment. Though ongoing, a certain amount of assessment is necessary before intervention can occur. On the basis of the preliminary assessment, it is necessary to establish goals with the client and, on the basis of these goals, to plan for intervention. In the next chapter we discuss how these goals are established and the planning process for group treatment.

Chapter Five

Helping Children Set Goals and Choose Problem-Solving Strategies

In the first part of this chapter, we shall extend the problem-solving paradigm from problem formulation through brainstorming and decision making to goal setting. In the second half of this chapter, we shall look at the planning process for selecting intervention strategies and the criteria that the group leader must consider in that process.

Goal Setting

George has to go to the dentist's office today. When he arrives at the office, as he feels his usual vague sense of discomfort or fear, his situational goal will be to remind himself to take a deep breath, relax, and think about the vacation he is going to take next summer with his dad.

Niki was told by her mother that she could not wear her torn blue jeans to school and would have to wear her new slacks. She swore at her mother, who grounded Niki for a week. The treatment goal she decided on was that whenever she disagrees with her mom's instructions and begins to get angry, she is to instruct herself, "Take a deep breath and calm down, Niki," and then to ask her mom if they could work something better out by talking about it.

Once the problem situation has been formulated, it is necessary to establish the specific actions to be taken or the cognitions to be altered in order to cope more effectively with the situation. These behaviors or cognitions may be regarded as a situational goal, as demonstrated in the first example above. The second example is a treatment goal, in which cognitions and behaviors are described that the child would like to perform in a set of similar situations. In this chapter we shall describe the criteria for defining both types of goals and how brainstorming and decision making are used to establish exactly what those desirable behaviors and cognitions might be.

Situational Goals. Once a situation, its responses, and the critical moment(s) are defined, the members can develop what they would like to achieve when the same or a similar situation arises. Most of the characteristics of situational goal statements are exemplified above. The situation and responses are described, a critical moment or series of critical moments are established, a time period within which the goal should be achieved is set, and a statement of what the child should be doing or thinking is made. Another characteristic of an effective goal statement is that the level of difficulty is somewhat greater than that of previously achieved goals. However, the goal should not be so difficult that, even with training, it is not achievable in the stated period of time. Finally, the goal should be for a change in the behavior or cognition of the person with the problem and not for a change in the responses of others in that person's environment. (There will be cases in which the environment is impinging on the children to such a degree that the group leader will have to take steps to deal with it before the children's goal for their own behavior can be determined. Such exceptions are discussed in the final chapter.) In the following example, the group leader helps the child to take responsibility for focusing on her own behavior and cognitions.

Erica told about a recent situation in which she was arguing with her sister, who became so angry that she shoved Erica, who fell against a lamp, which dropped from the table and broke. When her mother asked what happened, Erica just yelled at

her sister and called her names without any specific
description of the event. Mom sent Erica to her
room and told her she would have to pay for the
lamp. When Erica was asked what her goal could
have been in that situation, Erica replied to get her
mom to listen to her. When the group leader asked
the members what they thought of that goal, Anatole replied that she had little control over her
mom, but that she might be able to change her
own behavior in such a way as to increase the possibility that her mom would listen to her.

Clients often want to change the behavior or cognitions
of significant others in their lives rather than their own behavior. During goal setting, by repeating the notion that goals are
set for oneself and by letting the group discuss the consequences of setting goals for others, the focus of treatment usually becomes established.

Treatment Goals. In one group, Jed first set a specific
goal for the situation in which his brother teased him about
being so short. Later, however, the goal evolved as a goal for all
situations in which his brother or anyone else teased him. The
difference between a situational goal and a treatment goal is
that the former is established for a single situation while the
latter is established for a set of recurring but interrelated situations. Although goals are initially formulated for specific situations, most goals are eventually stated in terms of situations
that are likely to reoccur.

When Oliver sees kids his age playing and having
fun, by the last group session his goal is to ask
them to play with him in a loud clear voice and
friendly tone.

Should Henry have a number of unpleasant things
happen to him in the course of the day (as happened to him several times the previous week), by
the next session, his goal will be to think to him-

self, "Everybody has a bad day; I just have to make the most of it."

When Jeanette is playing with Madeleine or any other child who bosses Jeanette around and that child insists on playing the games she wants to play, Jeanette's goal is to tell the bossy person in a firm tone of voice that they are going to have to both decide together what they are going to play.

When Evie needs help with something she does not understand at school, her goal during the next three weeks will be to ask her teacher in a clear, loud voice, with good eye contact, to help her.

When Tiny feels the urge to have a cigarette, she will do sit-ups (which she has learned from past experience reduces the strength of the urge).

Training in Goal Formulation. The correct formulation of goals clearly points to the form of intervention to be used to train the child in the desired behavior or cognition. Let us examine several methods of training for effective goal formulation.

1. As in all procedures, the children are oriented to the importance of setting situational, then treatment goals, and the criteria for a well-formulated goal.
2. A commonly used first procedure is for the group leader to describe to the children a number of situations (such as the ones described above) for which the leader models correctly formulated goals.
3. The group leader provides one problem situation—a case study—for which the children must brainstorm as many goals as possible and afterwards evaluate together which of these best meet the criteria.
4. The group leader lists all the problem situations described above and asks the members to state what they would like to do if they were in that situation.

5. The group leader provides a list of improperly formulated goals and asks the group members to evaluate them.
6. The group leader writes each of the problem statements that the children have thus far developed on separate cards and puts the cards into a pile. Each child must then pick a situation and correctly formulate a reasonable goal that meets the above-mentioned criteria. The other members evaluate the goal and make alternative suggestions.
7. Homework is given in which the children pair up to decide on appropriate goals for each other in already-formulated problem situations. The homework is discussed at the next group session.

Once children have demonstrated they have learned the criteria for correct goal formulation, they will begin to formulate situational and treatment goals for their own problem situations. There are a number of ways to arrive at goals. First the group leader asks the members individually what they feel are the best responses in a given situation. Occasionally, especially if inadequate time is available in a group meeting, the group leader may suggest to one or more members the homework assignment of determining their goals in the situations they have already described. How realistic a given goal might be depends, at least in part, on an appraisal of the personal and environmental resources available to the child, the barriers to achieving those goals, and the potential long- and short-term consequences of the proposed responses, which the group leader will ask the child and the group to evaluate.

Once one or several goals for resolving a given problem have been formulated, the next step is preparing the group member(s) to design a plan to facilitate achievement of the goal. In the next section we shall discuss that part of the planning process.

Treatment Planning

A multimethod approach is basically a well-planned one. In Chapter Two we discussed the planning process of starting a group. Treatment planning involves determining the coping strategies to be used, the actions or cognitions necessary for a specific treatment or situational goal, and the procedures required to teach or implement them. The products of planning can be seen in group and individual treatment plans, in the weekly agendas for each meeting, and in the plans for maintenance and generalization of change. Planning draws on the information gathered at intake and throughout treatment and uses brainstorming to generate ideas from the group regarding appropriate actions with respect to problem situations. In the process of planning, group leaders draw upon their training, knowledge, and experience to determine the appropriate intervention strategies for implementing the necessary behaviors and cognitions to cope with problem situations. The leader also draws on the skills of the members in generating and evaluating treatment plans.

Generating New Alternatives. If the child has no clear idea of what to do in the problem situation, the group leader will use the group to generate a series of potential actions or cognitions that might remedy the situation, by means of brainstorming (Osborne, 1963). In general, brainstorming involves two or more people listing as many alternative solutions to the problem situation as can be imagined within a short, set period of time. Brainstorming may be used as part of the problem-solving process or as an isolated technique to generate ideas about anything. Even if individual children come up with their own ideas or strategies, the group may still brainstorm new ideas in order to increase the range of ideas available to the child. In addition to generating ideas about goals, brainstorming can generate ideas about the program, group reinforcers, maintenance plans, and so forth. Let us look briefly at an example of how the group leader uses brainstorming within the problem-solving format.

Group leader: Okay, Gary, if I understand you correctly, then your problem is that when other guys are smoking dope, you usually refuse the first time, but if they keep pressuring, you either accept it or you sometimes blow your cool. You told the group you'd like to quit and if you get caught smoking it, it's a parole violation, so the question for all of us is what does Gary do when someone keeps pushing him to smoke.

LeRoy: Oh, he could just refuse.

Group leader: Hold it, LeRoy! Let's first, everybody write down every idea you can think of that someone could do in a situation like that. Every idea is welcome—even wild ones. (pause) Is everyone writing? (pause) Okay, tell Gary your ideas. And we won't say what's good or bad about it until we hear all the ideas. Why don't you write them down, Gary?

Chuck: I think you should stay away from those guys in the first place.

Gary: There, the only problem with that is . . .

Group leader: (interrupting) Let's not say what's wrong with anything until we've heard all the ideas. Okay?

Ace: What about telling them you're straight, and you're proud of it?

Group leader: That's another possibility. Neil, what did you write?

Neil: I'd say that you're having a hard time quitting, and as difficult as it is for you, you gotta say no. And you just keep repeating it like a broken record. We talked about that a few weeks ago in the group.

Group leader: Okay, anyone else?

Tom: How about just going over to the guys who aren't smoking first, and then when someone comes along who offers you a drag, look around at the other guys, and say, no thanks, without an explanation.

Group leader: Uh-huh. (looks around)

Mel: (in a kidding tone of voice) Grab 'em by the collar, throw 'em on the ground and stomp on 'em.

Everyone: (laughs)

Gary: You guys may laugh, but that's what I wrote down. If he keeps bugging me, I'll just bloody his lousy nose.

Group leader: (with neutral affect) That's another idea. (pause) We seem to have run out of ideas, but I still have one.

Gary, you could use the feeling that you are getting angry to warn you that you are about to lose it, just as we did last week in the group, and then tell them any of those things the other guys suggested. (Pauses while he looks around.) Okay, then, why don't you summarize the ideas, Gary?

In this example the group leader had the members write down all their ideas before expressing them in order to maximize involvement of all the members and also so they would not forget their ideas. The leader was careful not to reinforce or discourage any of the ideas as they were described nor to permit others to do so. He also requested Gary to keep track of the ideas and to summarize them when they were finished. In addition, he provided his own ideas since this was an early session in the treatment sequence and he was not satisfied with the ideas generated by the group. He made certain that he first got the group's ideas. Finally, he prevented any of the members from evaluating until all the ideas had been voiced.

Rules of Brainstorming. Brainstorming has been shown to generate more alternative solutions of better quality than other procedures (Brillhart and Jochem, 1964; Meadow, Parnes, and Rease, 1959; Weisskopf-Joelson and Eliseo, 1961). As can be seen in the transcript above, brainstorming exercises proceed on two basic principles: deferment of judgment and the assumption that quantity breeds quality. The specific rules of brainstorming have been found to be effective components of problem solving in a series of studies (compare D'Zurilla and Goldfried, 1971). These rules are (1) the more ideas the better and (2) no criticism is allowed until the brainstorming is over. Formulated in a slightly different way, Archable (1977, p. 23) stated the rules as follows: "(1) What is the first idea that comes into your mind when I read the situation, (2) tell me anything you can think of no matter how silly it sounds, and (3) can you combine any of the ideas given by another member to make a new idea; can you take apart any of your ideas?" When a group member deviates from the basic rules, as did Gary in the above transcript, the group leader directs the member to keep his or her contributions within the boundaries of the basic brainstorming rules.

With adolescents and often with latency-age children, it is

usually not difficult to generate a large number of ideas with the procedures used above, especially with the help of the group leader. To increase younger children's abilities to generate alternative solutions, Spivack and Shure (1974) have developed an activity in which children are asked to simulate a real-life experience. Each child was given an animal trinket and asked to figure out ways to convince another child to let him or her play with a more desired trinket. The object of the game was to get the children, through simulation, to generate as many alternative solutions to the dilemma as possible. This is a common problem situation for younger children.

Archable (1977) has developed a board game to facilitate the group's generation of alternatives. The game takes the following form:

> The trainer read the story, set the kitchen timer, and asked for choices (alternatives). The trainer (verbally) reinforced each alternative the child gave ... The child received a point for each idea he (she) gave and a move was made on the playing board. When the latency between responses was greater than five seconds, the trainer prompted with one of the rules of brainstorming ... If necessary, the trainer modeled the responses from the prepared list of alternatives. All responses made after a prompt was given were reinforced. After five minutes, the bell rang. If the children seemed to run out of ideas before the time limit was up, the trainer continued to provide prompts, making them as specific to the theme as needed, to get additional ideas [p. 23].

Those children who receive the most points (and thus move the furthest on the board) may then select the first alternative that the group would focus on in identifying consequences. Here, the board game format is used to keep the members' interest and focus on generating alternatives and, later, on the task of identifying consequences.

Increasing Brainstorming Skills. We find it useful to present brainstorming in a game format. We often use a kitchen timer, set it for several minutes, and "race" the clock to see how many ideas the group members can generate before the timer rings. We also keep track of the largest number of ideas generated in any one brainstorming session and use that number in addition to the timer bell as an "opponent" to race against. In other groups, we have awarded tokens or points for each solution generated; the tokens are later exchanged for a group reinforcer such as playing a game or going on a group outing.

Many times we find that the children need to be taught to brainstorm. We have often used the "When I" game to increase the effectiveness of brainstorming. The group leader starts this game by saying, for example, "When my friends criticize me, I . . ." The child next to the group leader has to repeat this and add a phrase. Each subsequent child has to repeat all that was said prior to his or her turn and then add a phrase. To increase the alertness of those whose turn has already passed we alter the rules to include a "reverse" where the group leader or a child freezes the action and reverses the direction of the round robin. Thus, all the group members must be attending fully in case the reverse takes place soon after their turn.

The next step is for group members to present the general situations they are having difficulty with. The other members are asked to respond as they did above. For example, when working with socially isolated children we have used the phrase "When I see new kids around and I want to make friends, I . . . ". As above, each child must repeat all previous ideas and add a new one. If the group has difficulty brainstorming, this type of game could even be used as a substitute. For instance, in Gary's case, the group leader could have used "When someone pushes on me, it is in my best interest to . . ." and then to have gone around the room with Gary being last.

A group of children will not always generate solutions that successfully achieve a goal. The group leader must insure that such solutions are contributed during the brainstorming exercises. This can be done by the leader asking directive questions and contributing solutions during brainstorming, as in the above example. By contributing solutions, the leader is also modeling the kind of in-group behavior expected of the children and the types of responses that might help achieve the goal being discussed.

Deciding Among Alternatives. Once a set of possible alternative solutions has been generated, the group leader guides the members through an evaluative discussion of each of the alternative solutions. This discussion focuses on the possible consequences (potential outcomes and risks) of using each alternative. The excerpt from a sample group meeting below shows the members discussing some of the alternatives suggested earlier.

Group leader: Okay, Gary, now that you have summarized all the ideas, which ones do you think might be most useful for you, and why?

Gary: I have to go to the party because even the guys who don't smoke go there. So that's why I can't just stay home.

Ace: Yeah, I guess that's true.

Gary: I guess telling him to get the hell out of there or I'll shove the bloody stick down his throat is what I would usually do if I didn't want to smoke the damn thing. It would work, too. It always does.

Mel: Yeah, sure it works, but it doesn't exactly make you number one popular guy, either.

Ace: It doesn't for me, that's for sure.

Gary: I guess you're right, my big mouth always gets me in trouble. I suppose I should do what we talked about last week, tell myself to cool it, then just repeat "I'm straight now, and I don't need it to have a good time."

Group leader: What do you think he'll do or think about you if you do that?

Gary: Nothing, and I don't buy more big trouble, either—by smoking the stuff or by punching him out.

Group leader: Do the rest of you buy that?

Others: Yeah. Sounds all right to me. Stay in there, Gar'. I'll go along with that.

Group leader: Is there any risk involved for Gary?

Mel: I don't see it, if it's there.

Others: (agree)

Group leader: Then that's your decision? When someone starts pressuring you to smoke pot at a party, you say in a loud, firm, but not angry voice, you're straight now, and you don't need that stuff to have a good time. And if he persists you just repeat yourself like a broken record.

Gary: Yeah, that's about it.

This discussion results in the choosing of an alternative set of responses to those Gary originally used. In this case the alternative selected is a combination of the suggestions made by Gary, other group members, and the group leader; the combination being one that will usually maximize the chances of positive consequences and minimize the chances of negative ones (Goldfried and D'Zurilla, 1969). These alternatives, which the children would like to achieve the next time a similar situation occurs, can be conceived of as goals. They may be able to carry it off without any further training or, as is often the case, they will need to cognitively restructure the way they talk to themselves and to practice what they would say should a similar situation occur. How the group can be used to train them in these skills are the topics of Chapters Six and Eight.

One additional aspect of selecting a given alternative should be emphasized. The potential risk of performing that response should be weighed. In each of the above examples there may be a small risk to achieving the stated goal. Before encouraging the child to try out the newly formulated desired behavior, the child should be able to add "and it's a risk I have considered and am willing to take." In some cases, failure to consider the possible risk could be devastating to the child. For example, Rudy, who perceives he is having difficulty in disagreeing with his parents, chose as a goal to tell them about all of their behaviors with which he disagrees. Although some parents might even applaud such a response, many parents might become extremely angry or even punishing in response to this assertiveness.

With children like Gary, where aggressive behavior is rewarded through compliance of others, it is important that the discussion of alternatives focus on the potential long-term effects of aggressive behavior. We have found it useful to think in terms of *time horizons* as defined by Kunkel (1975). Time horizons can be described as periods of time into which a person projects when evaluating possible and existing consequences. The role of the group leader during this decision-making period is to help the children choose alternatives that will maximize achievement of immediate and long-term positive consequences.

Spivack and Shure (1974) and Archable (1977) both use games and activities in helping groups of young children identify the consequences of various alternatives. One of the many activities developed by Spivack and Shure involves pictures of children in potentially dangerous situations, such as standing in front of a swing. The teacher leading the exercise asks the children to state where the child pictured is playing and whether or not it is a good place to be playing. After asking if it is a good place to play, the teacher asks "Why?" and "What might happen next if the boys play in front of the swing?" To generate feeling statements, the teacher might continue by asking "How do you think the boys might feel if the swing hit them?"

Deciding on alternative behavior(s) may be accomplished in any number of ways. Researchers have reported decision making by voting on or assigning weights to each alternative (Becker and McClintock, 1967; Churchman, 1961; Edwards, Lindman, and Phillips, 1965). Robin and his colleagues developed a simple system of weighting alternative solutions in their work with parent-child pairs (Robin and others, 1977; Robin, 1979, 1980). The following is Robin's (1980, p. 153) description of the decision-making process. We have substituted the words *group members* for the words *family members*.

> [Group] members independently evaluate each
> solution by (1) projecting its positive and negative

consequences and (2) assigning it an overall rating of "+" or "−," depending upon whether its benefits outweigh its detriments. The individual's overall evaluations are recorded on the problem worksheet under separate columns for each [group] member. A lively exchange of opinion is encouraged in order to clarify the consequences of the solutions and to help [group] members appreciate each other's perspectives. Often, additional solutions are suggested during decision making, and these are evaluated along with the original solutions. Afterwards, [group] members carefully examine the worksheet for ideas rated "+" by everyone, and one such idea is adopted or several are combined.

Although we have presented a number of formal strategies for weighing or combining alternatives, we most frequently let the child choose, based on the structured group discussion and our personal assessment of which alternative(s) will (1) most likely be utilized by the individual child and (2) most likely achieve a positive outcome. As we have stated elsewhere, what may be an effective response for one child may not be effective for others in the identical situation (Edleson, Ordman, and Rose, 1983). A child may choose a response that others in the group feel is inappropriate. For this reason it might be necessary for the group leader to be somewhat directive in the selection of a response. Ultimately the children are the final arbiters of the responses they want to learn. Of course, if the goals are unethical, illegal, or impose on the rights of others, the group leader is always in the position of firmly stating an opinion and withholding training in the required skills. Val, when she wanted a couple of days off to go on a trip with her boyfriend, chose to lie to her boss about a sick grandmother in spite of the arguments made by the other group members about the risk involved and the ethical considerations. The group leader stated that neither she nor the others could agree with Val for reasons mentioned earlier, but that Val would ultimately have to make her own decisions and face whatever the consequences might be.

Weighing alternatives is a cognitive skill that encourages positive resolutions of situations involving interpersonal conflict. If, through practice in the group, a child or adolescent can look at alternative ways of dealing with antagonists or of evaluating situations, he or she will often be free of the restrictions of more stereotypical and often ineffective responses. At the very least, looking at alternatives reduces the often disastrous effects of impulsive problem solving. For these reasons, weighing alternatives before acting is a beneficial skill in its own right.

It is important to note that brainstorming and decision making may be used in response not only to problem situations but to a wide range of treatment activities. Some group leaders have used decision making when children could not determine their most pressing problem. Others have used it to think of as many ways as possible for the members to maintain what they had learned in the group.

Once a plan has been developed for interventions required to prepare children to cope with a given situation, the next step will be to implement that plan. In the next section we discuss the various kinds of plans that brainstorming can lead to.

Types of Plans

There are many types of treatment plans. As mentioned earlier, the major categories are individual, group, session agendas, and generalization plans, each of which is interrelated. Examples of each are presented below, along with their differences and similarities.

Individual Treatment Plans. Individual treatment plans refer to written plans drawn up for each individual. In a group of fifteen-year-old early offenders, the following plan was developed for Skip.

> *Behavioral Goals:* Skip was using the group to work on those behaviors that would keep him in school, at least until he was sixteen. He specifically

had to work on compliance with teacher requests, asking for help when he did not understand something, and doing homework. He also needed to work on making new friends of adolescents his own age who were still in school.

Monitoring Procedures: Skip would self-monitor the above procedures on a little card that he carried with him at all times. The teacher would initial his entries at the end of each day if she thought they were accurate.

Intervention: The intervention strategy was to use the modeling sequence within the group to demonstrate and let Skip practice the prosocial behaviors in specific situations he was constantly encountering. He would also be reinforced in the group for completing increasingly larger amounts of homework in school. He would be encouraged to meet with boys in the group outside of the meetings and to participate in prosocial activities with them, especially in baseball, in which he excelled.

A similar plan was drawn up for each person in the group and each was modified as the adolescent modified a target behavior, the monitoring procedure, or the intervention to be used. Where the problems are highly similar, it is often more efficient to use a group plan only.

Group-Treatment Plans. A group-treatment plan is a description of the group treatment strategy to be used and the justification for that strategy. A general plan is determined even prior to recruiting children and is modified as the characteristics and problems of the children become apparent. Initial group-treatment plans are reflected in the preliminary treatment contract developed as a point of departure for discussion with parents, children, and others concerned with the focus of the group. The major ingredients of the plan are the presenting problems, monitoring procedures, common goals, group composition, and group intervention strategies. An example of such a plan is given below for a group referred by a fifth-grade teacher.

> *Presenting Problems:* In a fifth-grade class there was a high frequency of fighting, name-calling, teasing, and occasional stealing among five of the boys in the class.
>
> *Common Goals:* By the end of the semester, the fighting, name-calling, and teasing would be reduced in frequency to at least half; stealing would be eliminated entirely; and mutual reinforcement and playing together cooperatively would increase.
>
> *Group Composition:* Put problem boys together in a group with two of the high-status but nonaggressive boys as models.
>
> *Monitoring:* The teacher indicated that she would be willing to count incidents of the above acts. She would keep a behavioral report card for this purpose that she would share daily with the boys and weekly with the group leader. Later the boys would self-monitor.
>
> *Preliminary Group Activities:* The group leader would meet weekly with the group for forty-five minutes after school, with the permission of the parents. After six weeks, the program would be evaluated to decide whether the group should continue. Meetings would be divided into two parts— problem talk and activities. Refreshments would be given at the first few meetings "just for coming"; later these would be contingent on completion of homework assignments negotiated at the end of every meeting. Individual and group charts would be displayed during the meetings. Paper

money, which purchases group trips and surprises, would be earned for participating in roleplays, group discussion, staying on task, and completing homework assignments, and also for the absence of stealing in the classroom. Persons with the most money at any one session would choose the activity for the next session. Roleplays would be used to demonstrate and practice how to avoid fights and to reinforce each other.

The group plan is used as a point of departure to be renegotiated, if necessary, as the original procedures prove to be inadequate or if, for other reasons, new procedures are required. The group plan, it should be noted, is a kind of treatment contract. Plans for sessions are derived from the group plan and are formulated as session agendas.

Plans for Meetings—Session Agendas. Most group leaders use the session agenda to plan their weekly meetings. The agenda is a list of activities that the leader expects the group to follow during a given meeting. The agenda is either put on the blackboard or mimeographed and distributed to the members. Most children and adolescents seem impressed with having a typed agenda that they can show to friends and family. Initially the agenda is planned by the group leader. Later the children are involved in the planning. At the end of a given meeting the leader may describe the tentative plan for the next meeting for the group's comments. Some group leaders have had special planning sessions between meetings with representatives of the group.

Thus the agenda is an excellent planning document as well as a tool for orientation. It also provides one more opportunity for children and adolescents to be involved in the planning process. Furthermore, the agenda makes it possible to set limits in a nonpersonalized way on off-task behavior, as in the following example.

Group leader: How many people would like to tell us what they did on their homework assignments during the week?

Larry: The last meeting was really fun. Could we play that game again?

Group leader: Gee, Larry, let's talk about that when we get to "evaluation" on the agenda. Right now we're talking about "homework"; that's item number one.

One example of an agenda taken from the above adolescent group is the following:

1. Review homework.
2. Review evaluations from the previous week and homework-completion-rate data.
3. Discuss problem of irregular attendance in group; then problem solve what we can do about it.
4. Plan for next week's meeting with guests from school.
5. Roleplay Harry's and Annette's situation in trying to talk to the teacher.
6. Present feedback and discuss talking with teachers in general.
7. Design homework for next week in pairs.
8. Evaluate.

Plans for Maintenance and Generalization of Change. The focus of a multimethod approach is not merely on change but on the maintenance and generalization of change. Since such a transfer of learning does not usually occur without taking steps to ensure its occurrence, a plan is established early in treatment for maintaining and generalizing beyond the time and place boundaries of the group. Initially, the focus is on development of the treatment plan but, as immediate change is obtained, greater emphasis is put on the generalization plan. Although maintenance and generalization plans are, in fact, a form of intervention, we have established them as a separate category to give them the attention they require. A typical generalization plan might include the following.

The group program will rely heavily on homework assignments given at the end of each session and monitored at the beginning of the subsequent session.

At the end of the fifth session we shall attempt to stimulate all the children to join nontherapeutic groups such as the Boy Scouts, 4-H clubs, or interest groups at school.

A program will be made available to parents for training in child management procedures with special emphasis on reinforcement procedures.

Increasing responsibility will be given to the children for their own treatment as the group progresses. They will serve as discussion leaders of the group from the fifth session onward. For this purpose they will be provided cue cards, which will eventually be eliminated.

These and other procedures for generalization are discussed in Chapter Twelve, as well as the principles and empirical foundation underlying them. The question of the principles to be employed to develop the above plans is answered below.

Principles of Planning

Once clients have decided what they want to do, say, or think in coping with a given problem situation, an intervention strategy can be selected. A number of overlapping principles for the selection of treatment procedures or strategies are described below. Many of these principles have been derived from Cormier and Cormier (1985, p. 297) and adapted to the group situation.

Goal-Attainment Procedures. Procedures are initially selected that are related to achievement of the goals agreed on by the child and the group leader. As we discuss various intervention strategies in the following chapter, we shall attempt to point out the specific goals toward which each of the strategies are oriented. Procedures that have the best empirical foundation are preferred.

Group-Related Procedures. The group leader must consider whether the given set of procedures can be used effectively in the group. Group-related procedures permit maximum involvement of all the members and provide increasing levels of responsibility to them. They also provide diverse roles for each member to play. Although most procedures fit this category, some lend themselves to group usage more readily than others. For example, modeling and rehearsal procedures take advantage of the many potential actors and models within the group and provide diverse sources of feedback. Systematic desensitization could be carried out in a group but usually fails to take advantage of the possibilities offered by the group since little interaction occurs among the members (see Wolpe, 1973). It should be noted that procedures selected for one individual must be compatible or overlap with procedures for other group members if the group is to be efficiently used. The decision should be based on significant overlap of appropriate strategies, and not on total overlap. If the appropriate strategies for a given child are not compatible with strategies for the majority of the group, referral to another treatment context may be considered. The procedures should also be feasible within the time limits of the group. Long-term procedures would be ill suited to time-limited small-group treatment.

Informed Consent of Parents and Children. Parents, as well as the referring agency, are informed about the major procedures to be used, and their approval is solicited. The children, too, should be aware of and approve the general thrust of the procedures. For this reason, paradoxical techniques and most punishment strategies will usually not be appropriate to the group setting.

Positive Procedures. Procedures should be selected that are basically positive. Reinforcement procedures are preferred to punishment strategies. This does not imply that highly disruptive behaviors might not be handled with such procedures as time-out from reinforcement, response cost, or extinction, provided that more positive approaches are primarily used.

Interesting and Fun Procedures. Procedures that are compatible with the interests of the children are selected. They should be exciting, interesting, and acceptable to the children or adolescents. Some procedures, such as those requiring role-playing or for which reinforcement is received, are inherently satisfying. Others may have to be paired with games or other devices in order to make them attractive.

Group Leader Competency. The group leader or one of two coleaders should be skilled in the procedure being used. If the procedure is essential but the group leader is not skilled in it, training may be procured or a "specialist" in the procedure may be called in to guide the process. All too often, group leaders and other professionals have tried out techniques with which they were minimally informed and untrained, with unacceptable results. If a procedure is being experimented with by the group leader for the first time, the children and their parents should be aware of the experimental nature of the procedure.

Gradually Increasing Demand. Procedures that do not overly burden the child are usually selected. If the task is overwhelmingly demanding, the child who must do school homework, take special lessons, engage in other after-school activities, and complete home chores may not be prepared to meet the excessive demand. On the other hand, as children's ability to perform the therapeutic task grows and their efforts meet with success, they can successfully cope with increasing requirements.

Increasing Child Responsibility. In the initial phases of treatment, the major responsibility for planning is with the group leader, who is initially best informed about potential strategies to be used. However, the children may provide a rich source of ideas about behaviors or cognitions that might best be used in a given situation and coping skills that might lie within the range of each other's competence. The group leader would draw on this source in the initial phases of planning and rely on it completely as treatment progresses. Furthermore, as the children learn the basic strategies, the leader shares responsibility for the selection of strategies with the group. Thus children's involvement moves from low to high as treatment progresses.

Maximum Flexibility. Plans developed early in treatment for strategies, cognitions, actions, or words are only tentative. As information accrues and plans are found to be inadequate, they are usually revised, sometimes eliminated, and occasionally substituted with new plans. A plan may be regarded as a point of departure to guide future planning.

Appropriate Timing. The best time to introduce strategies must also be taken into consideration. Although most strategies and orientation can be introduced early in treatment, the group must be sufficiently cohesive before intrusive treatment strategies can be introduced. Sufficiently high cohesion is usually indicated when the members indicate in group discussion or on postsession questionnaires that the group is interesting and/or enjoyable to the members.

It is also preferable to first orient clients to procedures before using them. Some procedures build on other procedures; for example, most procedures involving group members require appropriate and skilled feedback. As a result feedback training precedes many other more complicated strategies. Modeling and rehearsal strategies are components of both interactive and cognitive skill training and are also taught soon after feedback. Reinforcement strategies are employed throughout treatment and timing is also a factor (in this case, primarily when reinforcement is to be faded). As each of the intervention strategies are presented in subsequent chapters, the implications for timing will also be discussed.

Multiple Treatment Strategies. Finally, as we review the above principles, it is clear that one strategy is rarely if ever sufficient to deal with the complex problems children fall prey to. Problems are not unidimensional (Mahoney, 1974). The client usually requires assistance with a range of issues. Multiple treatment strategies also permit children to be the teacher of strategies in which they are competent, as well as the target person in procedures they must learn. In spite of the fact that intervention strategies are presented one at a time in subsequent chapters, their application is often combined into a well-integrated program. The multimethod approach receives its name from this combination.

Some Comments on Planning. Planning appears to occur in a linear fashion from data collection to the development of treatment and generalization strategies. Unfortunately, the paradigm is not always so perfectly followed. Often in groups that have been set up to deal with a narrow range of problems, such as self-control or social skills, many of the strategies are selected in advance. Children are selected whose problems fit the common intervention package. This does not imply that the intervention package is rigidly adhered to. As new common problems are discovered, the plan is often altered and new interventions added. Thus, in highly structured groups, ongoing planning may be reduced, but it is not eliminated. Furthermore, much of the planning of interventions occurs prior to the advent of the children.

Summary

In the first section of this chapter, we illustrated how goals are incorporated into the treatment process. We have noted how goals lead us further into the systematic problem-solving process, especially in the generation and evaluation of strategies for resolving problems. This in turn leads to planning for the implementation of those strategies. We described individual and group treatment plans, plans for sessions, and, finally, plans for the generalization and maintenance of change. Guidelines to be considered in planning were also presented.

In the next five chapters, we artificially isolate the modeling sequence, operant strategies, cognitive approaches, socio-recreational techniques, and group procedures for purposes of analysis and discussion. In reality, none are practiced alone in a multimethod approach to group treatment. These interventions provide the major strategies by which the children learn necessary skills for coping with the problem situations they have brought to the group.

Chapter Six

Changing Behavior Through Modeling, Rehearsing, Coaching, and Offering Feedback

The major treatment procedures for teaching the overt verbal and motor components of previously discussed social skills are modeling, rehearsal, coaching, and feedback. We have referred to these four procedures as the modeling sequence since they draw their significance from modeling theory and they occur more or less in the above order. In this chapter we shall discuss the modeling sequence primarily as it is used in the group setting.

Modeling, rehearsal, coaching, and feedback procedures together form a powerful technology for preparing group members in the use of new interpersonal behaviors. Similar procedures combined with other techniques may also be used to teach cognitive skills. Each of these four procedures will be discussed below. We shall begin with modeling, since this is the first step following assessment and goal setting, and provides the foundation for subsequent steps.

Modeling

Angela (group leader):   Okay, I'm going to pretend that I'm you and I'm going to show you one way you might approach your mom. You listen closely, Gretchen, and see what I do and say in this roleplay situation. Afterwards, we'll all talk about it and see what Gretchen and the rest of you find useful in the way I do it.

Angela (in role of Gretchen):   Well, Mom, this is really hard for me to tell you. It's about the scariest thing I've ever done. I am afraid you're going to be terribly disappointed in me. But you're the only one I can safely turn to at such a difficult time in my life. I need to tell you so that we can decide together what I'm going to do. (pause) You see, I'm pregnant. I need help desperately from you, Mom.

Pete: Yesterday, I was watching the way my friend, Jerry, was talking to girls. I learned a lot from him just by watching. He looks at them when he talks to them; he seems to be relaxed; he tells a lot of jokes; and he asks them about themselves.

Modeling, as exemplified by these two situations, is a process in which one person learns by observing the behavior, attitudes, or affective responses of another person. In the second example, Pete has just unobtrusively observed a friend who has enacted a complex set of behaviors he would like to learn. In the first example, the group leader has modeled a brief verbal sequence that the adolescent, Gretchen, is trying to learn, so that she can carry out that sequence with her mother. Modeling also occurs inadvertently, without planning, and the behaviors learned may not always be the ones we want taught. In treatment we attempt to gain deliberate control of the modeling process in order to teach children goal-related behaviors as effectively as possible.

Modeling procedures lend themselves especially well to the group-treatment setting. A group contains an abundance of potential models; new models can be introduced without seriously disrupting existing social patterns; and multi-person role-playing can be readily utilized. Group games can also be stimulated to encourage imitation. One example of a group game would be charades in which attractive models (such as a popular teacher or a local sports hero) are the characters to be demonstrated by one team and guessed by another.

The effective use of modeling procedures depends upon several factors. These include the child's skill to observe and imitate others, special attractive attributes of the model, similarity of the model to the client in various personal characteristics, the way in which the model is presented, and the incentives under which modeling and subsequent imitation take place (Bandura, 1975). Each of these factors that can be manipulated to enhance learning and imitation are discussed in the following subsections.

Skill in Observation and Imitation

One necessary condition of imitation is an attending response to the model's behavior (Bandura, 1975). If children are restless, if the cues are too vague, if the perceptive abilities of the child are limited, attention to the model may be drastically reduced. One way of increasing a child's attention to a model is to give him or her a structured observational role. For example, in a group of ten-year-old children, the group leader modeled how to ask an adult for help. Each child received instructions regarding what to look for. Mike was asked whether the model asked for help and how he did it. Jeremiah listened for voice volume and watched for body posture. Willard was asked to note facial expression. Lionel listened for words that expressed feeling. At the end of the modeling roleplay, each child related what he saw or heard as his assignment.

Another way of increasing the child's attention to the model is to provide reinforcement for careful observations of the model. In the above example, the group leader reinforced every descriptive statement made by members of the group with a token. One can also increase a child's attention by using simple instructions that are clearly presented. In the above example, the group leader wrote each set of instructions on a piece of paper and handed it to the child. All of these procedures served to make the modeling session as interesting as possible, which is another way of keeping the attention of the child. We try to involve adolescents in the process of determining suitable criteria for observation. For example, with a mixed group of fifteen- to seventeen-year-olds in a "job-finding" group, the leader asked the members to brainstorm what they thought was important to observe when the leader modeled the job interview. With younger children, similar criteria may be developed, but in order to make the task attractive, they are assigned the role of "detective," "reporter," or "spy." All children are provided with notepads as well as instructions for what to observe.

Frequently, however, additional training in attending to and imitating models may be required before giving children such observational roles. One way of increasing observation and imitation skills is through group games. As mentioned earlier in the book, charades are one vehicle for teaching children to both observe and imitate the behavior of others. A variation of charades is called "Who am I?" In this game the group leader, and later a child, imitates a social role, such as a father, mother, fireperson, policeperson, or doctor. The rest of the group attempts to determine what role the roleplayer is enacting. This activity creates the excitement of a game while preparing the children to develop the necessary observation skills for adequate use of models. A wider variety of group games and activities that may be suitable for enhancing observational and imitational skills are discussed in Chapter Nine of this book.

Incentives for Observing and Imitating

Although children tend to imitate certain models more readily than others, Bandura (1969) has pointed out that incentive control of observational behaviors is usually stronger than the effects of variation in observer characteristics and model attributes. For this reason modeling is frequently combined with reinforcement procedures. While these procedures will be covered more fully in a later chapter, we will briefly discuss here those procedures relevant to increasing the modeling effect.

Reinforcement of the model increases the likelihood that the child will imitate the model's behavior, especially if the model is rewarded in the presence of the observer. It also appears that a reduction in the frequency of imitated behaviors by the observer will result from the model's punishment. In addition to the consequences observed, it is important that the observer receive similar contingent rewards for imitation of desired model behavior.

The following example illustrates how both the model and the observers are reinforced for performance of the target behaviors. The leader of an adolescent group, attempting to improve the group's job-interviewing skills, invited to a session a peer who had just gotten a job. Prior to the meeting, the group leader requested that the model tell the members how he prepared for the interviews, what he did, the nature of the interviews, how long they took, and so forth. The members interviewed him further. The model in this case was recently rewarded by getting a desirable job and further reinforced in the group meeting by the attention and praise of his peers. In this first step, only general behaviors and approaches were modeled. In a subsequent meeting, the group leader modeled in a roleplay the specific job-interviewing behaviors the members were likely to require. At the end of the interview he had the prospective employer (a businessman invited for the purpose of the roleplay) inform him aloud that that was the best interview he had heard in a long time and that he would have hired the group leader if he were looking for a job. In general, it is the role of the group leader to see that whoever models is reinforced either with success or praise for the modeled behavior, or both.

Characteristics of Effective Models

The extent to which a child imitates behavior is partly a function of certain characteristics of the model. Adults and children, both filmed and live, have been effective models in studies involving children (Bandura, Blanchard, and Ritter, 1969; Keller and Carlson, 1975; Lovaas, 1967; Ritter, 1968). Some attributes of models may, however, increase the probability that they are imitated. These attributes include the high rewarding potential of the model, demonstration by the model of competence in areas highly regarded by the observer, and general renown or relatively high social standing with respect to the observer.

Bandura (1971) concludes, on the basis of an extensive research program, that the greater the number and variety of models available to children the greater the likelihood that they will find adequate models to observe and imitate. The group offers the possibility of both number and variety.

Who Are the Models?

In order to take advantage of the principles elucidated by Bandura, it is possible for the group leader to draw on a variety of persons for models. These are the group members, the group leader, invited guests, the individual client, and admired persons outside of the group. No one type of model possesses all of the above-mentioned desired characteristics. To compensate for deficiencies in one category of model, several are selected for any one set of behaviors. Let us look first at the group member as a model for others in the group.

Members as Models. In our experience, the more effective models show some of the observer's population characteristics (race, history of delinquency, youth, sex) in addition to the above attributes. For this reason the major source of models is usually the members themselves. The major drawback is that the members of many groups are children or adolescents who have a repertoire of socially maladaptive behaviors and only a limited repertoire of adaptive behaviors. This is especially true in groups whose members have similar problems.

Several practitioners have remedied this by composing groups that include both high- and low-status children. In intervention programs reported by both Chennault (1967) and Lilly (1971), low- and high-status children were paired to work on class projects such as filmmaking and skit production. As a result we have included relatively well-adapted children in most of our groups as models. Although parents of these children have occasionally objected, in the vast majority of cases, parents of models were pleased that their child was selected to be in the group and pointed out particular social skills they might also work on. On other rare occasions, teachers have also objected to pulling a child out of class "who really didn't need the help."

Generally the groups are sufficiently attractive that only two or three children, when asked to be in the group because they could be of help to others as well as learn some additional ways of getting along with others, have objected. In fact, most have been enthusiastic about the opportunity. In three recent projects we involved (with the cooperation of the school) every child in fifth- through eighth-grade classrooms in social-skills groups, and we had no difficulty in finding relevant targets for all of them. This also provided us with ample models for a wide variety of behaviors (LeCroy and Rose, 1986; Hepler and Rose, 1986).

Group Leaders as Models. Although group members may be one of the most desirable sources of models, certain aspects of target behaviors may not be found in the repertoire of any of the children. Under these circumstances, the group leader may also serve as model. The group leader—while different in age, education, often in socioeconomic status and race, as well as other characteristics—can demonstrate a wider range of new behaviors than can the children. In addition, the group leader often (but not always) has greater reinforcement power than any one member of the group. As a result, reports of social-skills training programs have, to date, relied most heavily on demonstrations by the group leader (Elder, Edelstein, and Narick, 1979; Cooke and Apolloni, 1976; Edleson and Rose, 1981). In these studies the group leader demonstrated a skill or set of skills to be used. Such demonstrations, via roleplays of hypothetical or real-life situations, permit the members to focus on a narrow range of behaviors, repeatedly if necessary. Thus the adult model provides a great deal more focus than the child would, with less risk that an undesirable behavior will be repeatedly modeled. In order to obtain both focus and a wide range of desirable (that is, imitation-inducing) characteristics, guests with such characteristics can be invited to the group and instructed in expected behaviors.

Guest Models. These guests are usually children who are a little older, a little more intelligent, a little more athletic, and of the same gender and race. In groups of mixed gender and race, models are also mixed. These models are the most attractive and the most likely to be imitated. In one group of junior high school students the leader brought in a high school student who was a few years older and a member of a local band that was very popular among the group members. The group leader had selected him because of the status he held with the group members and also because of his ability to demonstrate appropriate behaviors in social situations. The band member was, at the time, a well-liked student.

Adults may also be invited as guests. For example, a star basketball player from the local university, a singer from a local popular music group, and a well-liked small businessman from the local community were invited to serve as group models. These adults had high rewarding potential, renown in the community, and skills admired by the group members. As such, they were ideal potential models even though they were from another generational group.

Although their presence alone might have served as an important object of observation, the guests were instructed to present problematic or stressful events that they had handled somewhat effectively. They were told the kinds of behaviors the children were working on and asked to demonstrate these behaviors whenever possible. When the guests are children, they usually go through the same procedures as everyone else in the group, although they might roleplay as models somewhat more frequently and give feedback more often, at least in the early sessions.

In another example of guest models with adolescents, we added two former delinquents to a group of young juvenile offenders (Rose and others, 1971). These former offenders were now "making it," as they held jobs, drove cars, had girlfriends, and had no record of repeated offenses. Held in high esteem by the members, these former delinquents were hired as assistant leaders and, in general, performed the physical and verbal behaviors that the leader wanted members to emulate. The group members were aware of the models' special status as assistants and later, when several new members were added to the group, some of the old members were shifted to the assistant role.

In order to maximize the modeling process we have tried an ongoing open-ended treatment group in which distinct roles were enunciated: new member, regular working member, paid model or assistant, and even a role in which a former group member assumed major leadership functions in the group as an aide. Each role had different contractual arrangements in terms of expected performance and rewards. Although no data are available, the members were pleased with the arrangement, and it provided a wealth of well-trained and appropriate models.

Self-Modeling. In addition to observing others outside of

the group sessions, children can be encouraged to observe their own effective behavior. In many cases, a child may be functioning in a highly adaptive manner in a number of settings, with particular individuals, or at particular times.

We conducted a group for children who had difficulty in getting along with their siblings. It turned out that some of them were interacting successfully with one or more of their siblings while experiencing conflict with others. They were each asked to observe themselves as they interacted with the sibling with whom they got along or when they were interacting well with the conflicting sibling. By discussing what they had observed about themselves, many new ideas about how to interact more positively with other siblings were uncovered. The most powerful self-modeling technique is repeated self-observation on videotape. Before taping, the child is well-trained through the use of other models, extensive rehearsals, coaching, and feedback so that the taped performance is highly suitable for the problem situation.

Other Sources of Models. Puppets and fictional characters in plays and novels may readily serve as models for group members. Behaviors can be readily ascribed to these characters, or famous characters can be selected with well-known characteristics. They often make excellent models, especially for young children, because of their renown (such as the Muppets and Sesame Street characters) and their reinforcing quality. How these nonpersons are incorporated into the program is discussed at the end of the next section.

The Modeling Process

There are basically two approaches to modeling: unstructured and structured. The most common unstructured approach is to bring the group members into contact with desirable models and hope for the best. This can be structured slightly by telling the models which behaviors to demonstrate while in the group. The most common structured procedure is through role-played modeling in the group meeting (that is, demonstrating desirable behaviors in roleplays). Prestructured videotapes, skits, and puppet shows are other ways of demonstrating the model's characteristics to the audience. Let us examine some of these in more detail.

Real-World Modeling. Observations made outside of group meetings can be an extremely useful and accessible source of modeling. If the home situation of the group leader is not too foreign to the group members, they can spend time with the leader and his or her family. The members can be encouraged to observe the leader in social situations similar to those with which they themselves are confronted. The leader can also identify children in group members' classes and neighborhoods who can serve as natural models. By assigning observations of these models in particular situations, the group leader can draw on a rich and varied source of demonstrated behaviors.

In one group, all the adolescents were asked to find one person they really admired and to observe that person for a week. At the end of the week each of the members described the specific and general characteristics of the model. The members were surprised to find some characteristics they did not admire. Then each person targeted a subset of desirable behaviors, which the group leader and the members roleplayed for each other.

Roleplayed Modeling. The foremost method of modeling in the group is roleplayed modeling because of the amount of control the group leader has in providing the members with useful specific behaviors. The group leader or the member who roleplays can prepare in advance. The model can be instructed by the group concerning the behaviors he or she should perform. Members can be instructed what to observe while the model is roleplaying. The modeling demonstration can be repeated if the group leader or members think it is necessary. As a result of this flexibility, it is an extremely powerful modeling tool. Because of its importance, let us look at a detailed example of roleplayed modeling.

In a group of mostly shy and anxious children, ages ten to eleven, Margie wanted to know how to deal with her friend, Janet, who frequently walked away from Margie while she was in the middle of telling a story. Margie reported that she was upset with Janet and wanted to say something to her but she just did not know how to go about it. The group had discussed several ways of handling the situation when they asked the group leader to demonstrate what she would do in the situation.

Group leader: First I'll show everyone how to walk up to Janet and say most of the things that we decided would keep Janet a friend, but let her know that Margie doesn't like what she is doing and is mad at her because of it. I'll act as if I'm Margie and I need someone else to act like Janet would.

Emily: I will!

Group leader: Okay, Emily you can play Janet. Now the rest of you—Andy, Lee, George, and Margie—all have to watch carefully and tell me what I did after the play is over. Act like detectives and try to remember everything Margie says and does during the play. Like most detectives you have a pencil and notebook to write down what you see. Watch in particular whether what I say is useful. Look at how I say what I say. And look at my body posture and eye contact. Okay, are the detectives ready?

(The modeling begins.)

Group leader: Janet, can we walk back to class together alone?

Emily: Um, why?

Group leader: (looking directly in Janet's eyes) Janet, we're good friends, right?

Emily: (hesitatingly) Yeah.

Group leader: Yeah, usually we are and today I was telling you and Sue Ellen a story and you walked away in the middle of my story. I felt really bad when you walked away.

Emily: Well I wanted to see Helena, you know, the new girl.

Group leader: I know you did but it hurt my feelings. It would make me feel better if you could wait until I finish and then go do something else. This has happened before, too. I really think friends can tell each other when they are upset with each other, so that's why I'm telling you now.

Emily: Yeah, I'm sorry. I didn't realize that it bothered you. I'm glad you told me.

In this example, many of the principles of effective modeling, some of which have already been discussed above, have been demonstrated. The group leader drew on a problem situation relevant for Margie in particular and, at least to some degree, relevant for the rest of the group as well. The desired response was limited in scope and involved interaction with another person. The group leader instructed the observers what to look for and to jot it down if they saw it. The model was reinforced for her behavior. Since they were young children, the group leader made a game out of it by assigning the observers the roles of detectives.

What we did not see was that the group leader had the roleplayers actually move, physically, in order to duplicate the situation as nearly as possible. She also arranged a few props, such as books, and separated the roleplayers slightly from the observers. This is necessary to keep the drama-like quality of the roleplay and to maintain the interest of the members. As we mentioned earlier, it would have been possible for a member to model for the child instead of, or following, modeling by the group leader.

One variation in the selection of behaviors to be performed is the use of prestructured situations or vignettes rather than individualized situations developed by each child. In these vignettes the group leader has a list of situations that teachers, parents, and the children themselves in pregroup interviews had noted were problematic. These vignettes are particularly useful for children who have forgotten to fill in a diary or who find situational analysis too difficult because of intellectual, cultural, or motivational differences. Even if the group leader prefers a highly individualized approach, it is always reassuring to have a few vignettes at one's disposal. Hazel, Schumaker, Sherman, and Sheldon-Wildon (1981); Freedman (1974); and Rosenthal

(1978) provide samples of such vignettes in their roleplay tests, which are well suited to adolescents. We provide a similar list for younger children (Edleson, 1979). Vignettes have the advantage of using a central theme at every meeting, which all the members work on. It is also easier for the group leader to plan more effectively for situations to be handled at a given meeting. Many group leaders prefer to work only with vignettes while others prefer a mixture of individualized situations and vignettes. Variations in roleplaying from meeting to meeting are also necessary to maintain interest. One of the major variations is the videotaped presentation of a model roleplaying or acting out a given situation. Vignettes are very often presented in videotaped format.

Videotaped Modeling. The advent of low-priced videotape equipment has enabled group leaders to bring a wide variety of models into group meetings; this had been impossible in the recent past. Many studies have recently reported the use of taped models. Hazel, Schumaker, Sherman, and Sheldon-Wildon (1981) have developed an extensive program using videotaped models for teaching adolescents social skills. Their program, ASSET, consists of eight sessions on giving positive feedback, giving negative feedback, accepting negative feedback, resisting peer pressure, problem solving, negotiation, following instructions, and conversation skills. In each session, the group leader presents a series of videotaped scenes involving interactions between teenagers. Each interaction is shown with models deficient in appropriate skills and, following a discussion, several scenes are viewed in which appropriate, but not perfect, skills are demonstrated. Each of these scenes is also discussed and then members are given the opportunity to verbally and behaviorally rehearse the scene. This format is repeated throughout the eight sessions of training.

Two particularly good examples of combined self-modeling and videotaping are studies by Creer and Miklich (1970) and Dowrick (1982). Creer and Miklich (1970) worked with a ten-year-old asthmatic boy who spent most of his time watching television or reading. He was rebuffed in his attempts to join in activities with other children with teasing and name-calling, which he responded to with temper tantrums. In order to change his behavior, the researchers developed two videotapes. The first displayed inappropriate behavior, including a scene in which the boy was rejected by two boys with whom he had asked to play. The second tape showed appropriate interactions such as initiating conversations with other children. Over a two-week period, the boy viewed the two tapes on alternating days. After viewing the second film, the boy's appropriate behavior increased. By developing a videotaped self-model, the authors greatly enhanced the child's ability to increase his already existing adaptive behavior.

In a similar study, Dowrick (1982) developed a set of two-minute-long videotapes of effective-only behavior for each of eighteen developmentally disabled males and females who ranged in age from five to thirteen years old. Repeated viewing of the videotapes resulted in significant increases in the children's effective social and motor-coordination behaviors. We have attempted to incorporate this procedure of work with individuals into residential-treatment groups and school groups. Prior to group meetings, we videotaped group members involved in constructive behaviors in class, on the playground, and in unit meetings. These were played at group meetings and members were instructed to replay their own tapes several times a week as homework.

When videotape resources are available, we use them at least several times in every series of sessions to provide variety in models and in ways of delivering modeled behaviors. Videotapes can be reviewed a number of times as homework, which provides the children with multiple observations. Videotaped modeling does not, however, offer the flexibility of the tailor-made live demonstration. Using both live modeling and videotape presentations combines the advantages of flexibility and repetition.

Modeling Through Puppets and Stories. The popularity of television shows such as "Sesame Street" and the "Muppets" has shown the power of animated characters to communicate with children. The use of puppets may, at least for younger children, be a way of bringing a variety of models into a group meeting. Cartledge and Milburn (1981) have described a program of the American Guidance Service entitled "Developing Understanding of Self and Others" (DUSO). Among other things, the DUSO program utilizes puppets to model appropriate alternative responses in roleplays. It also uses animated characters to prompt group behaviors such as helping others, waiting to speak, and raising hands.

Fiction and nonfiction stories describing difficulties similar to those of the group members might also be assigned for group readings and discussions or individually, between group sessions. Cartledge and Milburn (1981) suggest that the American Guidance Service's *Book Finder* be used to locate stories with models of both inappropriate and appropriate behavior.

Modeling Through Scripts. Sarason and Ganzer (1969) have used written scripts in both modeling and rehearsal with groups of institutionalized delinquents. Understanding that most delinquents' models have been antisocial adults and older adolescents, the scripts were used to demonstrate the effectiveness of establishing new, socially acceptable, and, hopefully, exciting social models for the delinquents. In working with adolescent delinquents, Brierton, Rose, and Flanagan (1975) asked that the group members rewrite the Sarason and Ganzer scripts. It appeared that police in the original scripts were far gentler than those in Chicago, at least from the group's perspective. The very process of script revision involved the group in formulating a realistic appraisal and definition of their situation and in developing effective interactions to resolve the difficulties they were confronting.

Assignments to write an "ideal behavior" script can facilitate both observation of others and the generation of alternative ways of behaving. While scripts are mentioned here as a source of models for the group leader, we will discuss them at greater length later in this chapter when covering skills rehearsal.

General Versus Specific Modeling Strategies. As Bandura (1969) has pointed out, "Modeled characteristics that are highly discernible can be more readily acquired than subtle attributes which must be abstracted from heterogeneous responses differing on numerous stimulus dimensions" (p. 136). This does not imply that complex sets of skills cannot be learned. It does assume, however, that an instructional approach that uses combinations of hierarchical modeling and reinforcement of successive approximations if often required. But some children, because of previous learning or innate capacity, are able to learn a general approach to dealing with problem situations without learning all of the detailed intermediate steps. Practically, what this implies is that complex behavior patterns should, as in the above examples, be modeled globally first, and then broken down only into those smaller units that the child is having difficulty in duplicating. The smaller units are more readily modeled, rehearsed, and reinforced. An advantage of doing both is that some of the concrete behaviors related to a general approach may already be in the child's repertoire and not every one of the requisite skills may need to be modeled. Moreover, the capacity of a child to generalize from previous experiences can be tested in this way.

One additional principle of learning theory (Bandura, 1971) purports that practice in the modeled behavior increases the probability that a modeled behavior will be duplicated in the real world. The next procedure, behavior rehearsal, is based on that principle.

Behavior Rehearsal

After observing one or more modeled interactions, children are more likely than before to imitate them in their own lives. Before attempting to implement a complex sequence of new behaviors in the real world, practicing these skills in the supportive environment of a group meeting will further increase the likelihood of performance in the real world. Having both observed and practiced a new set of behaviors, the child is better prepared to deal with the situation and is probably less anxious. Such practice in a group meeting usually involves the group leader or members playing the role of significant others in the situation while the child plays his or her own role. This procedure is commonly referred to as behavior rehearsal. Although the rehearsal is usually first practiced in the group meeting, assignments are often given to rehearse or roleplay a given behav-

ior with a partner, a friend, or a family member in a setting outside the group.

Again, we will return to our sample group meeting. In
this excerpt Margie is given an opportunity to practice the modeled response in a roleplay. We pick up the group meeting at
this point.

Group leader: Well, Margie, you've had a chance to watch me
handle the situation. Why don't you give it a try?

Margie: Oh, okay, I think I can do it.

Group members: Good for you, Margie. You can do it.

Group leader: Okay, detectives, take out your notebooks and
keep track of what Margie does well and also anything you
might do differently. And Emily, you did such a good job as
Janet, why don't you play that role again. (Emily nods agreement.)

Margie: Here goes. "Janet, I'm your friend, you know. And
today, when we were talking with Sue Ellen, you . . . you
walked away in the middle of the story I was telling. I got so
mad at you . . . I'm still mad at you. You do that all the time."

Emily: "Well, I wanted to go talk to that other girl."

Margie: "Uh . . . well . . . uh, I felt hurt that you did that."

Emily: "Well, I didn't mean to hurt you."

Group leader: How about if we stop for a minute and talk
about Margie's roleplay? I saw lots of things she did well. What
about you?

In the above interaction Margie tried to use what she had
seen the group leader model earlier. She changed her previously
reported behavior and replicated in her own way the behavior
she had seen modeled.

Rehearsal is effective with a wide variety of child populations. For example, it has been used to increase sharing within
a kindergarten class (Barton and Osborne, 1978). Children who
had difficulty in sharing practiced asking others to share as well
as sharing themselves, when requested to by a classmate. Their

"positive practice" procedure increased sharing of toys three-fold.

Rehearsal techniques (often combined with modeling and other procedures) have also been widely used in teaching unemployed teenagers job-finding and interviewing skills (Azrin, Flores, and Kaplan, 1975; Kelly, Wildman, and Berler, 1980). In such programs teenagers have been taught to locate job openings and to present themselves more effectively in the job interview. In some programs the teenagers engage in extensive rehearsals of the job interview in order to increase their ability to convey information about job-related past experience, to direct questions to the interviewer, and to express enthusiasm and interest in the job.

Principles of Effective Rehearsals

There are a number of considerations in effective rehearsals, some of which overlap with effective roleplayed modeling. These include adequate training in roleplaying for the children, determining an appropriate level of difficulty, setting the stage realistically, and creating opportunity for multiple trials. We shall discuss these principles below.

Level of Difficulty. In early rehearsals the group leaders or members may model only one or two responses that the client attempts to duplicate in a later rehearsal, as in the above example of Margie. As the child becomes competent in single responses, the significant other in the roleplay provides an increasing number of counterstatements. The object is first to provide the roleplayer with an early success experience, but eventually to work toward the more complicated and extended conditions of the real world.

The child playing the significant other must also be instructed to keep the situation relatively easy in the beginning. The group leader acts as a director, making sure that the level of difficulty created by significant others is only gradually increased. All too often, in their flair for the dramatic or in a need to compete, the roleplayer playing the significant other creates an impossible situation to solve. In such a case, the group leader would stop the roleplay immediately, reinstruct the roleplayer, and begin again.

In addition to gradually lengthening the rehearsals and making them more complicated as treatment progresses, it is also possible to add new and more difficult situations related to the central problem of the child. For example, Gittleman (1965) employed this principle to its maximum when he arranged a series of vignettes for the aggressively responding child to model and then rehearse. These situations ranged from mildly frustrating to highly frustrating. As children succeeded at one level they went on to the next.

Some researchers have arranged an entire curriculum of problems that move from less difficult to more difficult. Hazel, Schumaker, Sherman, and Sheldon-Wildon (1981) and Goldstein, Carr, Davidson, and Wehr (1981) have created such a curriculum for adolescents. Group leaders have used some or all of the situations developed by these authors in their adolescent groups. Goldstein, Carr, Davidson, and Wehr (1981) advise that the content of the vignettes should be varied and relevant to the lives of the trainees. It is helpful to let the members themselves readjust the vignettes in the group meetings to fit their interests and circumstances.

Eventually, in long-term groups, new situations are roleplayed for which there has been no preparation or modeling. It is assumed that at one point in the treatment process, after numerous trials, the member will have learned enough basic skills to be able to handle novel situations, at least in the roleplays. Before members reach this phase extensive training is required. If the member cannot handle the situation, additional modeling and other preparation may be added.

Setting the Stage. In rehearsal, just as in modeling, the attempt is made to simulate the real world as nearly as possible. Actors knock at doors, enter rooms, use props, separate themselves from the audience, and where possible, rehearse under the most realistic conditions. In order to make it realistic, the group leader or the person rehearsing will set the stage by briefly reviewing the events that led to the situation, the situation itself, and characteristics of the scene in which the event takes place. Members may take a few seconds to imagine how they felt and thought in the situation at the critical moment.

Repeated Rehearsals. Obviously, one rehearsal is not sufficient to teach a child a given set of behaviors. Replications by others with similar problems, replications as homework assignments, and replications in pairs in the group are all ways of maximizing the number of trials. When there are four to seven children in the group, providing every child a chance to roleplay and arranging multiple trials requires a great deal of creativity and effort.

One way of using the group to carry out multiple trials is for the group leader to provide the stimulus situation for each child, one at a time, in rapid succession. The group leader can change the exact stimulus to fit each child's individual situation. This is often done as a review at the end of the meeting, as demonstrated in the following example.

Group leader: Jerzy, c'mon lend me that money; I'll get it back to you sometime.

Jerzy: No way, you don't pay anybody on time.

Group leader: Estelle, could I borrow your new dress? I promise I won't get it dirty.

Estelle: Sorry, but I don't lend my new clothes.

Group leader: Dale, let me look at the quiz answers, today, in class. You always keep them hidden. Be a good friend.

Dale: Nope, a good friend doesn't help a friend to cheat.

Group leader: Hey, that was great, shall we do it one more time? This time, I'll change the situations.

Obviously, this exercise works best if there is only one type of response being taught. However, it is possible even if repeated responses are required. It should be noted that in a period of a few minutes there were five rehearsals and model demonstrations, since each rehearsal by one child is a model for all

the others. This repeated practice exercise also requires extensive experience in roleplaying. Other procedures must be used in
early group sessions for children unfamiliar with roleplaying.

Preparing Members to Roleplay. It is our experience that
in early group sessions some children are very anxious about
roleplaying in front of the group. Others, usually adolescents,
will initially refuse to even participate in a roleplay. In the
event that one or more members refuse to roleplay or even if
they are initially anxious, we attempt to develop roleplaying behaviors incrementally. First, we try to introduce roleplaying
through games in early meetings. Such games as charades and
"Who am I?" that were mentioned earlier are ideal for such
preparation. Board games that instruct the participants to roleplay a simple situation are also helpful in this regard. It seems
easier for children to accept and follow through on instructions
from a game than from a group leader.

After some preparatory games we might ask reluctant
group members to simply state what they would say aloud without movement or affect. For example, Gary would be allowed
to say, "I would say to him that I didn't like what he was doing
and if he kept doing it, I would walk away." Another child
might be more comfortable in first rehearsing the lines of the
roleplay before rehearsing with appropriate movement, affect,
and voice volume. At other times we will instruct the group
members to rehearse in pairs without audiences, as a way of easing them into a more public display. We might also request the
more hesitant children to first play a significant person in another child's problem situation. The first roleplays are usually
one sentence replies, as in the last example. Gradually, an increasing number of multiple responses to responses of the
significant other are required. Occasionally, tokens or other
concrete reinforcers are used to shape increasingly difficult
roleplaying for younger children.

Another way of making children's first attempts at roleplaying easier is to help them through difficult moments with
coaching or prompting.

Behavior Rehearsal and Coaching. Early in the rehearsal
process, group members often experience difficulty with even

the most elementary steps of a new response. As stated earlier, the group leader may use several strategies in preparing the members for roleplaying and for easing them into a roleplay. In addition, a number of techniques can be used to coach the child through the first attempts at rehearsing new skills. Before discussing the various coaching strategies, we present a group meeting in which several of the strategies were utilized. The teenagers in this group were all experiencing some type of family conflict. In this excerpt, the group was roleplaying a solution to a problem that Joan was experiencing with her brother.

Group leader: Right now we are going to take some time to help Joan get ready to try out her solution. We're going to need someone to help Joan since she hasn't roleplayed a complicated situation like this before. That person will be her coach and give her suggestions if she gets stuck and forgets the way the model talked and acted. The coach will sit right behind Joan and whisper suggestions in her ear.

Jim: Since I was the model, I guess I could be her coach.

Group leader: Okay. Great. And we also need someone to play the part of Joan's brother—the person Joan was having a hard time with. Who wants to play her brother? How about you, Erik?

Erik: Well . . . I'm not sure I can do that very well.

Group leader: Do you think it would help if you also had a coach?

Erik: Yeah—then I think I could do it.

Midge: I think I know exactly what little brothers are like—brats! I can be Erik's coach.

Group leader: What do you think, Erik?

Erik: Yeah, Midge could help me. Sit behind me, too.

(Rehearsal with coaching begins.)

Joan: "Erik, you know I was real upset last night that you were playing your drums while I was trying to study for my test."

Midge: (Whispers to Erik: Tell her "So, what do I care!")

Erik: (playing the brother) "Yeah, so what do I care. You know my band is going to have its first gig in two weeks."

Joan: "Well, uh . . . uh . . . "

Jim: (Also whispering: "Tell him that you know it is important and make a deal.")

Joan: "Erik, I know your band is really important to you but so is my studying. Can we make some kind of deal?"

By assigning a coach to Joan, the group leader helped ease her into a first attempt at implementing a solution. By assigning a coach to Erik, the group leader helped to increase the level of difficulty of the responses given by Joan's brother in the roleplay. If the leader had wished to lower the level of difficulty, he or she might have acted as a coach or suggested that Midge help Erik respond in a less belligerent way. Initially, the leader acts as coach, especially if none of the members are particularly competent in the desired behaviors. As soon as possible, however, the leader involves other members, as in the above case.

We have used coaching in the initial phases of most complicated rehearsals. We also use coaching when helping group members to initially serve as group discussion leaders. Coaching need not be verbal, as in the above example. Cue cards or hand signals might be used instead. For example, in one group, large cards with such prompts as "I statement," "Feelings," and "Praise" were flashed to the roleplayer in order to cue certain types of responding. In another group we used hand signals in which pointing to the eye meant "give eye contact," pointing to the mouth meant "louder!", finger over the mouth meant "quieter," and a soft clap meant "keep it up, you are doing great."

Oden and Asher (1977) have reported an intervention strategy in which coaching was the central component. In their program, pairs of children were coached in social skills relevant to making friends. Then games were played in which those skills were practiced. In the final step, what occurred during the play period was reviewed with an adult coach. The program was demonstrated to be highly effective. As we pointed out earlier, coaching makes it possible to work on complex situations. Other structured rehearsal procedures also permit working on more global problems. These include role instructional training, scripts, and fixed-role therapy.

Variations on Rehearsals. As mentioned in the section on modeling, Sarason and Ganzer (1969) have used written scripts as a central procedure in an intervention program for delinquent boys. After extensive interviews and assessment roleplays with the boys, the authors developed a series of model scripts that covered a wide range of common problems, including how to interview for a job, how to interact with a law enforcement officer, and how to respond to peer pressure.

Models enacted the scripts while the boys observed. Then the boys were given an opportunity to enact the various scripts. Each roleplay was videotaped. The boys discussed the ways in which each roleplay related to their own lives. Reports from counselors and the boys, as well as follow-up data, indicate the scripted rehearsal procedure improved the delinquents' situations.

A variation on the use of scripts is role instruction, in which the child takes a "model role" and acts as if he or she were really that person. This procedure can be utilized during ongoing group interaction; that is, a new role may be played while the group discusses something.

Role instructions were used with Rusty and Millie in a group of thirteen-year-old children. Rusty had difficulty talking in groups and making friends. During one group discussion, Rusty was assigned the role of a highly participative member for ten minutes. Millie, on the other hand, annoyed the other members by her frequent critical and sarcastic remarks. She was asked to practice making only positive comments about other members and the group meeting for the same ten minutes.

Prior to the role-taking, the group leader gave detailed, individual instructions to the children about the roles they were to play. These were written on the chalkboard. At the end of the roleplaying period the entire group evaluated how well the roles had been performed. Subsequently, time periods were gradually increased to the point where an entire session might be spent in a model role.

One can add even greater structure to a role instruction exercise. The group leader might prepare in advance written role descriptions tailored to the specific difficulties of each group member. The leader would then develop instructions for each child and conduct the group meeting while members attempt to play their roles accurately. (This is similar to fixed-role therapy described by Kelly in 1955.) At the end of such an exercise we often ask the group members to develop a new script as home-work. In subsequent meetings the members play their self-designed roles and in this way are helped to make a deliberate selection of behavior patterns.

After an initial set of practice sessions, the children are urged to "try on" the behavior in the real world and to observe others' reactions. Children are encouraged in the first phase of treatment to maintain the fiction of playing a role in their own minds. The assumption is that to play "as if" reduces the threat incurred by performing new behaviors in the real world. The role can be explored without irrevocable commitment and be-cause of the intentional lack of detail, the children are free to develop their new roles in ways that feel comfortable.

Fixed-role therapy can be thought of as a form of guided behavior rehearsal followed by assignments in the real world. We have found scripts and fixed roles very difficult for children to use between sessions. Such techniques are, however, very use-ful with teenagers capable of carrying out complex assignments with little supervision. The younger the child, the more these techniques are limited to times when leader coaching is available.

One major procedure in the modeling sequence remains: feedback given to the children on their performance of a new alternative response. All rehearsal and coaching strategies are al-most always followed by feedback from the members and the group leader.

Feedback

Feedback refers to the process of providing a given indi-vidual with information, observations, and impressions about the individual's performance or general attitudes in real life or a roleplay. These comments may be made by fellow group members, the group leader, and/or significant others about the child's specific performance or general patterns. Feedback may be exceedingly helpful in learning new behaviors; however, if delivered arbitrarily, vaguely, or hostilely, feedback may be quite damaging to the person receiving it. Constructive or therapeutic feedback from multiple sources is one of the major advantages of the group provided that therapeutic criteria for delivering that feedback are adhered to. In our groups children are taught these criteria and helped to practice them as they provide feedback to one another on their various rehearsals. In this way they not only improve on the rehearsed behavior, they also learn how to give and receive both positive and critical feedback in real-life situations. Praise and criticism are important aspects of most interpersonal relationships.

When working on increasing effective assertive behaviors with adults, behavior rehearsal combined with feedback on performance has had superior results to practicing alone (McFall and Marston, 1970). Van Houten, Hill, and Parsons (1975) have shown feedback to also be effective in increasing academic behaviors and peer interaction rates of children. The importance of feedback in the learning process has led Bandura (1971) to conclude that everyday learning is usually achieved through modeling, performance, and self-corrective adjustments made on the basis of informative feedback on performance.

In this section we shall review the general guidelines for providing feedback, the specific criteria for evaluating the performance of peers, the techniques of giving feedback after a rehearsal or videotape, and the training for giving feedback. To illustrate many of the procedures we shall begin with the group presented at the beginning of this chapter, in which Margie is talking to a friend of hers about an incident that happened on the playground. In the example below, feedback is offered Margie by other group members and the leader. We begin just after Margie has rehearsed one possible strategy. The group is now offering feedback on Margie's roleplayed performance.

Group leader: Well, first, could you tell Margie what she did that you thought might be useful for her. You can look at your suggestion list if you need help.

Adam: She looked Emily right in the eyes, lots of the time, when she was talking.

Group leader: Good, I see others nodding in agreement. That's one thing Margie did very well. What else? Anyone else have any ideas?

George: Yeah, and she said it in a real mad voice and she looked real mad.

Group leader: Yes. How did she look mad?

John: She wasn't smiling at all. She had a straight face, and her mouth was in that mad kind of way.

Group leader: Right. What about what Margie actually said? Any ideas there? Think about what the model did.

Emily: Well, she told me that we're friends and what I did exactly that made her mad.

Group leader: Okay, lots of you seem to be agreeing with that, too. So Margie, it seems we all think you did a lot of good things in the rehearsal: the way you looked at Janet (Emily), the way your face showed you were mad, the way you told Janet that you're friends but that what she did made you mad. (to group) Okay now can you give Margie some suggestions on how you might have done it differently? What did you write down?

George: I agree with all the others, but I would have talked a little louder. If you're mad, it's hard to be mad and sound so quiet at the same time.

Group leader: That's something to think about. Any other things you guys saw you would do a little differently?

Andy: I'll tell you one thing she did wrong . . .

Group leader: (interrupting) You mean what you might do differently?

Andy: (laughs) Yeah, I forgot. What I would do differently, would be to be a little calmer, like the model, and not get quite so mad.

After the feedback was completed, Margie was asked to summarize what she had heard from the other group members and the group leader, and to consider what she thought she might change. As is usually the case, an additional roleplay was rehearsed in the group so that Margie could try to incorporate the new ideas she liked. She was also given an assignment of rehearsing the situation with her "buddy" before she tried it out in the real world as a homework assignment.

Guidelines for Feedback. We set down guidelines for offering feedback on a group member's rehearsal performance. Most of these guidelines are exemplified in the above illustration. The first guideline is that positive feedback is always given first in order that the child be reinforced quickly following a rehearsal of new skills. Positive feedback also creates an atmosphere in which criticism will more likely be accepted (Flowers, 1979).

The second guideline is that criticism of a performance is in the form of actions or statements the observer would do differently. "What I would do differently would be to speak a little louder and give a little more eye contact" is the desired form of a critical feedback statement. If a child fails to include such a suggestion when giving feedback the leader asks for one. For example, when in the above dialogue Andy said, "What you did wrong was . . ." the group leader said, "You mean, what you might do differently?" In this way, aversion to criticism is dramatically reduced.

A third guideline is that whether positive or critical, feedback is specific. When the client is too general, the group leader (and later the members) will ask what is meant by the general statement. In response to "You should be nicer," the group leader might ask, "How would she be nicer in that situation?" or "To be nice, exactly what would you do or say if you were in that situation?"

Another guideline is that in the early sessions the observers are provided with specific criteria for providing feedback. As we discuss below, they are trained in the use of these criteria.

Finally, the group leader, or preferably the member, reviews the feedback aloud. In a rerehearsal the members try out those new ideas that they evaluate as helpful or doable in the situation. In summarizing, the group leader stresses the positive attributes of the interaction. After the feedback, if there is still disagreement, the members with the problem are the final arbiters of what they would like to do or say. The above guidelines for feedback may also be applied following the viewing of tapes, which is the next subject.

Taping for Feedback. If available, video- and audiotapes serve as a valuable resource for group feedback. By playing back the taped version of parts of a roleplay that had already been discussed, one increases the accuracy and specificity of that feedback. Playback affords multiple opportunities to review a given situation. What the group misses the first time can often be caught in a subsequent review. Moreover, the roleplayer can also be an observer in the played back version of the roleplay. Children may often discover physical and other nonverbal attributes that may be interfering with the effectiveness of their performance.

In studies reviewed elsewhere in this chapter, videotaped review of performances has been a major component of intervention. As previously mentioned, Creer and Miklich (1970) used videotapes in supplying a ten-year-old asthmatic boy with models as well as feedback on his behavior. Chandler (1973) videotaped skits performed by delinquents to give them a better idea of their own behavior and the way others might view it. In general, videotaping, playback, and discussion are extremely time-consuming. We have used them incidentally to provide variation in the group and to increase cohesion, but because of time constraints, have not used them on a regular basis. If videotapes can be made accessible for reviewing outside of group time, adolescents can be assigned to view the tapes with their buddies at a considerable savings in group time (but at the cost of group leader feedback).

Criteria Checklists for Effective Feedback. In addition to the general guidelines discussed earlier, criteria checklists can facilitate the thoroughness of the information given to the roleplayer. These criteria are used early in treatment as a prompt, but as the group members become familiar with them, they are faded. The checklists may be used in their entirety or, as often happens with younger children, only a few may be used at a time.

As part of their ASSET program for adolescents, Hazel, Schumaker, Sherman, and Sheldon-Wildon (1981) have developed sets of criteria for guiding group members in both giving and receiving feedback. The ASSET program focuses on teaching these skills for use in everyday life. We have also developed similar sets of criteria (see Rose, Hanusa, Tolman, and Hall, 1982). These apply to both in-group feedback and feedback given and received in everyday life. We have included the more relevant of those lists in this section. They include checklists for giving positive feedback, for giving constructive critical feedback, and for receiving both positive and critical feedback. These lists only suggest dimensions that can be considered in performing and in giving feedback. Not every criterion must be met. What one chooses often depends on the situation.

Criteria to consider when giving positive feedback include the following.

1. Keep eye contact with the other person.
2. Face the person.
3. Talk loud enough to be heard but do not yell.
4. Smile when talking or at least do not frown.
5. Keep an appropriate distance from the other person.
6. Talk in clear and short sentences.
7. Offer feedback soon after the event.
8. Use "I" statements.
9. Touch or move toward the person being praised when appropriate.
10. Vary the type of statements used.
11. Do not mix praise with "put-downs," sarcastic or dishonest statements.

For many children receiving praise is as difficult as giving it. They are trained to receive praise by using the following general criteria: Acknowledge the praise where valid, or thank the person, and follow points 1, 2, 3, 5, 6, 7, 8, and 10 above. Do not deny honest praise or put yourself down.

For giving constructive criticism the following set of options has been developed.

1.   Keep a serious face.
2.   Ask to talk with the person for a moment.
3.   Praise what is positive.
4.   Acknowledge the limits on the other person.
5.   State how you feel ("I" statement).
6.   State what you think went wrong.
7.   State criticism tentatively.
8.   Be specific about what was done wrong.
9.   Give the person a reason to change.
10. Ask if the person understands; if not, explain again.
11. Ask how the other person feels.
12. Give suggestions for change.
13. Points 1, 2, 3, 5, 6, 7, 8, and 10 in first list above.

For receiving criticism this final set of options has been developed.

1.   Keep a neutral facial expression.
2.   Stay near the person.
3.   Listen to every word; try not to turn yourself off.
4.   Agree with the criticism if valid.
5.   Agree with that part that is valid.
6.   Agree, at least, that the other person sees the criticism as valid; for example, "I see that's the way you view . . ."
7.   Agree with the possibility that the criticism may be correct; for example, "It is possible that . . ."
8.   If surprised, ask for time to think about it.
9.   If criticism is too general, ask for specifics.
10. If not sure of criticism, state that you will watch for it in upcoming situations.
11. Ask others to confirm the criticism.
12. Say you understand and ask to tell your side.
13. Stay calm.
14. Don't interrupt.
15. Points 1, 2, 3, 6, 7, 8, and 10 of the giving praise list above.

In order to involve the children to a greater degree, some group leaders have found it useful to provide only one of the checklists and let the group develop the others in discussion. Although such a discussion is time-consuming, the children who develop the lists themselves are more likely to use them in practice.

Training in Giving Feedback. It will not always be the case that group members are immediately sufficiently skilled or motivated to give positive feedback or constructive criticism. We often find it necessary to teach members how to give positive feedback and phrase criticism so as to suggest alternative actions.

In teaching group members to give and receive both positive and corrective feedback we usually provide the above lists, sometimes in simplified language, depending upon the abilities of the members. After providing the list we will give examples and, as often as possible, spend group time teaching the members to develop both praise statements and constructive criticism. Such exercises focus on both giving feedback in day-to-day life and in giving feedback on roleplay performances in group meetings.

In groups of younger children and those with developmental disabilities we often train each member to watch for and give feedback on one specific criterion, such as eye contact or "I" statements. Over time, we add additional criteria. In this way we are shaping a member's ability to give feedback on several criteria. Almost every situation has specific criteria associated with the content. These are discussed in terms of the unique requirements of that situation before the rehearsal and are added to the list. In many cases the group leader will ask the group to consider only those criteria with which the given member is struggling. Going over the entire list may be too time-consuming to permit everyone to roleplay in one session.

One way we have taught praise and criticism skills is through the use of "round robin" exercises. For example, in one group of young children each child was asked to look at the group member on the right and to think about one good thing that this member did in the group or in class. After a few minutes of thinking, each member was asked to state that "good thing" and to attempt to use the list of criteria when doing so. Because this group consisted of younger children, the leader wrote simple prompt statements on the chalkboard to cue the members. The group leader also coached the group members in the use of the criteria. After the praise had been given the group members evaluated both how it was given and how it was received. Another variation is to put each child's name on an index card and request every group member to select a card at random. One at a time, each child then praises the child whose name is on the card.

Criticism must be handled more gingerly since many clients have had unfortunate histories as victims of criticism. The leader may initially model both the giving and receiving of criticism by first asking for criticism directed towards him- or herself. With very young children this might take the form of a round robin using the following phrase, "If I were the group leader, what I would do differently would be . . ." Using the same phrase, the children would then repeat the leader's statement and add a suggestion of their own. In groups of older children and adolescents, we have started in a similar way by asking that constructive criticism from each member be first directed towards the leader. The members and the leader write down one suggestion for change and then the leader responds to each one. The leader goes first. "Okay, Sheldon, one thing I would do differently if I were group leader would be to let us know or decide what games we were going to play the very first thing." Then the leader models the desired way of receiving criticism: "That's something I really should consider," "That's something I haven't thought of before," or "I'll give that some attention." Then, each adolescent follows in turn. If members have difficulty in coming up with a suggestion the group leader prompts them.

We have also started by asking all the children to write their names on a card and add one or two things they might do differently in the group or elsewhere. The cards are then mixed up and chosen at random by the members. The members are then required to provide the person on the card with his or her own constructive feedback. How each child gives and receives criticism is carefully monitored using the checklists provided. Finally, when cohesion is high and the members have had extensive experience with feedback in the exercises, they are permitted to give constructive critical feedback to each other following each of the roleplays.

It should be noted that we teach group members both positive feedback and constructive criticism for two reasons. First, they are prerequisite skills to facilitate effective rehearsals in the group and effective correction of errors in these rehearsals. They are also, and perhaps more importantly, extremely useful interpersonal skills that can facilitate conflict resolution or even, at times, prevent conflict in each child's and adolescent's life. For these two reasons, teaching positive feedback and constructive criticism skills is of central importance. As such, a significant amount of time is devoted in early meetings to developing these skills.

Summary

The modeling sequence—modeling, rehearsal, coaching, and feedback—usually follows the group's explication of the problem situation and the selection of alternative interactive responses. (If cognitive responses play a major role in determining adaptive or appropriate outcome, cognitive procedures may be used with or instead of the modeling sequence. These are discussed in Chapter Seven.) Although any of the procedures may be used alone or in combination with any other of the procedures, the usual sequence is summarized in Figure 5.

It should be noted in the above paradigm that rerehearsal often follows feedback so that the members can incorporate others' suggestions into their final rehearsal. If this last rehearsal is successful, homework is usually assigned in which the child agrees to use the skills learned in a specific situation before the next meeting. Chapter Eleven is devoted to a detailed discussion of assignments and readers are referred to that chapter for more detail.

As may have been noted, positive feedback is a major part of the modeling sequence. Also, when members have com-

Figure 5. The Modeling Sequence.

Modeling

↓

Rehearsal With Coaching

↓

Feedback

↓

Rehearsal Without Coaching

↓

Feedback

↓

Rerehearsal Without Coaching

pleted their homework, positive consequences are usually arranged. This arrangement of positive consequences and stimulus conditions for certain behaviors, in addition to how these are integrated into the group process, are the subjects of the next chapter.

Chapter Seven

Reinforcing Behavior Changes Using Stimulus and Operant Control

Every time one of the children assisted another child with her project during the meeting, the group leader gave her a token and praised her warmly. At the end of the meeting each child added up her tokens and put the number on the group thermometer.

During the group session, Larry, Rich, Roberto, and Toma were discussing some of the situations at school in which they got in trouble. The timer was set at random. Whoever was talking when the bell rang received five points.

As the adolescents brought in a situation to discuss in the group and described how they finished their other assignments, the group leader praised them enthusiastically.

In the simulated classroom activity, for each five arithmetic problems the children completed they received one raisin.

As the children in the social-skills group described in detail their conversation with one new person, they received the applause of all the other group members.

In each of these examples the group leader responded to a given set of behaviors with positive feedback (praise, tokens, material goods, or food). In each example, the reinforcement was delivered on the basis of some prior agreement. The relationship of behavior to consequence is referred to as a "response-reinforcement contingency." If such a behavior occurs under a given set of circumstances, then a given set of consequences will occur. In all of the above examples, all of the contingencies had been arranged in advance by the group leader or by the members. But even if there had been no prearrangements, consequences would have still ensued. As Homme and Tosti (1965, p. 16) point out, "Either one manages the contingencies or they get managed by accident. Either way there will be contingencies and they will have their effect." In general, that effect is to increase the probability of the behavior that precedes the reinforcement under the same or similar circumstances. Strategies involving the alteration of consequences of a behavior are referred to as *operant procedures.*

Those circumstances that precede or set the conditions for the given behavior are often referred to as *antecedent* or *stimulus conditions.* Treatment strategies are frequently employed in which these stimulus conditions are altered as a means of modifying a given behavior. Such strategies are often referred to as *stimulus control procedures.* In this chapter we discuss how modification of both antecedent conditions and consequences can be used in group treatment. We first look at the operant procedures.

Operant Procedures

Various types of consequences must be considered in group treatment. These include social reinforcement, activities as reinforcement, token reinforcement, group contingencies, material reinforcement, time-out from reinforcement, response cost, and punishment. In this section we shall elaborate on each of these types of consequences and how they are delivered in group settings.

Social Reinforcement. Of the available types of reinforcement, human response seems to be the most potent reinforcer of social behavior. Praise, a nod of approval, a touch, a wink, a smile, or criticism are major influences in our behavior. Even material reinforcement is enhanced when paired with social reinforcement from a person attractive to the child. Although most social approval is given noncontingently in most traditional therapies, in an operant approach the client must earn social reinforcement, at least in the early phases of treatment, by the production of desired behavior. The group leader praises or in some nonverbal way indicates approval of children for their accomplishments. The group members are also taught to show similar approval of each other for the same achievements. They are taught how to reinforce each other through modeling, instruction, and sometimes social-skill training exercises. Such a state of intense mutual reinforcement tends to create a reinforcing milieu.

An example of a social-skill training exercise commonly used with children and adolescents follows.

> The children are divided into pairs. The group leader says, "Write down one behavior you have observed your partner doing well in the group. For example, 'my partner has good eye contact when she gives feedback in the group.' Remember, be specific. Praise a behavior you can observe. Praise only that behavior your partner could be proud of and not embarrassed by." The group leader pauses a moment. "Okay, tell your partner." After a minute the group leader asks the members to tell the group what they were told they did well. The group discusses whether the above criteria were met. The partners are then exchanged and the exercise is repeated, but this time the children describe a behavior they have observed their partner performing outside of the group. (This variation assumes that they have extra-group contact.)

The exercise can be modified to help children to receive as well as give positive feedback by preceding the exercise with a brief discussion of what to say or do when receiving praise or other forms of positive feedback. The purpose of this exercise is not only to increase the mutually reinforcing statements made in the group but also to prepare the children to give feedback following roleplays. One can also adjust the exercise to include only compliments. This is usually followed by a homework assignment to give one or more persons honest compliments before the next meeting.

Peer pressure is a form of social reinforcement that largely controls the behavior of the peer group. One of the purposes of the group leader is to structure the peer pressure in service of prosocial goals. Obviously, this entails a good relationship between the group leader and the members. Goldstein, Heller, and Sechrest (1966) have pointed out that a highly reinforcing environment definitely increases the strength of the therapeutic relationship.

Activities as Reinforcement. An additional advantage of the group context of treatment is the wide range of highly reinforcing activities it provides, most of which are unavailable in the child-therapist dyad. Even such individual activities as making airplane models appear to be more reinforcing when other children are present. Using an activity contingently is one of the major means of intervention in group treatment. Children are reinforced for completion of homework, agreed upon in-group behaviors, and changes in extra-group behaviors with the opportunity to participate in such activities as games, crafts, dramatics, and sports. These reinforcing activities also create the stimulus conditions for other behaviors (such as cooperation) that in turn can be reinforced socially or with tokens. Activities are such an important means of intervention that they are presented in great detail in a separate chapter (see Chapter Nine).

Of course, not all interactive behaviors are desirable or prosocial. Children may enjoy running around the group meeting room screaming at the top of their lungs; they may prefer shoving and bumping each other in wild horseplay to sitting and discussing a serious problem. Even these chaotic behaviors can be used as reinforcers. As Premack (1959) observed, high-probability behaviors may be used as reinforcers for low-probability behaviors. For example, the children may be offered the possibility of discussion for five minutes, at the end of which wild horseplay may be permitted for an equal amount of time. As the discussion grows in interest over the course of several meetings, the horseplay reinforcement can usually be reduced and then eliminated as a reinforcer. Although usually effective with small children, we have noted a few examples of its successful application with older adolescents.

In an occupational therapy workshop, a group of fifteen- to sixteen-year-old adolescents with very limited skills and a disinclination to work on their complex problems had been meeting for several weeks with little success in obtaining even minimum progress. The usual reinforcers were not interesting to them nor did they respond readily to firm limit setting. Most activities proposed by any one child or the group leader were described by the children as "boring." It took a long time to get down to the work of discussing and resolving problems. The group leader offered the group access to the gym and a half-filled volleyball for ten minutes at the end of the meeting in a game without rules (except for the rule of no physical attacks on others), if they could do the social-skill training component of the meeting for fifteen minutes. They carried out the social-skill training with only minor aberrations. In subsequent meetings the group leader required more social-skill time to play "the game."

Material Reinforcement. For many children in our groups, praise or other forms of social reinforcement may not be adequate to modify or even maintain levels of behavior. For this reason material goods such as small toys, paper dolls, marbles, pieces of puzzles, and crayons may serve as effective reinforcers, especially for younger children. For both children and adolescents small pieces of food are the most common reinforcer. To be most effective, reinforcers should be small, low-cost, easily distributed, and highly valued by the potential recipient. Occasionally larger objects and the activities associated with using or repairing them may be offered, such as an old motor that the members can put together or a boat that needs to be repaired. In both cases, it may be possible for the adolescents to earn the parts of the motor or the boat, one piece at a time, and then earn blocks of time to use or repair them. One group leader rewarded the group members with a used bicycle, one wheel spoke or other part at a time, for each hour of homework the children completed. It took the group members nearly two months to earn the whole bike, but they produced many hours of homework for the cost. Furthermore, the bike provided a source of many diverse program activities, such as bike building and repair, bike riding, sharing, and reading about bikes. The principle is that in initiating a new behavior, the group leader must either deliver small reinforcers or pieces of a large reinforcing event or object at a high rate in order to build the desired behavior as rapidly as possible (Ferster and Skinner, 1957).

Another way to break a large reinforcer into small parts is to let the children earn points or tokens for behaviors that are specified in advance. The children can exchange their earned tokens at various intervals, either individually or as a group, for the desired item. This practice is commonly employed in younger children's groups and occasionally with younger adolescents.

Token Reinforcement. Tokens are symbolic units of exchange that, like money, may be used to purchase large items or activities. Tokens usually have a very small value. They may be paper script, poker chips, clicks on a counter, tally marks, stickers, points on a thermometer, or any other small indicator of achievement. Materials and activities are exchanged at a given time for a number of tokens, which is specified in advance. Since reinforcement is most effective when it immediately follows the performance of a given behavior, the tokens mediate the giving of the concrete reinforcer or activity. Tokens are usually paired with praise or other social reinforcement for a satisfactory performance.

In groups, one of the common ways of exchanging tokens for material reinforcement is to set up a group store with predetermined prices. The children have access to the store at regular intervals, for example, at the end of each meeting or at the end of several meetings. The items in the store might include gum, model airplanes, a certificate to be first in line for class, assistance with homework from the group leader for ten minutes, tickets for a sports event, coupons for a beauty parlor, or credit for buying a hamburger at a local fast foods restaurant.

In any particular store, items should be designed for the unique population being served. The child should be able to earn social as well as concrete reinforcement. Prices are usually determined by the group leader in terms of supply and demand. Bubble gum might cost ten points whereas a box of raisins might cost only two. Table 3 shows a menu developed for a group of thirteen- to fourteen-year-old girls who were referred primarily for lack of appropriate social skills.

Table 3. Store Items.

Items	Price
Listening to records, per record	5 tokens
Lessons in makeup, per 10-minute lesson	10 tokens
Sticks of gum	5 tokens
Used romance novel	2 tokens
Nail polish	15 tokens
Trip to the group leader's house	20 tokens
Dance lessons, per 10 minutes	20 tokens
Use of agency telephone, per 3 minutes	15 tokens
Going shopping with group leader	25 tokens

Most groups remain in the token economy only in the initial phase of treatment, which may be extended as long as eight sessions for younger children in schools and out-patient groups and much longer for children in institutions. As target behaviors become reinforced by peers and adults in extra-group situations or as the behaviors become self-reinforcing, tokens are gradually removed until activities occur noncontingently. The announcement that the award of tokens is being removed altogether usually provokes renewed discussion about being in the group. The importance of performing the target behaviors without the help of reinforcement is emphasized in the discussion by the group leader, as in the following example.

Peter: What do you say if we don't give any tokens at all for cooperating with each other, for giving good feedback, for completing the assignments, and all the other things you've been getting tokens for? You've probably been noticing that I've been giving fewer and fewer lately and that doesn't seem to keep you guys from doing what you agreed you should be doing.

Tim: Ah, c'mon Pete, why not? They're fun!

Peter: Anybody have any ideas why not?

Jerry: Well, maybe we really don't need 'em anymore. At least, I don't need 'em.

Eric: I don't need them either. They're just for kids, anyway.

Tony: Besides the group's nearly over. We won't get tokens anywhere else for doing those things.

Peter: I'm really impressed with the things you guys are saying. Dropping the tokens has to do with the reasons you guys are here. And you don't need them anymore. (Peter goes on to review their recent achievements.)

In all groups social reinforcement is used throughout the history of the group. Concrete reinforcement and tokens to obtain that concrete reinforcement are used in most groups, except for older adolescents (over fifteen years). We have found that reinforcement serves several purposes. The first is to increase the extra-group behaviors we are working on; second, it is a benign form of in-group control; and third, the cohesion of the group is almost always extremely high in groups using tokens and large amounts of reinforcement. To increase that cohesion still further, group contingencies can be used.

Group Contingencies. As we mentioned earlier, reinforcement is not only given to the individual—it may also be administered to the entire group. Occasionally, reinforcement is delivered to the group on the basis of each individual's achievement, such as when an individual receives points for completing a homework assignment that are then put on the group thermometer. Almost all preadolescent groups use a thermometer such as the one in Figure 6.

On other occasions reinforcement is delivered to the

Figure 6. The Group Thermometer.

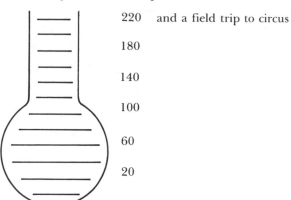

220   and a field trip to circus

180

140

100

60

20

Note: Each boy who completes his assignments puts five points on the thermometer. A bonus of twenty-five points is put on the thermometer if all the boys in the group complete their assignments. Additional points are earned for in-group cooperative behavior and for good feedback.

group for a combined effort, as in the case where the group received twenty minutes in the gymnasium because they all completed their homework assignments. In both cases, the group leader makes use of the additional group pressure to complete the desired behavior because of its import for other members. Group contingencies are more effective than individually administered contingencies in (1) improving classroom behaviors (McLaughlin, 1981, 1982) and (2) increasing positive peer social interaction (McCarty, Griffin, Apolloni, and Shores, 1977; Wodarski, Hamblin, Buckholdt, and Ferritor, 1973).

Obviously, group pressure exists to the degree that the opinions of peers are important to the individual (as it would be in a cohesive group). However, if the individuals have more important social alternatives the pressure may be ignored, or they may find the negative attention reinforcing of their nonconforming behavior, or they may even leave the group for more valued social relations.

For the highly vulnerable and rejected child, the group contingency may be the cause of increased rejection, especially if the child is relatively unskilled and has few successes. Under these conditions the group may blame the child for preventing them from obtaining maximum rewards. It is not sufficient to be merely aware of the problem; it is important for the group leader to create frequent opportunities for the rejected member to be the cause of large amounts of reinforcement from the group through contingent arrangements especially designed for highly probable success. For example, Melinda—a rejected child, according to a classroom sociometric test—was to receive ten points for the entire group every time she participated in the group discussion. The group leader permitted the members to address questions to Melinda and even to prompt her. This combination resulted not only in Melinda increasing her participation, but also in gaining the attention, acceptance, and cooperation of the other group members.

In summary, group contingencies should be used if the group is attractive for all its members and/or if the isolated member can be assured of success. It probably should not be used in the beginning phase of treatment but may be a powerful tool as the group progresses. Extensive research supports the assumption that behaviors can be maintained more readily with group contingencies than with individual contingencies (Wodarski, Hamblin, Buckholdt, and Ferritor, 1973; McCarty, Griffin, Apolloni, and Shores, 1977) and that group contingencies facilitate group development.

Combining Group and Individual Contingencies. In situations where the group is not sufficiently cohesive to warrant group contingencies, a variation is suggested that combines individual and group reinforcement. In this variation tokens are awarded to each child for performing a unique target behavior. Although the individuals keep whatever they have earned, the total is added to the group thermometer. Thus, the child uses personal earnings to make purchases from the group store, and the group also earns the right to move closer toward some commonly desired reward. This variation is often used with young children as a way of introducing them to the group-contingency concept. A similar approach combining individual praise and a group contingency was effectively used to increase the popularity of junior high school students (Alden, Pettigrew, and Skiba, 1970).

Types of Group Reinforcers. There is a wide variety of potential group reinforcers, which may be determined partly from the assessment survey and partly from the experience of other group leaders. One particularly powerful group reinforcing event for younger children as well as adolescents and children of both genders can be achieved through the use of a video-recorder or an 8-millimeter camera. Group behavior is filmed or taped, provided that certain standards are being met (such as, the children are cooperating with each other, they are playing a game and keeping to the rules, they are giving feedback to each other while meeting prescribed criteria, or they are seriously discussing a problem of one of the members). As soon as an undesirable or unacceptable behavior occurs, the tape recorder or camera is turned off in a very noticeable way, the timer is set for five minutes, and the cameraperson sits down. When the timer rings the filming or taping begins again. The group members can also earn time to watch the tape or, if facilities are available, to edit the film or tape. Often such an activity leads to the group requesting to design and create their own film. This privilege can also be earned as a group reinforcer.

Of course, not every group leader has such facilities available nor does every group enjoy filming. For this reason we have attempted to develop a menu of other potential group reinforcers. For adolescents in particular, the purchase of a junkyard car and the right to work on it has been quite effective. This assumes that the group leader has mechanical skills. Riding around one's neighborhood in a car chauffeured by the group leader is highly valued by some groups. Driving lessons have had notable success as a group reinforcer. Provided that the children have the necessary minimal skills, such activities as swimming, ice skating, cross-country skiing, bowling, horseback riding, and sailing have motivated children of limited interests. The juvenile offender is not able to obtain many of these activities by means of delinquent acts. For delinquents, such recreational activities must serve as far more powerful reinforcers than the delinquent act itself.

Another set of group reinforcers that we have used primarily with adolescents includes visits by high-status guests. Group leaders have invited disc jockeys, local singing groups and other local entertainers, newspaper reporters, and sports heroes from the local university or professional team for boys, girls, and mixed groups. Such persons have given of their time generously and at no cost when we explained the purpose of the activity. In some cases the potency of the group reinforcer can be increased by requiring the members to earn not only the visit but also lessons in the guest's sport or skill.

Other group reinforcers include dancing lessons by the group leader or a volunteer dance instructor, lessons in makeup and personal appearance, and restaurant meals (although in several cases desirable restaurant behaviors had to be shaped before this was offered a second time). Success in obtaining potent group reinforcers requires extensive exploration of the community and the interests of the children. We have been able to get many resources free or at minimal cost when our purposes were explained. But organizing such reinforcers can become a time-consuming activity.

Expanding Reinforcement Repertoires. Many children and adolescents who come into treatment have only limited interests. Programming and reinforcement for these children become extremely difficult. A number of strategies, however, can offset this problem. First, children can be placed in groups of slightly older children with far broader interests. The older children often serve as models for the less readily reinforced children. Where the majority of the group members have narrow interests, a high-status model with broad interests may be introduced into the group as a guest. The model may enthusiastically introduce new activities that often become much more acceptable to the group members than those presented by the group leader. Later the models will be invited contingently; that is, the children will have to earn through their behavior the opportunity to have the visitor at their meeting.

In a somewhat similar procedure, children are noncontingently confronted with a broad range of potentially reinforcing activities. These are usually paired with activities that are already reinforcing. This procedure has been referred to as reinforcement sampling (Ayllon and Azrin, 1968). For example, a group of early juvenile offenders was given the opportunity to go on field trips to an employment agency, a museum, and an auto-repair shop. None of these places were initially interesting to the adolescents, and therefore were useless as reinforcers. The field trips were taken in a van that made a detour through their neighborhood, which was highly reinforcing. Moreover, following the trips, they ate hamburgers at McDonalds. Later, as they found these new activities satisfying, they had to earn the right to go on the field trips, which had become highly attractive activities. A group of black girls talked to a series of successful black women in various fields. The talks were preceded by self-selected music on tapes, and followed by ice cream. After a while the girls began to choose the talks as valuable experiences in themselves, so the talks could be used as reinforcement for other activities.

Shaping. Shaping involves the reinforcement of successive approximations of a desired behavior. First, relatively easy-to-perform behaviors are reinforced, and as these are mastered, more difficult behaviors must be performed before reinforcement follows. To use shaping, clear identification of the end behavior and the successive steps to achieve that behavior must be specified. Generally the group leader must determine in advance at what levels reinforcement for one behavior ceases and reinforcement for new behavior begins. These levels are usually discussed and sometimes negotiated with the group members.

In the following example of shaping, the group leader worked with young and somewhat disorganized members in the returning of monitoring notes from parents. The notes indicated that the members had completed their homework. In this group the children would either lose the notes or get them so crumpled and dirty they could not be read. To teach them to get the notes home and signed, the group leader had them practice folding them carefully and putting them deep in their pockets. He reinforced them each time they were successful. When they all had successfully demonstrated the skill, he had them bring the notes to a colleague in another room in the building. The colleague signed them and the children brought the notes back to the group leader, who again reinforced them. Finally, they were instructed to bring the notes home, get them signed, and bring them back to the group leader the next day. When a child showed his note to the group leader, he was immediately reinforced. The time elapsing between the sending of the note and the time of return was increased to about three days before reinforcement was given. Finally, the group leader reinforced them only for completing the entire sequence of getting the notes home, performing the desired behaviors, getting the notes signed, and returning them at the next meeting a week later. In this way the entire sequence was gradually shaped. The reinforcement in each of these cases were tokens that could be used to purchase goods or toys in the group store.

This particular training process involved a combination of instruction and reinforcement of successive approximations of the desired end behavior. This case involved a series of different behaviors rather than one complex behavior. By strict definition, shaping should involve only the reinforcement of successive approximations of one complex behavior. In practice, as in the above example, many other procedures, such as coaching and instructions, are combined with reinforcement in the shaping of children's behavior.

Schedules of Reinforcement. Thus far, reinforcement has been discussed as if it always follows every presentation of a given behavior. In fact, this regular arrangement of behavior and consequences rarely occurs in groups. Many other arrangements, each presenting a unique contribution to the modification or stabilization of behavior, also exist. Ferster and Skinner (1957) provide an extensive description of the effects of various arrangements on the speed and acquisition of a response, the strength at which it is maintained, and the rate of decrease of an established response. Only those schedules that we are readily able to arrange with any frequency in groups will be reviewed here.

In establishing new behaviors, the group leader attempts to immediately reinforce every occurrence of the desired behavior. This ideal, rarely achieved, is referred to as *continuous reinforcement.* Perfect continuity is not usually achieved in the group setting for several reasons. First, the group leader and the members cannot help but miss some occurrences of a behavior because so much interaction is going on at any one time. Second, the group leader may observe the behavior but may be too busy with another child to reinforce it. The only exceptions to this are highly visible behaviors with low frequency, such as the act of assisting another child by a usually uncooperative child. At best, then, the group leader can only approximate perfect continuity of reinforcement.

Some behaviors that occur in the group can better be reinforced if they occur within a given period of time. This is referred to as *fixed interval of reinforcement.* To implement this, the group leader sets a timer for a given period, usually five to ten minutes. When the timer goes off, the leader can then reinforce each person in the group who has performed at least one target behavior. This is easiest to do if all the children have the same behavior to work on, for example, speaking in the group or praising another group member. The greater the diversity of target behavior among the members the more difficult it is for the group leader to keep track of them. One novel arrangement (designed by the ten-year-old children in one group) was to put the word indicating the desired behavior on a sign which was hung on a string around each child's neck. The children, in pairs, reinforced their partner with a token if the desired behavior occurred in the given time period. This plan had the side effect of providing the children with an opportunity to reinforce each other. Then they decided to put the stars received for reinforcement on the signs "just as football players put footballs on their helmets."

If the behavior is a high-frequency behavior, such as participating in the group discussion, the group leader may reinforce the child only after a given number of occurrences. This *fixed-ratio schedule of reinforcement* is probably just as difficult to observe as continuous reinforcement and therefore is also seldom used in groups. More frequently used is a *variable-ratio schedule of reinforcement* in which the child is reinforced after a varying number of responses. For example, every several times Charlene requested (instead of demanded) something from another child or the group leader, she received a reinforcer. Ideally, the frequency of reinforcement should have been random. The leader estimated that the frequency ranged from two to six performances before reinforcement was given. Originally, Charlene had received tokens almost every time she made an appropriate request. The advantage of the variable-ratio schedule was that it was a procedure for thinning the reinforcement received. Thinning serves to stabilize the behavior learned in the group.

Another schedule commonly used in groups is the *variable interval schedule.* In this schedule, the group leader sets the timer at varying lengths of time. One group was working on giving eye contact to each other. The group leader had set the timer at five, seven, three, ten, two, and sixteen minutes. When the bell rang he asked the observer to reinforce each child who had had eye contact with at least one other child during the period between bells. In order to thin the reinforcement still further, the demand for desired-behavior occurrences would increase and intervals would grow, possibly to an entire meeting. Finally, no reinforcement would be given at all.

Although behaviors tend to build up more quickly under rich reinforcement conditions, such as those mentioned above, the same behaviors tend to disappear more quickly when reinforcement is suddenly terminated (Ferster and Skinner, 1957). For this reason, any treatment plan usually gradually changes schedules of reinforcement from high-frequency (rich) to low-frequency (thin) and from regular frequencies and intervals to random frequencies and intervals before terminating reinforcement completely.

The focus thus far has been on strategies for increasing desirable behaviors. We next focus on strategies for decreasing undesirable ones.

Differential Reinforcement of Other Behavior. Several girls constantly complained at home, in school, and in their group meeting about the most insignificant events. This resulted in their rejection by other girls, both in the classroom and in the group. The group leader negotiated with the girls that she would reinforce them with tokens every time they described an event in positive terms, stated something they liked, or otherwise indicated approval of an activity or a person. The leader and other group members agreed they would not respond to the complaining.

In the above example, the group leader is differentially reinforcing behaviors other than the behavior she wants to reduce in frequency. Since this response usually results in weakening a behavior without some of the side effects of more aversive or intrusive procedures, it is commonly used in group treatment. In the above example, it should be noted that the group leader negotiated the plan with the children involved. Moreover, the other children were receiving high frequencies of reinforcement for other behaviors. One of the difficulties in this procedure is deciding on behaviors that are incompatible with the target behavior. In this case, we have found it useful to ask the group to brainstorm about what might be reinforced. They have often come up with creative possibilities. For example, Karen had indicated that her target behavior was "not butting into other people's affairs, especially when they are arguing." Brainstorming positive alternatives resulted in Karen being reinforced for walking away from others who were arguing.

Another form of differential reinforcement reinforces an individual if, during a given time period, the undesired behavior does not occur. For example, during the group session of highly aggressive twelve-year-olds, the timer was set for every ten minutes. When the timer went off, the group leader reinforced all children who had not hit another child during that period. Although this procedure avoids the problem of having to define the behavior to be reinforced, it results in reinforcing a nonbehavior, which fails to conceptualize for children what they should be doing under the circumstances.

Extinction. Extinction is the process of weakening a response by nonreinforcement. A group example of extinction is the following. The group leader and the other children ignored all manifestations of obscene gestures that Jerry made in the group. The application of extinction procedures in a group is complicated by the fact that not only the group leader must refrain from responding to a given behavior; all the members must also hold back any attention for the target behavior. If the members continue to attend to Jerry's obscene gestures, in spite of the nonresponse of the leader, the frequency of the behavior is likely to be maintained or even increased. Thus, whenever extinction is the treatment strategy, the group leader must include the group in the discussion of the application. If the members are unskilled in the use of extinction, the leader must train them through exercises, instructions, modeling, and rehearsal. Once trained, the group members can be asked to assist in this strategy on other occasions. Successful ignoring of a maladaptive behavior of one of their peers throughout a designated portion of a meeting usually results in the group receiving reinforcement.

For groups whose members have contact with each other outside of the group, extinction can be reinforced if the members agree—in Jerry's case, on the playground and in the classroom where his gesticulating had been getting him into trouble. The disadvantage is that any one child can provide reinforcement of the undesired behavior with a giggle or a snort. Unless the group is committed to helping Jerry, the procedure should probably not be used in his group. Another disadvantage of extinction is for children who receive little reinforcement in the group for other behaviors. In this case, the maladaptive behavior would tend to persist longer than the ignoring behavior of the group. For this reason, if extinction is to be used in the group, care must be taken that the child is receiving a high frequency of reinforcement for other behaviors.

Generally, extinction is used for behaviors that are not too disruptive and that do not result in hurting another child. If extinction is not working or if the behavior is too disruptive or damaging to others, more intrusive actions may need to be taken. One such procedure is time-out from reinforcement.

Time-Out from Reinforcement. With younger children, one of the most common strategies to control disruptive behavior in families or in the classroom is time-out from reinforcement. This procedure can also be used (primarily with latency-age and younger children) in the group. In this procedure the child is removed from all reinforcing stimuli for a brief period of time in response to a disruptive or aggressive behavior. To be effective, time-out usually lasts from thirty seconds to five minutes in a quiet place where reinforcers are limited. The reason for the briefness of time is that the group leader wants to keep every child in the therapeutic interaction for as much of the treatment period as possible. Moreover, longer periods do not seem to be more effective than short periods. The time-out usually begins when the child has ceased disruptive behavior. For example, every time Harry destroys or damages even a small part of another's work, the group leader escorts him, in a matter-of-fact way, to a seat just outside the glass door. The group leader states calmly that the rule is "we do not destroy other people's work." At the end of the time period, the child is brought back to the activity. In groups, the procedure has some special difficulties. First, if there is only one group leader, the child is difficult to monitor during the time-out. With two leaders, one can monitor while the other continues the group activities. Second, it is often difficult to find a suitable time-out place that has few if any reinforcers. The people who pass by in the hall and the coats of the other children in the cloakroom all serve as delightful diversions. A chair in the room that does not face the group or the outside window may be the best place. In general, time-out is a strategy of last resort in groups, although some group leaders report using it with great frequency in early sessions with acting-out groups of children. If frequent time-outs are being used, the group leader needs to examine whether the group is sufficiently reinforcing.

The advantage of time-out over more intrusive punishment procedures is that group leaders do not model the very aggressive behavior they are trying to eliminate. To maximize its effectiveness, the group leader will often train the members to take time-outs in a roleplay. The group leader will then reinforce the children for appropriate time-out behavior. Usually this is followed by a discussion of how one can avoid time-out in the group.

Although time-out is usually used with younger children, Tyler and Brown (1967) describe how time-out was used to control the recreation-room behavior of adolescent residents of a training school cottage. Whenever a resident broke the rules, he was put into his room for a short period of time. The study was divided into four phases. In the first and third phases, time-outs were used. In the second and fourth phases, reprimands were used. The time-out confinement was much more effective.

In general, time-out works best in a highly cohesive group where there is a great deal of ongoing reinforcement. The child is much more concerned about leaving such a situation than leaving a less attractive one. Also, time-out is often ineffective with the scapegoat in the group or the highly rejected child. One way such a child can escape his or her tormentors is to behave in such a way as to receive a time-out.

Response Cost. Response cost is the removal of positively reinforcing stimuli from the environment following a response. In some groups every time a child utters an obscenity he is fined several tokens. The advantage of a fining system is that all undesirable behaviors can have certain specified fines attached to them that are administered on a continuous schedule. A grave disadvantage is that the whole token system may degenerate into a punishment system. It seems that it is far easier for staff to fine than to reinforce. If data are kept on the frequency of fines and positive reinforcement, one can usually monitor the effectiveness of the group leader on the basis of the ratio of fines to positive reinforcement. As a rule of thumb, we advise our group leaders to keep it as large as four reinforcing tokens to every fined one. Our clinical observations suggest that this ratio is sufficient to maintain a positive reinforcing climate in the group.

Some group leaders have used a procedure similar to response cost by reducing free time or some desired activity, such as sports time in the gym. If this is used contractually it may be an effective procedure, unless the group continues to lose most of the activities that it values. In that case the group loses its attraction for the members. If the procedure is used merely when a behavior occurs that the group leader does not like, the reduction of cohesion is even more drastic. Frequent use of the removal of group activities has the added disadvantage of removing positive training opportunities. Such activities should not be removed lightly.

Administration of heavy response costs does not appear

to be as effective as administration of light response costs. In a
study evaluating the effectiveness of a token system for pre-
delinquent boys, Phillips (1968) discovered that large token
penalties given to the entire group failed to reduce their maladaptive behaviors. On the other hand, the same behaviors were
quickly eliminated when a group member, in his role as man-
ager, levied lesser fines. This is more evidence of the power of
member-administered contingencies wherever and as soon as
possible.

Stimulus Control

Whenever Ginny sat next to Nina in class, the two
of them fought or argued and often got into trouble with the teacher. The group leader arranged
that Ginny and Nina be placed on opposite sides of
the room in all of their classes. As part of their
contract, the girls eventually agreed to separate
themselves for several weeks.

Ron told the group that in order to avoid his impulsive eating at home, he and his mother removed
all foods from the house that could be eaten without preparation, such as potato chips, crackers, and
soft drinks. If the rest of the family wanted to eat
these things, they purchased them in small quanti-
ties and threw away leftovers.

Allan, Mike, Bryan, and Juanita—the four members
of the study-skill group—all agreed to study at a
clean desk with no music playing and with a set of
presharpened pencils readily available. Furthermore, each would have a list of things that they
agreed to do before they got up from their seats.

In the above examples, the children, the group leader,
or the parent deliberately arranged the environment to decrease
the probability of undesirable behaviors and increase the proba-

bility of desirable ones. Success in completing the target behavior would usually be followed by some form of reinforcement in order to maximize the effectiveness of the procedure. Research indicates that modification of the antecedent conditions alone rarely results in stable change (Gambrill, 1977). To be most effective in changing behavior, consequences of the given desired behavior should also be modified. The prearrangement of the antecedent conditions or stimulus control procedures are especially useful when behaviors exist, but do not occur with sufficient frequency or in appropiate situations (Gambrill, 1977).

Commonly Altered Stimulus Conditions. In self-management training, children are most often trained to rearrange their own environment. The training may also involve instructions, modeling, and reinforcement. For example, adolescents with sleeping disorders were advised to get out of bed after ten minutes of not being able to sleep and to perform some boring task until they felt tired. They were to repeat this cycle until they fell asleep (Bootzin, 1973). In a group of smoke-enders, the adolescents agreed to stop seeing friends who smoked, to avoid situations in which they had previously smoked a great deal, and to go into situations where smoking was prohibited, such as the movies or the nonsmoking sections of restaurants. Success and failure were discussed in the subsequent meeting. Adolescents with problems in studying were presented with a list of ideas that included the following: sitting in the front of class, taking careful notes, organizing their notes immediately after class, and asking themselves questions at a specified time after their readings and lectures concerning the content of the readings and lectures. The list was derived from the literature (Groveman, Richards, and Caple, 1975, pp. 28-29) and from an exchange of experiences by the group members. Members chose and publicly stated what they intended to do (following the suggestion of Flaxman, 1976) and reported what had occurred during the week to the group.

Physical Proximity. One form of stimulus control often used with aggressive children is physical proximity. It involves the group leader in sitting next to the potentially aggressive child. This is often sufficient to keep the behavior under control. However, as soon as the child shows signs of becoming aggressive, the group leader prompts the child to perform an alternative behavior. Such a procedure provides the aberrant child with somewhat greater attention than other children, though the others often consider it a form of protection from the aggressive behavior. It usually can only be used in a small group or in a larger group with more than one leader. In general, we have found this procedure effective in reducing disruptive behaviors when one child is the main source of such behaviors. Although more intrusive than extinction, physical proximity is not as intrusive as time-out from reinforcement, where the child is totally withdrawn from group interaction.

Instructions. A number of verbal antecedent conditions can be employed in the course of treatment. The group leader makes frequent use of instructions, requests, cues, and demands for behavioral change. Of these, instructions are the most common. Instructions are frequently used in teaching other procedures, such as relaxation, which in turn mediate the modification of target behaviors. To be effective, instructions must be clearly stated and relatively brief. In addition, the children should be checked to see if they understand the questions, and compliance with the instructions should initially be followed with reinforcement. In order to shift responsibility to the child, instructions are usually faded in the course of training in a given set of behaviors. Wherever possible, instructions are paired with modeling as well as reinforcement to increase the likelihood of compliance. We have also found that excessive use of instruction tends to limit its effectiveness as a change tool.

Commands. One additional procedure that involves verbal antecedent conditions is clear limit setting or commands. Used primarily in response to disruptive behavior, a clear command to terminate a behavior and begin a more appropriate one may be regarded as both a consequence of one behavior, and antecedent to another. Although ineffective as a long-term intervention strategy, telling a child in a stern tone of voice that the group leader expects that he will get back in the window at once, that he is to immediately stop punching Jeffrey, or that the volume of voices needs to be reduced may create conditions that make possible the use of more effective long-term strategies. Often disruptive behaviors occur for which no treatment plan has been formulated. An occasional firmly stated command may be a useful holding action. On the other hand, excessive use of commands as opposed to other more positive strategies mentioned in this chapter creates a highly aversive atmosphere and weakens the effectiveness of the occasional command. It has been our experience that beginning group leaders tend to rely far too heavily on instructions and commands or to completely avoid the use of commands even when the situation demands it.

Summary

The modification of both operant and stimulus conditions are powerful tools in the modification of behavior. In this chapter we have described the types of reinforcers commonly used in group treatment. These include social reinforcers, activities as reinforcers, and group reinforcers. We also dealt with schedules for introducing these reinforcers in groups. For those children who have a limited variety of reinforcers at their disposal, we recommended strategies for expanding their repertoire. Most of the above procedures are used to increase the frequency of desired behaviors. We also described those operant procedures (in terms of their unique group application) that are used to reduce the frequency and/or intensity of undesired behaviors. These include reinforcement of behaviors other than the one we want to reduce, extinction, time-out from reinforcement, and response cost. Finally a number of group applications of stimulus control procedures were illustrated. One particular set of stimulus conditions that impinge on overt behavior are self-instructions and cognitive self-statements. Strategies for training children in groups to employ these and other cognitive procedures are discussed in the following chapter.

Chapter Eight

Helping Children Cope with Stressful Situations: Cognitive and Relaxation Techniques

Group leader: Okay, Romy, now that I have demonstrated how you might think to yourself while working on the puzzle, why don't you give it a try in a loud whisper, so we can tell what you're thinking?

Romy: (in a stage whisper) First, I have to organize this mess. I'll make a plan. Now follow the plan. Okay, that's good, keep it up. It's getting a little boring, but I'll stick to it. Keep going, Romy. Now remember one step at a time. That's it. Oh, Oh! I slipped up. It doesn't matter, I'm still doing a good job. I just better go a little more slowly.

Group leader: Okay, that was great, Romy. What did the rest of you observe that Romy did well in instructing herself on how to do the puzzle?

———————————————

Lavette: Everyone at school thinks I'm weird. Maybe I am.

Lynn: What do you think you do that's so weird?

Lavette: Nothing I know of, but a kid just yesterday said I was weird. I hate it. It makes me feel awful. Sometimes, I think I really am weird.

Lynn: What do the rest of you think? Is Lavette weird like that one kid said?

Sandy: I don't think she's weird at all. I don't see anything she did in class that's weird.

Leslie: Me either, you're a neat kid, Lavette. You're sorta quiet, that's all. It's a lot better than being a loudmouth like that Martie kid.

Diane: Yeah, you're nice to other kids and you're fun too. If anyone is weird it's those kids who go around calling everyone else weird. I get called weird lots of times. I just ignore them.

In the first example, Romy has cognitively rehearsed what she would say to herself while working on a puzzle. The group leader then encouraged the group to provide her with feedback. These are two of several steps in the cognitive procedure called self-instructional training.

In the second example, Lavette has accepted as true the "weird" label that some of her peers have thrown at her. This cognitive distortion has caused her a great deal of anger, anxiety, and self-doubt. Lately she has been unwilling to play with other children at recess for fear that someone would call her weird. The group leader, Lynn, has begun the first step of disabusing her of her distortion by using the group to point out the inaccuracy of her self-statement. Later, Lavette will be taught how to deal with those situations in which a classmate labels her "weird."

As these two examples have indicated, there are at least three major goals of cognitive change strategies. The first is to correct cognitive distortions and to improve the client's self-evaluation. The second is to reduce anxiety associated with these cognitive distortions. The third is to change overt behavior. In the second example above, the group leader not only used cognitive procedures to help Lavette change her self-evaluation, but used the changed self-evaluation to help her to deal with put-downs from her peers and to become an active participant on the playground.

In the first example, the group leader demonstrated, or cognitively modeled to Romy in a roleplay, what she should say to herself while working on the puzzle. The leader then had Romy practice, or covertly rehearse, what she should be saying to herself during this frustrating task. The task was a vehicle to improve her self-control and problem-solving skills. Thus, cognitive behavioral strategies, alone or in conjunction with other behavioral strategies, are used to mediate the achievement of overt adaptive behavior and improved self-evaluation, and each of these mediate the achievement of the other.

Several overlapping cognitive paradigms readily lend themselves to use in the group. The first is self-instructional training (developed primarily by Meichenbaum, 1977) in which the group leader trains the members to instruct themselves in the performance of a given task or sequence of behaviors as the behaviors are being performed. The second is cognitive restructuring. The children may also learn certain general principles, such as problem solving, creative processing, or frustration tolerance as a result of learning to work systematically on a variety of complex tasks with the help of self-instruction. One major technique for teaching self-instructional statements is cognitive modeling in which the group leader or one of the members models or demonstrates how one instructs oneself in a difficult situation. A second technique within self-instructional training is cognitive rehearsal in which a child practices or rehearses aloud the recently modeled sequence of self-talk. Usually, several or all of the group members practice the modeled instructions in front of the group. A third technique is self-reinforcement in which individuals praise themselves after successfully rehearsing or carrying out a set of self-instructions and the accompanying overt behaviors.

Another overlapping cognitive strategy has been labeled, among other things, *cognitive restructuring* (originally developed primarily by Ellis, 1974, and heavily contributed to by Beck, 1976, and Meichenbaum, 1977). In this procedure cognitive distortions or illogical statements adhered to by the child are identified and replaced. The major steps in this strategy are group evaluation of the cognitive distortion, as was demonstrated briefly in the case of Lavette, and replacement of the distortion with logical or self-enhancing self-statements. Cognitive modeling of the new response, cognitive rehearsal, and self-reinforcement may also be used in this process.

Self-instructional training and cognitive restructuring can be considered as learning strategies of coping cognitions and coping behaviors. Another coping strategy that is not solely cognitive but that clearly makes use of cognitive techniques in its application is relaxation techniques. These are among the effective change strategies commonly used with groups of children and adolescents, especially with children who are tense, anxious, or depressed. The children are also taught to apply these relaxation techniques in response to a cue of feeling stress, anxiety, anger, or pain, depending on the problem they are working on. Relaxation is taught primarily through a technique of alternating tension and relaxation of muscle groups. The techniques of teaching this alternation are overt and cognitive modeling, self-instruction, and behavioral rehearsal.

In this chapter we shall discuss the concrete steps employed in self-instructional training, cognitive restructuring, relaxation training, and related strategies as they are uniquely employed in a group context.

Self-Instructional Training

The most common cognitive procedure used with young children, both individually and in groups, is self-instructional training. Proposed by Meichenbaum (1977) and extended by Kendall (1977), this procedure has recently gained wide support from clinicians as well as researchers. However, its clinical application has, thus far, outstripped its research support (Cormier and Cormier, 1985).

Self-instructional training has generally been used with children characterized by a high frequency of hyperactive, aggressive, and impulsive behavior. It has been used to develop skills in such areas as resistance to temptation, delay of gratification, problem solving, reading, and creativity. We have used self-instructional training in groups to supplement overt modeling-rehearsal strategy (discussed in Chapter Six) for children with a limited repertoire of social approach responses and other friendship skills. We have also employed self-instructional training to help children complete such tasks as school homework or chores at home, as shown in the upcoming example.

Self-instructional training, as we have applied it in groups, consists of five major steps. Once a target behavior has been identified, we provide the children with a rationale and explanation for its use. In the second step, the group leaders serve as models and perform the desired behavior while talking to themselves aloud. Third, the group members perform the same task while the group leader instructs them aloud. Fourth, members then separately perform the task while they each instruct themselves aloud. This is also done in pairs with one child acting as a coach. Then the children separately repeat the task without a coach while whispering the instructions to themselves. Finally, all the group members together perform the target task while instructing themselves silently. Since all of the phases lend themselves to a demonstration or a performance by the entire group or subgroup, it is particularly efficient for groups. Let us look at each step separately.

Providing a Rationale. As in most procedures discussed in this book, the first step in self-instructional training is to provide the children or adolescents with a rationale for its use. The following explanation has been used with adolescents; variations of the explanation have been used with younger children as well.

> Today, we are going to learn a technique for helping ourselves get through difficult situations. As you know, almost all of us talk to ourselves. I certainly do. For example, last week I was supposed to give a speech to the staff at the agency. I was really nervous about it. So as I went into the meeting room I told myself to be calm and to remember that I knew more about my subject than anyone else in the room. I kept reminding myself to look at them and not at my notes since I knew what I was going to say. When I made a slight mistake, I

reminded myself that everyone can make a mistake and to just keep going. It really helped.

We are going to learn special ways of talking to ourselves that might help us all to get through difficult situations. First, we are going to look at the steps that need to be performed in each situation. Then, I'm going to demonstrate what each of you could be saying to yourself to get through each of those steps. Next, you will practice those same self-statements, first aloud and then to yourself. Are there any questions? (Group leader answers questions.) There are many different kinds of tasks during which we can talk to ourselves, such as, when Helena is having trouble with her homework, or when Joshua is being yelled at by his teacher and he is trying not to get angry, or when Nicky has to do her chores after school.

In the above example, not only did the group leader explain the procedure, she demonstrated how it might be used in a problematic situation of her own. Finally, she drew on situations she knew to be problematic to the group members to link the procedure to their own experiences. Following the presentation of a rationale, the group leader helped the members to analyze the problematic task by breaking it down into its component parts. It should be noted that tasks are both interactive (as in going through the steps of making a speech) and noninteractive (as in doing one's homework).

Task Analysis. In this phase, the group leader attempts to ferret out the most common critical moments in the problem situation that seem to interfere with the performance of the task. Initially, the leader may suggest a number of critical moments and check with the group as to their accuracy. Later, the members will be able to propose and discuss such critical moments themselves. In a group of hyperactive children, the members and group leader identified the following critical moments.

1.   The task seems overwhelming, and you don't know if you'll ever finish.
2.   The task seems to have so many steps, you feel you'll never finish.
3.   You made a small mistake, and you feel you're getting upset.
4.   Your mind is wandering, and you are having trouble concentrating.
5.   You are speeding up and making a lot of mistakes.

     The group members then discussed what they might say to themselves in order to cope more effectively with these critical moments. Since the group's repertoire of ideas is sometimes limited in the early group sessions, many of the suggestions for self-talk may have to be initiated by the group leader. In subsequent sessions, the members will increase the proportion of their own ideas. In this way, the children can be maximally involved in learning the self-instructional paradigm.
     In response to the above examples the members and group leader came up with the following suggestions for self-instructions:

1.   There's a lot to do, but if I take one step at a time, I won't be overwhelmed.
2.   Even if I make a mistake, I can correct it and finish on time. Besides everybody makes mistakes sometimes.
3.   My mind is beginning to wander. (in a loud voice) Stop! You can do it, take a deep breath, concentrate. Keep going, one step at a time. Good!
4.   A bit too fast, slow down, that's better. It's not a race.

     Cognitive Modeling. In cognitive modeling, the group leader or an experienced group member models the various self-instructions internally while explaining aloud what is happening in the situation. The group leader asks the members to take notes on what is said so that after the demonstration they can point out the most and least useful self-statements. (With younger children, tokens are often distributed for identifying self-statements.) In the following example, continued from above, the group leader, Maggie, models handling the problem of doing homework.

Maggie: (I'm sitting at the table, I feel overwhelmed.) I tell myself, "Maggie, list the things I have to do." (As I review the lists I see that there are a lot of steps. I begin to get anxious.) I tell myself, "Take one step at a time. Now what's the first step?" (I'm working for a while, then I make a little mistake.) "That's okay, Maggie, a mistake is not so terrible; it means I have to go a little more slowly." (I'm beginning to make a little progress.) "Well, Maggie, you're doing fine. I knew you could do it. Keep it up."

In the discussion that follows the demonstration, the group leader encourages the members to point out the self-instructing statements.

Maggie: Okay, what did I tell myself?

Lizzie: Well, you told yourself to get with it, to get your act in gear.

Helena: And to do one thing at a time.

Maggie: Yes, anything else?

Dina: Well, you told yourself when you were doing good and it wasn't so bad to make a mistake.

Maggie: You all are really listening. I think you got everything. Is there anything else I should have done but didn't do?

Lizzie: You could have told yourself to stay cool.

Maggie: That's a great idea.

(Next the group leader briefly discusses the principles that can be generalized from the specific statements.)

Maggie: Now, if we get into a situation like this, it's helpful to remember some general ideas. First, if you are doing okay tell yourself so. Second, if you make a little mistake, it's not so terrible. Tell yourself that. If the situation looks overwhelming, take a moment to organize yourself, tell yourself what you have to do, and just take one step at a time. And Lizzie's suggestion to keep telling yourself to remain calm when you start to tense up is also a good one to remember. There's another one that we didn't mention. It doesn't hurt to remind yourself specifically what you should do or say. We'll see examples of that later on.

Following the modeling and discussion, the group leader introduces cognitive rehearsal.

Cognitive Rehearsal. Cognitive rehearsal is the roleplayed practice by the members of the same situation simulated by the model. If possible, the child is given an actual task to perform while responding aloud or in a stage whisper with the appropriate self-instruction. Usually each child in the group will perform the rehearsal. Those for whom the given task presents no problem serve as an additional model for the other members.

It is also possible for each child to perform the task with another member performing the role of group leader. This arrangement provides additional practice in a short period of time. However, even if the group leader circulates around the room, a number of serious errors may be missed and go uncorrected. We have resolved this by rehearsing, first, one at a time, and then doing it in subgroups the second time. By practicing aloud, then in a whisper, and then privately to oneself, many additional rehearsals for each member will be possible. Finally, still further trials may also be assigned as homework. Let us examine a specific cognitive rehearsal.

Maggie: Who would like to go first?

Helena: I'll give it a try, because it really is my problem.

Maggie: Great! I'll give Helena the situation and tell her how she is feeling. Then Helena will tell us, aloud so that we all can hear it, and in an assertive tone, just what she might do next. The rest of you will listen carefully and note what she does well and what she might do differently. In fact, if you write it down it will help you to remember. Are you ready? (Everyone nods.) Okay, Helena, you see a pile of books on your desk. You think,

"I've got to do my homework, but it's such a mess. I don't know what to do."

Helena: Ah, ah, ahhh. Well, I'd better get organized before I start. (with a big smile, on remembering) I'll make a list of everything I have to do.

Maggie: (under her breath) Good, so far. (then in a loud tone) You look at the list and you think, "Wow that's sure an awful lot."

Helena: Something about "step." Oh yeah, I've got to take one step at a time.

The rehearsal goes on until the situation has been completed. This situation, as most others, was quite brief. The group leader asks the members to offer feedback to Helena and then asks Helena to rehearse it one more time. Group feedback usually provides information from the members to the child who rehearsed, whether or not the agreed-on responses were obtained and regardless of the quality of those responses. In addition, in older or more sophisticated groups, feedback would focus on the self-statements' fluency, completeness, logical consistency, realism, and tone. Once feedback is completed, the task is repeated. The second time, the roleplayer takes into consideration the suggestions for corrections. After the second cognitive rehearsal, the group leader goes on to the next person in the group. When all the members have practiced the task aloud, the next step—fading—takes place.

Fading. The previous step may be regarded as the "thinking out loud" phase. Fading prepares the children to instruct themselves privately. The first step in the process of fading is for the children to rehearse whispering the self-instructions as the group leader describes what is happening. Since the whispering is not too intrusive, it is possible for all the children to whisper at the same time. However some group leaders prefer to carry out this phase in pairs with one of the pair monitoring the whispering of the other and providing feedback to the other. The whispering step may be modeled first by the group leader, or better yet, by a member who seems to understand the process.

In the next step, the group leader continues to describe what is happening while the members respond silently. This step is readily carried out as a group exercise. Finally, the fading is completed by having each member covertly imagine what is happening while covertly giving themselves instructions for responding to the imagined events. It is an amusing sight to behold an adult and six or seven children with heads slightly nodding and lips slightly moving, going through the exercise for four to five minutes in stiff silence. It also occasionally elicits uncontrolled laughter.

Multiple modeling trials, multiple rehearsal trials, fading the verbalized self-talk, teaching the general principles of effective self-talk, and providing the children with an opportunity to teach others are all strategies for increasing the likelihood of transfer of the new cognitions to the real world. Two other strategies are also used. Meichenbaum (1977) suggests that varied tasks be employed and that the difficulty of the tasks be increased over time. The group provides a great source of variation. The group members are also instructed to look for more complex situations to put into their diaries and bring back to the group. The group leader may, at the same time, design "canned situations" with gradually increasing levels of difficulty. Of course, the final means of effecting generalization is to assign the responsibility of carrying out the newly learned self-instructions in the real world. Although such assignments are not readily monitored, the children describe their experiences to the group at the beginning of the subsequent session.

Variations. The group approach, itself, is a variation of Meichenbaum's self-instructional approach. One can invent a number of variations to keep the interest of the group high and the learning effective. It may be necessary to first train children for whom self-talk is a mystery in conscious self-talk while they are playing. The task would be to practice self-talk while performing the steps of a relatively unstressful game, such as the following one.

Alberto (group leader): I've got some new rules for Simon Says, guys. Before you imitate what I am doing, you have to say aloud, "He said 'Simon says,' so I can do it" or "He didn't say 'Simon says,' so I can't do it." Now let's try that. Okay, "Simon says 'sit down.'"

Group together with Alberto: You said "Simon says," so we can sit down. (They sit down.)

Alberto: Right, let's try again only this time I won't help you.

Another variation involves the use of audiotapes: the group leader prepares several tapes with self-instructions followed by silence to permit compliance with the instructions. Each child then puts on the earphones of a mini audiotape recorder and listens to the instructions while performing the desired task. Later, the children must repeat the task without the tape recorder while covertly giving themselves the instructions. Each child may use several different tapes in this way in the course of the meeting.

Still another variation is to have the children rehearse in triads with one person describing the situation, one person describing the internal stimuli, and the third person describing his or her response. Gradually the additional players are faded. A similar variation was utilized by a group of girls who put on a play in which every character had a self-instructor whispering loudly in her ear. The girls liked the exercise so much they decided to repeat it the following week with the girls in each pair dressing alike.

A number of authors have suggested supplementing self-instructional training with operant procedures (Kendall and Finch, 1976, 1978; Nelson and Birkimer, 1978). We have reinforced children (especially younger children) for correctly stating a self-instruction. We have assigned each member of the group the task of delivering tokens when a self-instruction was given by a person practicing a given task. This resulted in more careful observation as well as a more complete performance. When the group members were working on the situation, each person would give one self-instruction. If the instruction had not already been stated, the person who stated it would be given a token by the person on the right. Then the next person on the

left would give a self-instruction, and the member on that person's right would deliver the token. These procedures appeared
to increase the attraction of the procedure and the interest in
the group. With five- and six-year-olds the same procedures were
used with M&M chocolate candies.

Although self-instruction may successfully help children
to perform difficult tasks and to solve problems more effectively, occasionally many children are so obsessed with distorted cognitions that they are unable to deal with any situations
until their distortions are corrected. Several sets of strategies for
correcting such distortions have been referred to as cognitive restructuring.

Cognitive Restructuring

There are several approaches to cognitive restructuring.
One of the earliest is Rational-Emotive Therapy (RET) developed by Ellis (1974). Another is a more behavioral approach
developed by Meichenbaum (1977) and Goldfried, Decenteceo,
and Weinberg (1974). We have adapted the latter approach to
group treatment of children. Since much of the approach bor-
rows from Ellis, RET is first briefly described below.

RET assumes that all problems are the result of magical
thinking or irrational ideas. Some of these ideas lead to self-con-
demnation, others to anger, and still others to a low tolerance
for frustration. The RET therapist helps clients to identify
which irrational ideas they hold, as evidenced by their statements to themselves in stressful situations, their emotional reactions, and their behavior. Thus the major intervention strategies
in RET are verbal persuasion and teaching. In a group, the RET
therapist uses the members as the major source of feedback,
persuasion, and disputation of the irrational ideas. Ultimately
clients are taught to dispute their own irrational beliefs, for
which there is no supporting evidence, and to recognize the effects of holding such ideas. Some of the more commonly occurring of Ellis's irrational ideas, which we have encountered with
many children and adolescents, are the following:

1. The idea that it is an absolute necessity for all individuals to be approved of or loved by virtually every significant person with whom they come in contact.
2. The idea that one should be thoroughly competent, adequate, and successful in every possible area, if one is to consider oneself worthwhile.
3. The idea that it is terrible when things are not the way one would like them to be.
4. The idea that all one's troubles are due to external circumstances and that there is nothing one can do about it.
5. The idea that if something is extremely difficult, troublesome, or fear-inducing, one should be thinking about it all the time.
6. The idea that it is better to avoid problems and difficult situations than to face them.
7. The idea that there is a perfect solution to all problems and that if one does not find it, it is catastrophic.

In the multimethod approach we draw on the above irrational beliefs to identify and dispute distorted ideation. The list of irrational ideas is also helpful in justifying why some thoughts appear to be self-defeating or self-enhancing. (For definition of these concepts, see below.) For the most part, the paradigm proposed here has drawn primarily from the work of Meichenbaum (1977) and Goldfried, Decenteceo, and Weinberg (1974) for the following reasons. Ellis appears to assume that the irrational ideas he describes are universal while the other authors cited tend to individualize their approach and to determine the unique irrational components for each person in each situation.

Another difference between Ellis and Meichenbaum is the former's preference for the label *irrational*. We prefer Meichenbaum's labeling of thoughts as either *self-defeating* or *self-enhancing*. *Self-defeating cognitions* refer to thoughts that defeat one's purposes, while *self-enhancing cognitions* refer to thoughts that facilitate the attainment of one's purposes. The major problem with using the concept of irrational beliefs is the danger of the children labeling themselves irrational or "crazy."

Although, in recent years, Ellis has proposed additional techniques to supplement his major strategy of therapist- and self-disputation of irrational ideas, the Meichenbaum approach to cognitive restructuring lends itself to a much wider variety of potential group and behavioral interventions. Finally, less emphasis is placed on identifying negative statements and more emphasis is placed on teaching coping alternatives in the Meichenbaum approach. In fact, if one is unable to identify the specific self-defeating ideation, one can move immediately to training in coping alternatives.

There is a great deal of similarity between self-instructional training and Meichenbaum's approach to cognitive restructuring. The major difference is the addition in cognitive restructuring of logical analysis of cognitions and the application of disputational procedures. The group analyzes a given member's thinking in a specific situation and disputes the logic or the usefulness of certain cognitions. Once identified as self-defeating, these cognitions then become the immediate target of change. Later, as a list of new self-enhancing cognitions are developed, together with the group, the self-defeating cognitions are replaced by the self-enhancing ones. Training to replace self-defeating statements with self-enhancing ones is done with cognitive modeling and cognitive rehearsal, just as in self-instructional training.

In order to clarify cognitive restructuring, let us lay out its steps and examine each of them in detail as they are used with children and adolescents within the context of the small group. The steps are as follows.

> providing a rationale
> training in the basic concepts
> identifying self-defeating and self-enhancing statements
> logically disputing self-defeating thought patterns
> shifting from self-defeating to self-enhancing statements
> modeling the shift to self-enhancing cognitions
> rehearsing the shift to self-enhancing cognitions
> group feedback
> fading

In the following sections we describe in detail the steps of "providing a rationale" through "shifting from self-defeating to self-enhancing statements." "Cognitive modeling," "cognitive rehearsal," and "fading" have already been described under self-instructional training. Chapters Three and Four described methods for identifying self-defeating thought patterns. In addition, we have added a subsection on "variations" of cognitive restructuring that are particularly suited to the small group.

Providing a Rationale. As Cormier and Cormier (1985) point out, the importance of providing an adequate rationale and overview cannot be over-emphasized. It is a gradual process in which the assumptions are taught slowly. This is especially true for children, who may require many examples before they accept the basic tenets of the approach. The following rationale, adapted from Meichenbaum (1977), is one way to begin. Variations of this rationale have been used with both children and adolescents.

> One thing you will learn in this group is to take a look at how our thinking and how we talk to ourselves influence how we feel and how we act. We can make ourselves more frightened by telling ourselves we are frightened. We can make ourselves feel bad about ourselves by calling ourselves names or putting ourselves down in other ways. We can also get rid of bad feelings by thinking about ourselves differently, by telling ourselves to take a deep breath and relax, by telling ourselves to go more slowly on a difficult task, or by reminding ourselves to take one step at a time. Sometimes we tend to exaggerate, to make terrible tragedies out of one small failure. And then we allow ourselves to put ourselves down because of the tragedy that we created in our head. We can often make ourselves feel better if we reexamine stressful situations with the help of our friends here in the group and if we find new, more accurate ways of thinking about problem situations and our responses to them.

At this point, the group leader asks if the members know of any ways in which they think about situations that have made them feel angry or unhappy or have kept them from doing anything about some situation. After a discussion of these examples, the leader goes on to provide an overview.

> In this group, one of the things you will be doing together is looking at situations that make you unhappy and at the ways in which you think about those situations. If what you are doing or thinking isn't working for you, the group will try to help each of you find better ways of thinking and behaving in those situations. The process of learning can be fun as well as helpful. There is a board game called Think Better, a game like Monopoly, that you will be playing. The group will also do lots of dramatics or role playing.

Training in the Basic Concepts. In providing the rationale, at least two specific concepts are presented to the children. Children can readily learn the basic concepts if they are presented in a clear and orderly way with ample practice in their use. In this section, we shall define those concepts and later describe how they are taught to the children or adolescents. Two central concepts are self-defeating statements and self-enhancing statements. These concepts and supporting examples are shared with children, for whom the vocabulary used to analyze thinking may be unfamiliar, in the following terminology.

Self-defeating statements are ways of talking to ourselves and describing situations that interfere with achieving our goals or make us anxious or unhappy. For example, Barry would like to talk to the new boy in the class. He says to himself, "Oh, that kid won't like me anyway." Barry walks away sad and lonely, just as he does with other children in the class. The statement leads to inaction, self-doubt, and anxiety. As such, it is self-defeating.

Self-enhancing statements are essentially accurate appraisals of a given problem or stressful situation. They may also include self-supportive statements and self-instructional statements that help solve a given situation one step at a time. Usually self-enhancing coping statements do not stimulate strong negative emotions. For example, when Fred was criticized by his teacher in a way that felt unfair, he thought, "Wow, that doesn't seem fair to me; I'd better ask her exactly what I did." Although there was clearly emotional arousal in response to the situation, it was followed by a problem-solving statement. In another example, when Alice fell for the third time that day, she thought, "This isn't my day; I'm glad all days aren't this way." In this example, Alice did not let the third fall get the better of her.

Training in Identifying Self-Defeating Statements. To facilitate the identification of self-defeating statements, a number of somewhat overlapping concepts may be used to describe what an individual is doing. These concepts, derived from Meichenbaum (1977), Beck (1976), and Ellis (1974), include exaggeration, catastrophization, absolutizing, prophesying, putting oneself down, selective perception, and excessive self-demand. Depending on the intellectual skills of the children, these concepts may or may not be shared with the group, but they are helpful for the group leader to analyze the unique aspects of a given self-statement.

Exaggeration is a common characteristic of most self-defeating statements. It is the practice of taking a relatively insignificant situation and giving it more importance than the facts of the situation call for. For example, Jayne received an average grade on a quiz. Although she did better on previous tests, she thought to herself, "I'm doing terribly in this course." Such an evaluation is an exaggeration, and will probably increase anxiety.

Catastrophization is a form of gross exaggeration that makes a tragedy of some trivial event. In the above example, Jayne's saying, "I'm failing the course, my life is ruined," would be an example of catastrophizing.

Absolutizing refers to statements that suggest that a given situation will continue unchanged regardless of changing conditions and that nothing can be done to alter that situation. Such statements are often identified by the presence of absolute terms, such as "never," "always," "cannot," or "impossible." Examples of absolutizing statements are Barry's earlier statement that no one will ever like him, or Diane's statement that she never gets what she wants. Such statements ignore all exceptions and exclude the possibility that changing circumstances lead to different opportunities. They also often generate a feeling of hopelessness, which is clearly unrealistic and, hence, self-defeating.

Prophesying refers to the self-statement that predicts future unfortunate and unknowable outcomes. Many of the absolute statements and catastrophic statements also fall into this category. The danger of prophesying negative outcomes is that such statements may serve as self-fulfilling prophesies. "I'm going to fail, I know I will" and "I'm sure I won't be able to sleep tonight" are both samples of prophesying that may result in undesired consequences.

Self-put-downs are self-descriptions that are essentially negative and critical and for which there is inadequate evidence. Any positive component (unless sarcastically expressed) is absent from such statements. Usually such statements describe quite general rather than specific behaviors or cognitions. When Henry spilled the milk, he thought, "What a dumb, clumsy idiot I am. I can't do anything right." (Note also "exaggeration" and "absolutizing" in this example.)

Selective perception refers to the response of focusing on one small negative event and discounting the rest of the situation. The child who made one mistake on his quiz and did well on the rest says to himself, "See, I made a mistake. I hardly know anything." This is an example of selective perception (as well as exaggeration.)

Excessive self-demand is reflected in statements in which a child demands unrealistic achievement levels. Often the words "should" or "must" are included in the statement. "I must get that bike. It would be awful if I didn't." "I must get a hundred percent on all my tests." "I should always be good."

Identifying Self-Defeating and Self-Enhancing Thoughts. Once self-defeating and self-enhancing statements are defined, the group leader presents the definition and examples stated above to the children. The leader then asks the children for their own examples in each category.

For further practice, the group leader distributes the following exercise to the members and asks them to identify self-defeating and self-enhancing statements. With older groups, the leader might also require each member to explain why the cognition falls into one of the above-mentioned subcategories.

Exercise 1

1. John, who is having problems at school, thinks to himself, "Everybody hates me. I'm just no good."
2. Arnie has to make a report in class. As he gets to the front of the class, he feels nervous and has a lump in his throat. "Okay, Arnie, you're a little uptight, but you've been this way before and you still could do your thing."
3. Annette was criticized by her mother for getting dirty on the way home. Later that night her dad said she was not working very hard on her homework. Annette said to herself, "Gosh, I sure am a dumb, terrible, awful person."
4. Charlene said to herself when the same thing happened to her, "This isn't my best day. I'm sure getting yelled at a lot. I wonder what I could do differently to save the rest of the day."
5. Tony's mother yelled at him for not making his bed. He said to himself, "She hates me, nobody loves me."
6. Tina is playing her favorite solitaire game. Her dad tells her to come and help set the table. She thinks to herself, "I'll do it quick, and get back to the game as soon as I can."
7. Mannie was picked on by the kids in class several times that day. When lunchtime came, he discovered he forgot his lunchbox. Mannie thought, "Everything bad happens to me. I can't do anything right."
8. Alissa's mother said that the new boy in class was on the phone. As she approached the phone, she said to herself, "I won't be able to speak at all," and panicked.

Following the discussion by the members, the group leader instructs the members to change all the self-defeating statements into self-enhancing statements. These are compared and evaluated by the members and leader. Then the members are asked to identify at least one self-defeating statement that they are accustomed to making and a recent situation in which it occurred. In the following example, Paul, the group leader, leads this step of the process.

Paul: Eddie seems to have a good situation. Tell the rest of the group what you often think, Eddie.

Eddie: Mine's sort of like that one on the list, you know, where Mannie says that everything happens to him. That's what I think a lot. I really have a lot of bad luck. That's why I'm always so worried. I'm sure something lousy is going to happen again.

Jack: Like what, Eddie?

Eddie: Well, last week I lost my hat. I was really afraid to tell my mom. I didn't find it for two days. That was awful.

Paul: Anything else happen to you?

Eddie: Well, not recently, but that was bad enough.

Paul: I wonder if that's a common experience for kids your age, even for kids my age.

(Group members laugh since Paul is almost forty.)

Jack: Yeah, I lose things all the time. Yesterday, I even lost my math book.

(Others in the group begin to tell about losing things.)

Paul: It seems to me that a lot of you, maybe all of you, have bad things happen to you now and then like Eddie. Some of you don't seem to find it as awful as Eddie does though. I guess this is a good thought to take a look at.

Disputing Self-Defeating Statements. In the above example, Eddie went on to tell of other things that happened to him. In the discussion that followed, it became clear that he was not unique in the amount of bad luck he had, but only in the way he responded to unlucky events. Later in the discussion, Paul inquired as to whether he had any good luck.

Eddie: Well, sure, I got an A in Math. And I got to go fishing with my dad. And I found a quarter just yesterday.

Jack: You told us you caught a pretty big fish. And you found your hat.

(Others in the group go on to tell Eddie about other good things that happened to him.)

Eddie: I guess I do have a lot of good luck. I never thought of it that way before.

Paul: Well, I guess we can safely say that you get your share of both good and bad luck, just like everyone else. It seems that the thought of having bad luck all the time is your self-defeating thought and the one you're going to have to work on. What do the rest of you think?

In the course of the discussion of self-defeating statements, the arguments of other members of the group are often sufficient to convince children that their self-defeating cognitions are indeed interfering with their lives. To make sure a client has arguments that attack the viability of the self-defeating statements readily available, group leaders may demonstrate the kinds of arguments that might be used. They would then have members rehearse the counterarguments aloud.

Replacing Self-Defeating Thoughts. Continuing with the above example, Paul has reviewed with the group all of the counterarguments to Eddie's self-defeating notion that he has particularly bad luck all of the time.

Paul: You've heard what the group members have said, Eddie. Why don't you give us those same arguments in the most convincing terms you can.

Eddie: Well, when I say to myself, "Boy do I have bad luck," I should say, "That's not true. I have lots of good luck, like when I found the quarter and caught the fish. Lots of kids lose things and have things happen to them." (looking at Paul)

Paul: (softly) Everybody . . .

Eddie: Oh, yeah, everybody has bad luck at times, but you can't wait around and worry about it.

Paul: What did he do well, guys?

The group then evaluated how Eddie handled the situation and Paul asked him to do it again, incorporating any new ideas from the members that he had liked.

Variations. Simply practicing aloud for too long a period may, unfortunately, be a boring technique that could easily turn a child off to the rest of the learning process unless the procedure of argumentation is presented in an attractive way. A number of ways of doing this are: using videotapes of the process, arguing with oneself in front of a mirror, using reinforcement by other group members for each counterargument, and round-robin group argumentation. However, the "boxing-match debate" described below has been one of the most attractive means of convincing children of the self-defeating quality of their ineffective ideations.

In this debate, a boxing match is simulated. First, the child with the self-defeating notions is assigned the role of the "great debator" and is provided with two coaches who "remind" the debator of the arguments as they are needed. Another group member is the "self-defeator," who is also assigned two coaches. The self-defeator is instructed, along with coaches, to argue the side of the self-defeating ideas.

The debate is set up like a boxing match with one person, often the group leader, serving as referee. The debate is carried out in a series of two-minute rounds with a minute break between rounds for the two debators to get additional tips from their coaches and, if necessary, from the group leader.

The leader or referee declares a "technical knockout" after the client convincingly puts down the self-defeating statements with good logic and assertive voice tone. The leader encourages the other members to cheer as the great debator bounces around the ring with hands held high in victory.

This is an extremely popular procedure because of its dramatic quality. One can add to the drama by audio- or videotaping the debate. The great debators can observe and listen to the tape of their arguing against the self-defeating statement as a homework assignment. In this way, tapes serve as a self-modeling procedure.

A similar program worked particularly well with a group of first- and second-grade gifted and talented children who had been referred to the group because of social-skill deficiencies. These children carried out the debate with great enthusiasm and flair. It has also been effectively used with developmentally delayed populations, although fewer arguments were generated on both sides.

We have thus far described two cognitive strategies for training children to cope with their thinking and the stressful environment to which they must respond. An extremely important coping strategy that is maintained and practiced by means of self-instruction is relaxation. Relaxation may be viewed in various ways: as a procedure that contributes to the prevention of nonfunctional affective responses, such as anxiety and depression; as a coprocedure in the use of certain cognitive strategies, such as systematic desensitization (Wolpe, 1973) or group exposure (Hand, Lamontagne, and Marks, 1974); and finally as a learned response to stress-inducing or otherwise problematic environmental events. In the following section, we discuss how relaxation is taught in groups and how children can use it in the real world.

Relaxation Training

Relaxation procedures are widely used for the treatment of anxiety and stress disorders. Their efficacy has been extensively evaluated by Barrios and Shigetomi (1979) and Borkovec and Sides (1979). Although the specific ways in which relaxation works are not well understood, the results of most comparison studies are positive (Hillenberg and Collins, 1982). We have extrapolated from research with adult clients in individual sessions and have modified techniques somewhat to suit children and adolescents in group settings. In this section we explicate the group application of progressive relaxation training, specifically as it applies to teaching children. We present two basic approaches, one for older children and adolescents and the other for young children and those who are developmentally impaired. We also discuss a number of variations on these two approaches, specific uses of the group, and strategies for generalizing the procedures to the real world.

Since many of the children with whom we work suffer from excessive anxiety and stress, either in specific situations or chronically, the use of systematic relaxation has been increasingly incorporated into the multimethod group programs. The ability to relax on command creates a physiological set of responses that appears to be incompatible with anxiety and impulsive responses. Once a child is well trained in the relaxation response, even thinking the word, *relax,* at moments of high stress seems to provide the pause necessary to prevent uncontrolled anger or rage. Relaxation can be taught as a useful skill in its own right or as an adjunct to cognitive procedures.

In addition to being incompatible with negative emotions and impulsive behavior, skill in relaxation has often enhanced a child's self-esteem. Children learn to take pride in their achievement as they demonstrate this esoteric skill to family and peers. In some groups the relaxation activity becomes a highly valued group reinforcer. Finally, for many, just practicing relaxation on a regular basis seems to reduce chronic anxiety and stress.

Teaching Relaxation in Groups. For older children and adolescents, relaxation is taught primarily through demonstration, instruction, and practice. As training progresses, the instruction becomes self-instruction. One muscle group at a time is tensed and then relaxed. At the completion of the tensing of one muscle group, the group leader checks each of the children by attempting to lift the affected body part to see whether the muscles appear to be tensed correctly. After the relaxation phase of the exercise, when the given muscle group appears to be correctly relaxed in all the members, the group leader goes on to the next muscle group. There are many patterns of giving instructions in the literature, although alternate tension and relaxation prevail in most of them. The order and the size of the muscle group are the major variants. The set of procedures we have most commonly used with older children and adolescents is described below. It is also used with some adjustment in language for younger children. In the following example, the group leader begins, as with all new procedures, by orienting the children to the purposes of the procedure to be used.

Last week we talked about the different ways of using relaxation. This week, as we agreed, I shall be teaching you how to use relaxation in those situations that make you feel tense, nervous, and angry. The first few times we do this, you may find it difficult to follow the instructions—you may itch, or feel the urge to giggle or move. (Note that the group leader gives the members permission to do what is highly likely to occur anyway.) Don't worry about it. You may feel some degree of relaxation or even a whole lot at times or in certain parts of the body. Sometimes, when it is a whole lot, it might even scare you a little bit. But you may learn to really enjoy it. Now listen to me carefully and try to follow the instructions as best as you can.

Okay, loosen any tight belts or other tight clothing. Take off your glasses and remove your contacts if you forgot and brought them along. Lie on your back with your feet slightly separated. Place your arms alongside your body with your palms up and your hands open.

Bring your attention to your right hand. Now slowly make a fist. Feel the tension in your fingers and your hand. Now give your attention to your right arm. Try to feel the muscles and then concentrate on tensing the muscles in that arm. Increase the tension as much as you can from the hand to the top of the shoulder. Stretch the arm, but don't lift it, as you will then tense other muscles. Keep your attention on the tension in your arm, and try not to let any other thoughts come into your mind. Remain this way for five seconds. Slowly release the tension in your fist and then your arm. Your hand should be slightly opened once again with your palm up. Try to think about what is happening in the arm. Each of you may feel differently. Some of you may feel the arm becoming quite heavy and sinking into the mat. Now focus on your left arm. (The group leader goes through the same steps with the left arm.)

Now concentrate on the right leg. Push the heel away and draw the toes toward you in order to avoid a foot cramp. (The group leader examines each of the feet in order to make sure the exercise is correctly done.) Then slowly increase tension until the maximum tension has been achieved from the foot to the thigh. Stretch the leg but do not lift it. Wait five seconds in this tensed condition while focusing on the leg as much as possible. Now slowly release the tension in the leg. Some people feel the leg become heavy. Some feel it sinking into the floor. (Then the group leader goes through the same steps with the left leg.) Now relax the right arm as much as possible, now the left arm, now the right leg, and once again the left leg.

Now turn your attention to the area around your waist. To tense this area, you tighten or contract the stomach (abdominal) muscles and draw them slightly upward. Then draw the buttocks towards one another. (With some children the word "buttocks" will stimulate laughter. In this case avoid this area the first few times.) Forget the rest of the body and concentrate on this one tensed area. Slowly release the stomach muscles and the buttocks, and let stomach and buttocks sink heavily into the floor.

Now direct your attention to the muscles of the chest. Gradually tense these muscles. Now move your shoulders toward each other from behind, tensing the back and rib muscles. Now gradually relax the chest, the shoulders, the back, and the rib cage. Let your lower and upper body sink into the floor. Relax your arms and legs once again.

Now focus on the neck. To tense it, pull back the neck towards the nape; hold it a few seconds and slowly let it loose. You may note a difference between the tensed neck and the resting neck. Move your focus to the face. Clench your jaws together; tense the cheeks, mouth, and eyelids; wrinkle the forehead. One by one release the tension in each of these—the jaws, the cheeks, mouth, the eyelids, and finally, the forehead. Let these muscles feel the pull of gravity. Open your mouth slightly.

Go slowly once more through the entire body relaxing once again but without tensing the feet, the legs, the pelvic area, the chest, the back, the arms, the shoulders, the neck, and the face. If possible let your body sink still further into the mat. Now hold it for a minute (later, two to five minutes). (Then the group leader ends relaxation with the following instruction.)

Don't jump up and run off. Move your fingers slowly; now your toes; now your arms and legs, just a little; now a little more; now your shoulders. Move your head back and forth. If you feel like stretching, stretch. Increase the depth of your breathing. Sit up, stretch some more; hold it momentarily. Now, if you feel ready, stand up.

Before beginning such procedures it is important to check out any history of injury. Muscles that have been injured may be prone to knotting up when they are tensed. In these cases, avoid the tension phase for the previously injured and nearby muscle groups. Also current medication should be noted. If any is being taken, the parent should check with the physician whether the medicine might in any way interact with the relaxation state.

Variations in Teaching Procedures. As noted above, there are many variations in relaxation procedures. Longer versions that consider, for example, the voice box and very minute muscle groups have been described by Jacobson (1929). We have found these to be especially useful when there is an impasse and the child is unable to relax a particular large muscle group, or in situations in which a very minute muscle group seems to be the focus of the tension. In most cases, however, the above paradigm is sufficient. For most children the entire relaxation paradigm is too long to be handled in one session. We find it useful to do the arms and legs in one session and the trunk and head in another session, and then practice relaxing the entire body in several additional sessions. In the remaining sessions we practice a highly abbreviated version in which no tension is used at all. Both arms are relaxed at the same time. Then both legs, the upper and lower torso, and the facial features are relaxed. (Bernstein and Borkovec, 1973, go from seventeen to seven to four muscle groups in the course of a treatment that focuses solely on relaxation as the major intervention.)

The above procedures seem to be suitable for most older children and adolescents. For many younger children (usually under the age of twelve) or those who suffer from physical or emotional impairment, the above paradigm may not be sufficiently simple for the children to master these highly complex skills. For this reason the group leader should know several ways of modifying the commonly used paradigm to fit the unique requirements of young, extremely active, or emotionally or physically handicapped children (see Cautela and Groden, 1978, pp. 43–44).

Relaxation for the Very Young. For very young or developmentally disabled children, we follow the post-readiness procedures elaborated on by Cautela and Groden (1978, pp. 46–47). They give the child a simple test to determine whether they can sit quietly for five seconds, give eye contact for three seconds, imitate simple procedures, and follow simple instructions. If not, the program works on these basic skills. Once these skills are available to the children, they are taught the position for relaxation. The children are asked to sit with their heads squarely on their shoulders and their hands on their laps for five seconds without vocalizing or moving. With older or better-functioning children a somewhat longer period may be used. Then the group leader teaches them to relax first the large motor areas, such as the arms and legs, and later, smaller motor areas, such as facial muscles or the throat.

The initial steps are particularly important. For example, all the children are asked to assume the relaxing position. The group leader gives each child a tap or reinforcer if it is correct. Then the leader asks all the children to make a fist and to extend their right arm as straight and far forward as they can. Each person is to look at the leader who is demonstrating the behavior, then to the neighbors on the left and the right to see how each of the others is doing. By then, the arms are sufficiently fatigued to let them fall back into the relaxing position while gradually opening the fist. The group leader then goes around the room checking each arm by picking it up slightly and letting it fall like a limp rag doll. Cautela and Groden refer to this as the "limping procedure." The group leader asks the children having trouble making a fist to tighten their outstretched hand around the leader's finger. It is also helpful to have the child open and close the hand several times. If the problem is persistent, squeeze toys are recommended (Cautela and Groden, 1978, p. 68). The same procedures are followed for the second arm. Usually this is enough for a first session.

While in their chairs, the children lift up their legs. If necessary, the leader pulls the leg gently while instructing "stretch your leg out, toes inward; point your toes towards your nose." After holding it a few seconds, the children are instructed to gradually relax the leg, slowly bend it down, and slowly straighten the foot. This usually requires several trials. Cautela and Groden suggest that they "let it feel like a Raggedy Ann or a loose clown." The second leg is tensed and relaxed in the same way. That is sufficient for the second session.

Similar adaptations to the earlier paradigm are made for the rest of the body. The paradigm may be followed except when special problems arise. With younger or handicapped children, the tempo is much slower, the language much simpler, the demonstrations more vivid and more frequent, the repetitions more numerous, the reinforcement more continuous and more concrete, and the involvement of the children in the leadership role less likely than with older children and adolescents.

Using the Group. Almost all the procedures described above, for both older and younger children, can be taught in a group or in the classroom. Even in the small group, at some time the group leader should observe each child separately in order to detect individual problems. This may occur within the group context while the others are observing each other in pairs.

Often a relaxing atmosphere is created by dimming the lights, playing a relaxing record, and putting up a "do not disturb" sign on the outside door. This tends to cut down on horseplay and other silly behavior.

Wherever possible and as soon as possible, the better functioning children and adolescents are put in the position of teaching or monitoring each other. This is usually done in pairs. Thus every child goes through the daily relaxation procedure twice: once as relaxee and once as relaxor. Before the children get to that phase, the group leader demonstrates the necessary steps repeatedly. Furthermore, children must be "certified" as coaches before they will actually be permitted to give the instructions to another child. Even when children are giving the instructions to other children the group leader is close by, circulating among the children and carefully observing and prompting. To provide multiple models the instructional pairs are frequently rearranged.

On occasions when particular children have demonstrated unusual skills, they may coach the entire group. In this way, the opportunity to coach becomes a powerful reinforcer for mastery of both the relaxation skills and the teaching of them.

Another commonly used group technique for stimulating interest in the relaxation procedures is the use of the game Simon Says. The children are asked to duplicate the command only if preceded by the words "Simon says." Thus if the group leader says "tense the muscles in the hand," the group members would be expected not to respond. If however the leader says, "Simon says tense the muscles in the right hand," compliance would be expected. Normally Simon Says is an elimination game. Since elimination from the game would defeat the purpose, those who make mistakes get a point. The object is to get as few points as possible. In this game all the children are in a semicircle facing the group leader or the leader's designate. For some children the game is so exciting that it interferes with relaxation, and has to be avoided or not used too frequently.

With young children, frequent reinforcement should be given by the group leader in the initial phase of learning. In addition to praise, tokens are often put into a paper cup lying next to the child as the group leader inspects each child to note success in carrying out an instruction. Lack of compliance is almost always ignored. Persistent lack of compliance may be discussed later as a group problem.

With adolescents, only social reinforcement is given. Sometimes, permitting those members who do any of the steps well to demonstrate to the entire group may serve as an effective reinforcement (if group cohesion is high and the norms are essentially protherapeutic). In fact, adolescents can be reinforced by the leadership responsibilities mentioned above as coach or group demonstrator.

Generalization of Learning. To generalize relaxation skills, a number of different relaxation positions are taught (following the suggestions of Cautela and Groden, 1978, pp. 77–78): sitting, standing, and walking, as well as lying down. Relaxation is also taught in different settings, such as in the classroom and halls, in the community, in all the rooms of the home, and wherever the child experiences tension. Field trips can be taken to places where it is helpful to practice relaxation.

A wide variety of persons are used to teach relaxation: all the group members, the group leader, and if possible, parents and teachers. In those classrooms where the teacher practiced relaxation once or twice a week, it was noted that the use of relaxation was maintained. The same was true where parents used the procedure with the children at home. For this reason, significant people in the children's lives are encouraged and sometimes taught to do the relaxation procedures.

Earlier in the chapter, it was noted that the children are taught to identify stressful situations. After teaching relaxation techniques, these situations are reviewed. The children are then asked to imagine the situation and to go through the short steps of relaxation as soon as the critical moment in the stressful situation occurs. Thus, following a strategy proposed by Paul (1966), the initial onset of feeling stress or anxiety becomes the cue to use relaxation in stressful situations outside of the group.

Practicing Relaxation at Home. Of course, homework practice is an essential part of any generalization package. Sixty percent of the research projects reviewed by Hillenberg and Collins (1982) required homework practice. Most of the researchers who used homework claimed it was essential to teaching the procedure. Unfortunately, no one investigated the difference between training with and without homework although we have some anecdotal evidence, which was cited above, of the advantage of homework. Even in studies with adults, homework compliance was difficult to obtain. With children and adolescents, it is probably even more difficult. The use of tapes, which the children borrow along with a tape recorder, seems to enhance compliance as well as the use of daily buddy contacts in which partners practice with each other. Some group leaders have special daily relaxation sessions that are carried out with the help of aides immediately after school, for ten minutes. These daily sessions are gradually faded until the homework seems to be done without such a structure. Finally, the use of reinforcement for relaxation is gradually faded. Concrete reinforcement is faded first and then social reinforcement becomes more sporadic. However, we have found that premature elimination of all social reinforcement creates the risk of losing all home practice.

There is often too little time in groups to give relaxation training the attention it deserves. In this case it may be useful to incorporate the family or the school in obtaining additional training for the children. Of course, relaxation training is usually only one of many strategies of intervention used in the group to achieve common and individual group goals. The appropriateness of the relaxation strategy and the extent of its use depends on the nature of the target behaviors. Certainly where the children complain of chronic or acute anxiety or stress, relaxation training should be a central feature of the program.

Meditation. Because of its counterculture implications, meditation often has a particular allure for the adolescent. Since no consistent difference in results is noted in research literature between meditation and relaxation for the treatment of anxiety and stress (Everly and Rosenfeld, 1981), it is possible to offer the group members their choice, provided that the group leader's skills are well-developed in both areas. Since our experience with meditation and other similar procedures is limited, we recommend for the interested reader the work of Carrington (1978a, 1978b); Goldman, Domitor, and Murray (1979); and Goleman and Schwartz (1976).

Summary

In this chapter we have presented a number of cognitive procedures that can be readily used in groups. These included self-instructional training and cognitive restructuring, both of which draw on cognitive modeling, cognitive rehearsal, and group feedback. The group is an efficient vehicle for helping children to recognize cognitive distortions and to brainstorm more suitable alternatives. The group is also an efficient means of providing a rationale for each of the procedures used. A number of group exercises are used to help children identify self-defeating statements and to learn self-reinforcement. Relaxation can also be taught readily in groups, and group members can improve their relaxation skills by relaxing each other. Variations of relaxation procedures commonly used in groups were discussed as they apply to various populations.

Throughout the last three chapters on intervention we suggested a number of games and other sociorecreational activities to enhance the quality of the learning experience and to provide variety in the various interventions used. Since such activities are central to the multimethod approach, the next chapter is devoted to their conceptualization and principles of application.

Chapter Nine

Using Games and Activities to Achieve Treatment Goals

Billy (friend of group member):   Is that group you belong to any fun?

Jean (group member):   Yeah, you bet! Although we have to work on our behavior and stuff, we also play all kinds of games like Scrabble, charades, and Monopoly. And we made up our own board game, too. We even played soccer lots of times, but only for a few minutes each time.

Freddie (group member):   We put on plays and we got to videotape one and show it to our moms and dads. It was about kids just like us.

Al (group member):   Don't forget the trip we made to the TV studio. They showed us how the pros do it.

Billy: Wow! You guys do have fun. How do you get in that group?

Every group has its work: reviewing and developing homework, modeling, rehearsal, feedback, exercises, problem solving, group discussion, practicing relaxation, and cognitive restructuring. Although, depending on how it is presented, much of what is done may be fun to the children, in the beginning such activities are often insufficient to motivate consistent interest and even regular attendance. For this reason, incorporated into every session, especially the initial sessions, are such group activities as games, sports, dramatics, storytelling, crafts, photography, and trips.

239

The purposes of these activities are multiple. First, as mentioned above, they are used to increase the attraction of the group in the early phase of treatment. Second, they create a variety of problematic or stressful situations in which the members can reveal and/or practice their coping skills. Choosing roles, selecting activities, losing a game, failing to complete a task, and meeting demands for cooperation and requests to clean up are all situations that may require new behavior—such as assertion, humor, interviewing, problem solving, self-organization, and decision making. The group leader uses these situations to reinforce effective coping, to assess coping strengths and deficiencies, and to try out new skills (in a homework assignment). The leader also monitors the use of newly learned skills and coaches their use in the ongoing group process. Third, group activities provide a variety of new roles and leadership opportunities for members. These roles can be coached during the group process and rehearsed, either as homework or in the treatment part of a group meeting. This is one of the few opportunities for many of our clients to be a helper of others, a star player in a given sport, or a coach, and to fill other attractive social positions that may not be available to them in the normal classroom situation. Finally, group activities provide a rich opportunity for direct observation of children interacting with one another under various stress levels. It can become a major source of observed behavioral data for assessment and evaluation.

The purpose of this chapter is to discuss the major principles of analyzing, designing, and implementing program activities as a major treatment resource along with the behavioral and cognitive change strategies already described. To facilitate this discussion, we draw on the concepts presented by Vinter (1974b, pp. 233–246) who drew in turn on the work of Gump and Sutton-Smith (1965, pp. 755–760). The concepts *physical field, activity behavior, constituent behaviors,* and *prescriptiveness* have been used by a number of researchers for the analysis and implementation of the potential of program activities (Garvin, 1981; Ross and Bernstein, 1976; Rose, 1972).

Analyzing Program Activities

The activity is analyzed in terms of the physical field, the required behaviors (constituent performances), and the informal behaviors associated with it. These three components are defined and their implication for assessment and treatment are described below.

Physical Field. Physical field refers to the minimal physical space, materials, and equipment required to carry out a given activity. The only material required to play the card game War is a deck of cards, and it can be played in any space large enough to hold the players and light enough to read the cards. Checkers requires a set of twenty-four checkers and a square board with 64 squares; space must be sufficient to hold the players and boards. Baseball requires at least an empty lot in the way of space or, better yet, a baseball diamond. The equipment is a ball and bat and, ideally, some gloves and bases. Listing materials and space requirements when planning an activity will help avoid many potential program failures.

Often the group meeting room is quite circumscribed. It usually is a small classroom or a lounge. Occasionally a stage or even a gymnasium may be put at the group's disposal. The limits of this space should be considered when planning activities. Where the available space is not sufficient for desired activities (that is, activities that provide new opportunities for learning), new space may have to be negotiated. Field trips dramatically expand the physical field and provide a new environment in which to try out behaviors learned in the group. If attempted too early, however, the unlimited space involved in many field trips may fail to restrict acting-out behavior of many of the clients, as in the following brief excerpt from a group leader's record.

We went from the usual meeting room to a large cafeteria. The semblance of control I had in the meeting room was lost in the cafeteria where they ran about uncontrollably, stealing food and passing it from the counter line to the others in the dining area.

Restricted space limits movement, but it also can facilitate the control of certain behavior. The group leader in a central location can use both eye contact and touch control to help keep a group on task (Redl and Wineman, 1956). Yet the real world alternates between broad spacious areas and highly restricted ones. Children must learn to perform activities in all kinds of physical fields. Thus, the group leader usually begins with the restricted space of the meeting room and gradually introduces larger areas, for which the children are prepared in advance.

The materials available also control and enhance skill training in specific ways. The availability of tools makes certain programs possible. Access to a television or film camera opens up a wide range of activities. Various kinds of sports equipment and crafts supplies all expand the nature of what can be done in the group. In preparation, a group leader may make an inventory of the materials available in order to assess which items can be readily used and for what kinds of activities.

Another aspect of physical field is the time required for a given activity. Often a session can have as little as five to ten minutes available for an activity, including the instructions. It would be difficult to carry out most activities in such a limited time without modification of the rules. Some games, however, can be squeezed into a short time period, carried over to another session, or completed as a homework assignment.

Constituent Behaviors. Those behaviors that are essential to a given activity and are required of the participants are constituent behaviors (Vinter, 1974b). Game-playing behaviors such as rolling dice, moving a piece one space at a time, and taking turns in the same order are examples of constituent performances. Activities are generally selected in which the constituent performances can be linked to behaviors that are targeted for change.

Informal Behaviors. Informal behaviors are associated

with but not essential to the performance of a given activity. In playing baseball, cheering one's team, arguing with the umpire, and urging another teammate on may be considered informal behaviors. If solely restricted to consituent behaviors, the opportunity for learning would be indeed limited and the activity itself would be experienced as quite dull.

Dimensions of the Activity Setting

Vinter refers to the physical field and constituent behaviors as the "activity setting" since these conditions are necessary for activities to occur. He identifies six basic dimensions of the activity setting as a scheme for determining the appropriateness of specific program activities for common and individual treatment goals. These dimensions are the level of prescriptiveness of constituent behaviors, the level of external or institutional control, opportunity for physical movement, the level of competence required for performance, the opportunity for and intensity of interaction, and, finally, the reward structure. Each of these will be discussed below.

Level of Prescriptiveness. The extent to which rules of an activity regulate or otherwise circumscribe behavior is referred to as the level of prescriptiveness. Activities associated with all group activities vary considerably in their degree of prescriptiveness. In some activities, such as a chess tournament, virtually all behaviors, including those of the onlookers, are prescribed. In games without names, in which children merely alternate who chases whom, a low level of prescriptiveness can be said to exist. Since clients differ radically in their ability to handle regulation of any sort, the level of prescriptiveness is highly pertinent to group activity planning and selection. For clients who find it difficult to submit to control of any sort, activities with a low level of prescriptiveness are selected initially: for example, the games of tag, catch, hide-and-seek, storytelling, and freestyle painting.

It is possible to increase the level of prescriptiveness as the attention span of the children and the cohesion of the group increase. For example, the game of tag can be replaced by Blob (described under "Active Games," below), which later can be replaced by Capture the Flag (also described below).

Some prescriptions are inherent in the materials or tools required to perform the activity or in consideration of safety. Power tools can be used only in highly prescribed ways. In some activities, such as dramatics, materials may be used in unprescribed and often highly creative ways. A circle of cardboard becomes a crown. A tennis ball may become a giant piece of gold, and so on. In general, a low level of prescriptiveness permits a greater use of imagination and creativity. Nevertheless, children in treatment groups generally require activities across the range of prescriptiveness, since varied levels provide varied stimulus conditions for a wide range of potential target behaviors.

External or Institutionalized Controls. External controls refer to the "source or agent of controls that are exercised over participants during the activity" (Vinter, 1974b, p. 236). These controls are performed by the group leader, by the participant, by umpires or team captains, and sometimes, more informally, by the person who is "it." Initially, however, most activity controls are regulated by the staff, except in highly familiar activities. Self-regulated controls are ideally the ultimate aim. To this end the group leader is constantly shifting control of activities to the group members and among the group members. For example, the role of discussion leader is delegated to the members in early sessions, often with the coaching of the group leader. The coaching, too, is ultimately faded. Team captainships are distributed among all the members before any one individual gets a second turn. In dramatics, the role of director is shared by all who desire it. The directors may have to be coached to varying degrees.

Because control is a major problem for many clients, the issue of the controller is given a great deal of attention in planning activities. Early juvenile offenders in one group were characterized by their inability to accept the controls of adults. The group leader chose activities, at first, in which all control came from the rules of the well-known game, soccer. In another group, one member in particular tyrannized the others. In this group, the leader primarily offered activities in which equal participation was dictated by the rules—in this case, board games in which everyone got an equal turn. In addition, the use of a kitchen timer, as a nonpersonal controller, assured that no person in group discussions, skits, or roleplays went over the allotted time. In general, stimulus control of behavior that emanates from the inherent limits of space, materials, available time, or the rules of the activity are preferable to verbal instructions issued by the group leader or other authority person. Such indirect control limits power struggles between the authority person and the adolescent in particular.

The implication of the above discussion is that in planning for new activities, the group leader reviews indirect and direct sources of control in each activity and ways in which these might shift over time. Although most children need to adapt to both adult and material control, programs with different sources of control are recommended. As in the examples above, timing is important. With children in revolt, nonpersonal control is necessary, at first, just to maintain them. For children who are anxious and unsure of themselves, clear adult-given control is usually desirable at first. Later, control can shift to the group and then, the self.

Provision of Participant Interactiveness. Activities vary in the amount, distribution, and intensity of interaction. All three variables are of concern to the group leader in planning programs. For example, in individual craft activities the group members are together but the amount and intensity of interaction is extremely low. This might be a comfortable early activity for children with a great deal of anxiety in interpersonal interaction with their peers. Later, subgroup games might be introduced in which the members do puzzles in pairs or put on three-person skits. Only later will the group leader suggest an activity that involves the entire group in intense interaction with each other.

Group discussion has the potential for intense interactiveness and broad distribution of participation. However, unless the group leader or the member who serves as discussion leader keeps track of who is speaking, the distribution can be quite limited. The same is true for skits or group planning. For this reason, the importance of broad participation is discussed in early sessions and is strongly encouraged through the selection of programs and through reinforcement throughout treatment. We have found with adults, at least, a high correlation of participation with outcome (Rose, 1981).

Provision for Physical Movement. Provision for physical movement refers to "the extent to which participants are required or permitted to move about" (Vinter, 1974b, p. 236). Since most of the work of the group affords limited movement, many group leaders select activities that maximize physical movement, such as active games or sports. However, if the group leader is helping the children to manage classroom stress more effectively, a predominance of low movement may be required. In this case, such activities as simulated class or educational games or computer use may ultimately be more effective in terms of goal achievement than the more active games. Often, if the group is held immediately after school, the group leader may, even in this situation, begin with a brief high-physical-movement activity. It is also possible to increase physical movement in quiet work activities. In overt modeling and behavioral rehearsal, it is useful and more realistic to have the actors get up, knock on imaginary doors, and otherwise go through the physical actions of the roleplay as well as the verbal behavior. Moving to different parts of the room from time to time even during discussions tends to reduce the restlessness that often accompanies long discussions.

Competence Required for Performance. In most activities a minimum level of competence is required for the members to carry on the given activity. Some activities, such as the card game War or tag, require very little in the way of competence to play them, while games such as bridge or chess, or playing musical instruments require a great deal of competence. In general, the group leader takes into consideration the existing competencies of group members in drawing up a list of potential activities. The leader might also include either low competency activities as well, or those activities in which competencies can be readily taught. Programs that remain too long at the lowest competency level often lose members' interest. Moreover they do not provide as readily the variety of stimulus conditions required for performing goal behaviors. The art is finding those activities that permit diverse levels of competency, as in the following example.

> In a group of fourteen- to fifteen-year-old adolescents referred for high levels of anxiety and a high frequency of self-put-downs, cognitive restructuring was the major means of intervention. The group leader discovered that one of the children played the violin and two others could play simple chords on the guitar. His proposal for a bluegrass band with two washboards as well as the above instruments was met with unanimous acclaim. Ten minutes of each meeting were set aside for rehearsing the band and teaching the washboard players the minimal skills necessary for their part of the activity. Even though the minimum competency level was quite varied, all seemed to enjoy the activity. What is more important, the practice afforded the group the opportunity to discuss their excessive self-standards and the consequent anxiety that seemed to interfere with their enjoyment.

Some activities are highly attractive to children but the children do not possess the minimal skills required to engage in them. In this case the group leader may modify the rules so that a lower level of minimal competency is required to participate. In the above example, had there been no fiddler, the group leader could have used a tape. In a group of seven-year-olds who wanted to play baseball but who could not hit the ball at all, the group leader had each batter throw the ball as hard as he could into the infield and then run for first. Before each ten-minute game, the leader also provided batting practice until the members were hitting often enough to get rid of the throwing rule.

Reward Structure. Rewards and costs are inherent in the structure of any activity. Activities, however, vary as to the quantity and nature of rewards, the ratio of rewards to cost, and the opportunities for a broad distribution of rewards. In competitive games the major rewards go to those who win, unless the group leader also rewards good plays, good passes, good assists, or good tries. In crafts rewards may only be associated with finishing a high-quality product unless the group leader provides praise for small steps, good ideas, helping others, careful use of tools, and similar small achievements. It is clear that the reward structure is determined not as much by the activity as by the way the group leader uses that activity and maximizes the rewards for the children. Teaching the group members to reinforce each other as well as themselves is also a way of increasing the reward structure of all activities. Rewards from others or from oneself also reduce the satiation effect of reinforcement from the group leader.

The six dimensions for analyzing an activity setting are not without limitations. The dimensions are probably not complete nor are they mutually independent. Moreover, it is almost impossible to take them all into consideration at one time. Nevertheless, we have found them extremely useful in evaluating various activities and in planning for and selecting activities. The various types of activities below will be analyzed in terms of the dimensions described above.

Types of Program Activities

Many types of activities are used in group treatment. Several have already been described. In this section we shall identify the major categories of group activities commonly used in group treatment and some of the conditions under which they can best be implemented. These include games (sports, action, paper and pencil, card, board, and social skill), handicrafts, drawing, charades and dramatics, simulated classroom activities, photography, and field trips.

Games

Games provide an opportunity for the occurrence (and reinforcement) of such behaviors as taking turns, giving feedback, following rules, and learning how to lose and how to win. Most games are highly prescriptive, but the control is lodged in the rules rather than with the group leader. The game format is especially useful with disruptive and resistant adolescents. Although they rarely show initial interest in the work of the group, these adolescents are often swept up in an exciting game. As Cartledge and Milburn (1981, p. 100) point out, "Games provide an opportunity for the child to learn the consequences of his actions without having to suffer them. In a game mistakes and exposure of ignorance are more tolerated. Games usually encourage laughing and joking, which can be instrumental in relieving anxiety and facilitating involvement."

By identifying a number of game categories one can facilitate planning and decision making in the selection of game activities. First on this list are major athletic games such as baseball, basketball, football, and soccer. Second are group action games such as dodge ball, Mother May I?, or Red Light/Green Light that require less space, fewer rules, and virtually no special equipment. Third are paper-and-pencil games such as Tic-Tac-Toe and Hangman, which can be played in a highly confined place with nothing more than a piece of paper and a pencil. They are also characterized by almost no physical movement. Fourth are card games, which have the same characteristics as paper-and-pencil games except that cards replace the paper and pencil. Among the most commonly played card games are War, Old Maid, Concentration, and Fish. (See Giannoni, 1974, for a variety of card games for children.) Both card games and paper-and-pencil games can require a wide range of levels of competency. As noted in the above examples, usually—but not always—games with a low level of competency and a high opportunity for frequent rewards are used in group treatment. Both types of games have the added advantage for group treatment of being readily played in a short period of time.

Cooperative games in which the rewards do not come from winning at the cost of someone else's losing is a fifth category of games. Although most of the games mentioned above are competitive in nature, with a few rule changes most of them can be converted to cooperative games. Examples of cooperative games are balloon volleyball in which the object is to keep the balloon in the air as long as possible or tug-of-peace in which the object is to make letters on the ground with a long clothesline.

Sixth are board games such as Monopoly, Scrabble, or Chinese checkers. These require a board and other materials. In most other ways they are similar to paper-and-pencil and card games. They are, however, somewhat more difficult to end before their natural completion time (for example, within an allotted ten-minute period). Games in general afford an interesting and sometimes exciting way of integrating social-skill training with sociorecreational activities. In the following subsections we discuss each of the game categories in more detail.

Major Athletic Sports. Most of the children in our groups have had little success in major sports. When these games are played in school, many of our clients are customarily assigned to unimportant roles requiring minimal competencies. When they do get a turn because it cannot be avoided, they are greeted with derogatory remarks about their lack of skill. Nevertheless, the members often initially prefer these games because they are what they know and these games have high peer status. Because of the children's lack of minimal competencies and because of the extensive time these sports require, they are rarely incorporated into group-treatment programs. In the short time available in group treatment, there is little likelihood that a given child will make major inroads into skill development. Soccer and basketball appear to be more desirable sports than softball, as they permit broader participation, encourage greater cooperation through extensive passing, and require greater physical movement. Moreover, a minimal level of competency can be quickly acquired. It is also possible to have a short game of ten to fifteen minutes without the members feeling disappointed. Finally, it is possible to modify the reward structure by giving points for good passes, effective dribbling, keeping one's position, and good tries. In spite of their therapeutic potential, there are many problems with major sports and there is little time to resolve most of them. Group leaders, therefore, tend to make far greater use of other active games.

Other Active Games. It is far easier to squeeze in games like Capture the Handkerchief or dodge ball in the ten to fifteen minutes allotted to activities than to attempt to play softball or soccer. Moreover, the minimal level of competence required to play them is far lower than that in the major sports. Furthermore, the levels of participation are usually more intense and more broadly distributed. As a result, the reward structure permits far more frequent reinforcement. The games we have frequently used and the reasons for using them are described in detail below.

One of the most commonly used games with preadolescents is Capture the Handkerchief. In this game two teams with the same number of members are selected by the group leader. Each member of one team is given a number, and duplicate numbers are given to members of the other team. The group leader stands between the teams and holds a handkerchief aloft. While calling one or more numbers, the group leader drops the handkerchief. The children with the assigned numbers run up to the handkerchief. The object is to grab the handkerchief and get back to one's own side before being tagged by the person with the same number on the opposite team. A point is given for either getting back to one's own side safely or tagging one's opponent with the handkerchief.

Blob is a "new" game that is attractive to young adolescents and children alike (Fluegelman, 1976). It starts out like tag except that the first and all subsequent persons tagged are added on to the person who is "it," forming a "blob." The game is continued until all the members are caught and become a part of the blob. The time of the game can be limited by restricting the area in which it takes place. Other tag games are particularly popular with young children as well, such as hopping tag, three-legged tag, or blindfold tag.

Indoor track meets consist of the javelin throw (in which

a straw is tossed) and the discus (in which a paper plate is hurled). Another activity is the low jump, which involves crawling under a stick while holding onto a partner who must also get under the stick. The stick is lowered on each successive turn. Yet another activity, the slow race, requires consistent forward motion, but the last person to cover three feet wins. In such an activity the poorly coordinated have as much chance to win as the more athletically inclined. Although there is limited interactiveness in the constituent behaviors, there is a great deal of excited interactiveness in the informal behaviors. As a result these games are enjoyed by all age groups, although adolescents often resist them in the beginning.

As separate activities or as part of the indoor track meet, relays are commonly used in group meetings. Most relays take up very little time and can be readily squeezed into a busy group schedule. Often more than one can be played at a group meeting. In most relays the basic idea is to divide the group into two or more teams with an equal number of members. Each team lines up at a common point. At a given signal, the first person in line on each team begins to carry out a designated activity while progressing to and from a designated destination. Upon returning, the first team member tags the second team member, who repeats the activity. A team wins when all the team members have performed the given activity and returned to the team. The most common relays we have used in group treatment sessions are described below.

1. *The forty-yard swim.* Each team is given a tablespoon of water. The object is to walk to the destination and back without spilling the water. If it spills the tablespoon is refilled and the person starts over.
2. *Barefoot marbles.* Two marbles are placed in front of each team. The first players begin by picking up the marbles with their bare feet and running to the destination and back without dropping them. If one is dropped it must be picked up again before resuming the race.
3. *Footsie race.* Each team has a long piece of rope on the ground in front of it. The players are blindfolded and bare-

foot and must feel their way along the rope, one at a time, to the destination and back to the team.

4. *Shoe relay*. The shoes for each team are put in a pile across the room. The first players on each team run across the room and find their shoes, put them on, run back, and tag the next person, who does the same.

5. *Crab relay*. Each person leans back on hands and feet and walks like a crab.

6. *Balloon relay*. There are many variations to this relay. One can pass the balloon over the shoulder to the next person on the team who passes it under the legs to the next person. The first person can run to a chair and sit on a balloon until it breaks and then run back. The first person can bat the balloon until it hits the wall opposite the team and then bat it back until it is caught by the next team member.

7. *Potato carry relay*. The first person carries the potato (or balloon) in a spoon to the destination and back to the next person without dropping it.

Cooperative Games. Most of the above games are competitive. It is possible to use games that are designed to be cooperatively played or to make cooperative games out of competitive games by rule changes. The advantages of cooperative games are that they tend to increase group cohesion, reduce interpersonal hostility, and increase cooperative behavior. Because of the norms of most adolescents, cooperative games tend initially to be less popular than competitive games, but once played, the resistance seems to disappear. There is a long history of research demonstrating the positive side effects of cooperative games. Some examples are given below.

Deutsch (1949) was among the first small-group researchers to demonstrate experimentally that cooperative learning results in greater harmony than does competitive learning. Shortly thereafter, Stendler, Damrin, and Haines (1951) confirmed this finding with a study of seven-year-olds. What made children cooperative or competitive was primarily a function of their social situation. Sherif's (1956) study suggested that when "normal" twelve-year-old boys were placed in situations where one group could achieve its purposes only at the expense of the opposing group, group members became hostile to the other group. Sherif points out that the probability of achieving harmony is greatly enhanced when individuals or groups are brought together to work toward common or cooperative ends. Aronson (1975) tested this hypothesis in the classroom. After a series of studies, he concluded that cooperative interdependent learning led to improvement in self-esteem, to feelings of increased importance in school, and to increased group affection and friendship. All of these gains were made without interfering with academic achievement.

Orlick (1978, 1979) studied the physical medium of play and games as a means of influencing positive cooperative socialization among children. A number of games were designed for children to interact in a cooperative way to meet a challenge or to achieve the goal of the game. Behavior observations supported the assumption that cooperatively structured games elicited cooperative social interaction among elementary school children.

In addition to the previously mentioned balloon volleyball and tug-of-peace, we have used a number of other cooperative games in treatment groups. Many of them involve changing the rules of standard games. In "one-basket" basketball the object is to get everyone to make one basket but not more. After a member gets a basket, the member is no longer permitted to shoot but must dribble or pass to another member. This can be played without teams, and no body contact is permitted. A similar game has been developed for softball with no teams. All members bat until they get a hit and then they go out in the field, where all positions are rotated.

Chinese checkers can be modified to become a cooperative game by making the object the achievement of a tie in getting the marbles to the opposite side. The members seem to help each other to get their marbles in place.

For the reasons mentioned above, cooperative games seem to be preferable to competitive ones. However, there are reasons to use competitive games as well. First, achieving skills in competitive games may enhance the child's status at school, where such games are often played. Second, since losing and winning are important parts of these school activities, children have to learn to deal with both. The group provides a protective setting for these behaviors to occur and an opportunity for the children to receive immediate feedback regarding how well they managed these behaviors. Moreover, most activities other than games are noncompetitive. A reliance on these as well as on noncompetitive games tends to de-emphasize competition.

Social-Skill Board Games. Most board games are extremely popular with children. Drawing on that interest, we have extensively used board games designed to provide practice in specific social skills. Board games add variety to the typical social-skill routines of modeling, rehearsal, coaching, and group feedback. Several of the many variations of social-skill games are detailed below. It is possible to select existing games or to design one's own game, often with the group's help.

To evaluate, select, or design a social-skill game one should consider the following elements, suggested by Heitzmann (1974): (1) an aspect of chance such as can be obtained through throwing dice, drawing a card, or spinning a wheel; (2) elements of surprise or novelty; (3) inherent fun and humor; (4) opportunity for broad participation (everyone has a turn and everyone's turn is equal); (5) a variety of possible activities; (6) well-defined limits and rules; (7) clearly understood goals for learned behaviors; and (8) opportunities for immediate and frequent feedback. Figure 7 is an example of a simple format for a social-skills board game that has been commonly used with children from six to twelve years of age. It is possible to simplify it for younger children or to make it more complicated and dramatic for adolescents. Let us examine the elements in the game.

There are basically five different kinds of squares. The most important are the roleplay squares, which instruct a member to pick a roleplay card; in response to this square the member draws a card from a pile labeled "roleplays." A list of such roleplays are developed for each group. These roleplays can be taken from any of the roleplay tests referred to in Chapter Four. An example of the instructions on one such card would be the following:

Figure 7. Format of Social-Skill Game.

Pick role-play card	Rest here	Ask others a personal question	Go back 3 spaces	Start
Pick problem	Roleplay cards here	Think cards here		Say twister
Pick fun card				Pick think card
Go back 3 spaces				Pick fun card
Praise all in group	Treats here	Fun-Game cards here		Pick role-play card
Pick think card				Ask group feedback
Pick role-play card	Pass here, get M&M	Pick think card	Tell joke	Ask member for help

Roleplay a situation in which a friend asks you for money. The friend has borrowed before and has never paid you back. The group leader will play the borrower, and the group will give feedback to the bearer of this card.

Simpler instructions are required for younger children. The group leader provides the additional instructions as required. For children who cannot read, pictures are provided on the cards and on the board. The group leader helps the children to interpret the pictures.

A second type of square is the cognitive-affective exercise (think cards in Figure 7). For example, one card asks, "What's the last situation that made you angry? Describe the situation, what you thought, and how you felt." Other cards might have the child distinguish between a list of self-defeating and self-enhancing statements.

The third type of square asks players to pick a fun card, which provides surprise activities. These cards suggest such activities as singing a song, saying a tongue twister, or telling a bad joke. The fourth type of square provides such game instructions as "Start here," "Go back three spaces," and "Rest here." A fifth type of square, which is not always used, is the reinforcing square in which a child receives a raisin, nut, piece of candy, or a token if he or she lands on it or passes it. This square has made the game highly attractive to younger children.

The leader acts as a player and as a source of constant feedback on how each player is doing. The leader also regulates the tempo of the game and may adjust the game if it does not quite meet the members' interests or the goal orientation. The leader may require the members to respond more quickly and may add new instructions or new cards.

These board games have been used with all ages. One board game for emotionally disturbed adolescents, designed by Stermac and Josefowitz (1982), was evaluated for its effectiveness in modifying social skills and "bizarre" behavior. In one quasi-experiment (without a control group) the authors found a significant increase in social skills and a significant decrease in "bizarre" behavior from pretests to posttests. (Interjudge reliability was .93 for social skills and .81 for bizarre behavior.) A similar board game was used by Quinsey and Varney (1977) for incarcerated adult offenders.

Cartledge and Milburn (1981) point out several important issues in the use of social-skill games. First, at some point the connection needs to be made between fun games in the group and their application to the world. There are at least two ways of achieving this. One is through a discussion following and/or prior to the game, and a second is through feedback from the group leader. Second, the game should be designed to allow ample opportunity for members to make specific social responses relevant to their targeted problems. Winners should be determined not by chance but on the basis of performing the target behavior. In fact, the games should be designed or adapted to minimize lose-win situations unless the target behaviors are commonly found in competitive situations. Third, the game should be designed so that no member is eliminated. (This is a good rule for all games.) An excluded member should be given a new start to provide maximum opportunity for continuous participation.

In conclusion, social-skill board games are probably one of the most important activities used in group treatment. In some groups almost no other sociorecreational activity is used. Variation is brought into the program by having the group members continually redesign the game to include new features. Because social-skills games help fulfill many treatment goals, they provide a well-integrated sociorecreational treatment program.

Handicrafts and Drawing

These art activities are often used to increase manual dexterity and spontaneity. They are usually characterized by a low level of physical movement and interactiveness unless the group leader designs the activity to increase physical movement and interaction among members. For children who become anxious when interacting, arts are an ideal starting point, with the gradual addition of interactive activities, such as subgroup or group projects.

Arts-and-crafts activities vary in the degree of minimal competency required. However, many activities require only the lowest levels of competency to participate in and to enjoy. Making simple boats or birdhouses from presawed parts are almost always successful even with the least handy participants. Similarly, fingerpainting and abstract drawing require few initial skills. Of course with increased skill and increased interest more complicated works can be created. Occasionally one or two members have special skills in these areas. If these are children who lack recognition in other areas they may be encouraged and, in fact, trained to share their skills with other members of the group.

As we pointed out earlier, the problem of low interactiveness can be overcome in middle and later sessions by using subgroup and group projects. A dramatic example is "making a monster." In this activity either the entire group or two subgroups are given an assortment of materials (feathers, paste, string, scissors, hair, cloth, paper clips, and whatever the group leader finds in cleaning out a desk). Each person makes a part of the monster and adds this on to the group monster. Although this activity is greatly favored by younger children, occasionally adolescents also play it enthusiastically. One of its virtues is that it provides the stimulus conditions for waiting one's turn and for cooperative behavior. Other group projects include a group mural or a group clay sculpture.

The group can combine crafts with other activities, such as laying out and coloring the prototype of a social-skills board game, or making scenery for a play. Of course before one can make scenery for a play, one must develop a play. This is not the only use of dramatics.

Dramatics

For many children with few social skills, game skills, or crafts skills, dramatics is often a means to accrue status in the group or at least to take pleasure in a leisure-time activity. Drama provides a high level of reinforcement for players and stagehands alike. It provides variations in role, not only as actors, but as writers, stagehands, directors, set designers, and so forth. Each of these permits the manifestation of a wide variety of skills. This is especially important where not all children are willing or ready to assume the role of an actor. Drama allows a wide variety of prescriptiveness, from the low level of the spontaneous skit or charades to the high level of the formal play. Drama evokes varied stimulus conditions for many different kinds of behaviors. Group leaders, by their selection of plays, skits, or types of charades, can allow almost every child to act out roles the child must learn for the real world. Dramatics can either be squeezed into the narrow time limits of treatment groups or can be expanded for special sessions if treatment requires it. With adolescents it is possible to use dramatics as the major treatment activity if roles are used to practice goal-oriented behaviors.

In developing and selecting scripts for children the following suggestions are helpful. Themes should be familiar to the children from their daily lives. No part should be too long or require memorizing too many lines. Coaches or prompters should be generously used to hold memorization to a minimum. Prompt cards are also helpful. In treatment, performance quality is not the primary goal, as it would be in a little theater group. However, it must be high enough for the members to take some pride in the final product. Narration is especially helpful in shortening scenes, in reducing memorization, and in adapting an existing script. In a particularly large group, choruses and crowd scenes can provide parts for those who do not want to perform a part all alone.

The play is only one form of drama. Skits, spontaneous roleplays, charades, and other forms of pantomime are even more frequently used than play production. Each has its own particular advantage. For example, skits and spontaneous roleplays contain no parts that require a great deal of advance planning. The group leader or a member can merely sketch out the parts on slips of paper and the actors can develop the specific content as they go along. The group leader or an experienced member may serve as a prompter if one is needed. The skit can be audiotaped or videotaped and presented to the parents as an example of what happens in the group and to friends as a means of increasing the status of the children in their peer group. Such taping can also saliently reinforce the performance of target behaviors or completion of behavioral assignments.

Charades are often used as preparation for putting on skits or for eventually rehearsing behaviors. However, they are also an important activity in their own right with both children and adolescents. Charades are usually a team game, although they can be played as individual performances as well. One team selects a phrase (from a theme, movie title, or tv program, for example) and then secretly works out its dramatization, syllable by syllable, word by word, or the entire phrase. As the first team performs the given phrase, the second team attempts to guess it. Many variations are possible, but in most versions the game permits wide participation, requires low to moderate competency, provides opportunity for leadership behavior and cooperative behavior, and can be performed in a limited time period and in a limited physical space.

Charades or acting without using words are one type of pantomime. A number of other pantomimes are commonly used in treatment groups. They also provide most of the advantages of charades. In Pantomime this Object, a broom or stick is used as a prop. Each child uses the object to pantomime a guitar, horse, violin, or whatever the child (or the group leader) chooses while the members guess what the object is. Then the stick is passed on to another person who pantomimes a new object. In Occupational Pantomime, different occupations are pantomimed, while the rest of the children guess the profession. What Kind of Store? is performed in the same way.

The charade activities mentioned above are primarily for younger children. For more experienced or older children, Challenge Pantomime would be more suitable. The group leader or a team of group members make up complex situations that tell a brief story. A pair of volunteers are given the situation, which they then pantomime for the rest of the group. Those who did not write the scenario try to tell the story when the charades have finished. A situation prototype might be the following. "You are at a carnival and are eating ice cream. A friend wants you to go with her on a frightening ride. You don't want to go. Show what happened." Similarly, group members can pantomime stressful situations the group leader knows they have actually experienced, such as the following. "You have broken your mother's favorite mug. She comes home and you try to explain." "Your best friend is playing with a person who always puts you down. You see them together. Show how you would respond." This version lends itself to a discussion and demonstration of nonverbal behavior, emphasizing its importance in communication. Although there are many opportunities to link dramatics to the group's work, as in the last example, one of the most effective linking strategies is the simulated school activity.

Simulated School Activity

Many children referred to treatment have difficulty concentrating in the classroom or manifesting other classroom "survival" skills, such as remaining in their seat and raising their hands when they want to speak. (One may not agree that these skills are essential or even desirable for learning but they are often required in the classroom and failure to comply may be costly to the child.) Since it is often difficult to carry out treatment during class, it may be helpful with children (usually of twelve or under) to simulate the classroom. In order to create interest in simulated school activities, they are initially heavily reinforced. As the children are successful in the various goal-oriented activities in the group and in the classroom, concrete reinforcement is eliminated. During the classroom simulation the group leader usually plays the role of the teacher, although a number of leaders have invited colleagues, older children, another teacher, or even a group member to play the teacher's role. As the simulation progresses the "teacher" must attempt to simulate as nearly as possible the real classroom's atmosphere. The following is an example of such an activity.

> The group leader showed the boys a picture of some men on a boat in the middle of a lake. "This is going to be a writing exercise in which you make up a story about what you see in this picture. You can write anything you want. The only rule is that you stay in your seat. When the timer goes off anyone in his seat will receive one token and anyone writing will receive another token. The timer should go off about four times in the next ten minutes. Any questions?"
>
> The boys worked hard all ten minutes and received the maximum number of tokens. "You guys did a great job. Now comes the hard part. You have to listen to each other while each person reads his story. What does a person who is listening look like?" Following a discussion of the behavioral characteristics of a listener, each boy read his report. The group leader reinforced them intermittently for giving the appearance of listening.
>
> At the end of the exercise he said, "You fellows are marvelous listeners. What do you say we try that out in class this week? Just hand this lis-

tening card to your teacher each day and she'll check off whether or not you did a good job of listening. She knows about the card and said she would be glad to do it." The group members then discussed the assignment and what they had to do to get the cards checked and back to the group leader. Everyone agreed it was a good idea.

Photography

This activity requires at least one camera—even a homemade pinhole camera—some film, and some understanding of the importance of light and movement in the process of taking pictures. In the beginning, the restrictions of light and movement, the kind of film, and the kind of camera increase somewhat the level of prescriptiveness. If the group develops an interest, both prescriptiveness and level of competence can be increased. Since the activity permits, but does not require, little interaction and broad participation, it is ideal for early implementation in most groups. Moreover, it requires only a little time to have a successful experience. We have found it especially useful for economically deprived children who have never had access to photographic equipment. Of course, if there is only one camera, time must be carefully negotiated in advance to prevent violent arguments from erupting. The activity can be expanded to include developing and printing as well.

Another more sophisticated use of photography would be motion picture taking or videotaping, if the equipment is available. These activities may be integrated into other activities, such as dramatics, field trips, or roleplays. Members might also set up an exhibition of photographs that they have developed and mounted themselves. They could publicize and sell tickets for it.

Field Trips

Field trips provide the occasion for practicing newly learned skills in the real world and ample reinforcement for a wide variety of roles and behaviors. These excursions involve group planning, decision making, cooperative behaviors, obtaining information, and teaching others. Because of the great popularity of excursions, they are often used as group contingencies for continued assignment completion.

Most group meetings provide a highly restricted physical field. The excursion dramatically expands the physical field, as the transportation system, shopping mall, bowling alley, museum, or stadium becomes the vastly enlarged area of operation. As a result the children or adolescents are confronted with new and often unexpected experiences. It is an opportunity to try out in the real world the many behaviors learned in the group under the supervision of the group leader and the other group members. When the group returns from the field trip, one of the important points of the agenda is to review, one at a time, the achievements of each of the members in demonstrating his or her unique target behaviors.

Some common examples of field trips for younger children are visits to the local zoo, a farm, a factory, an elevator in a tall building, a forest, a children's museum or exhibit, a fire station, a police station, the next level of school, the major city library, a veterinarian's office, a pet shop, or a children's concert. For adolescents, one might add to the list a visit to the nearby university campus, concerts, college sports events, employment offices, government offices, a courtroom in session, shopping centers, and a hospital. We have used trips for both age groups from both lists. It depends more on the interests than on the age of the children.

Although this is the end of our activities list, the numbers and types of programs for children and adolescents are vast. Literature available to the group leader includes *Games for Girl Scouts* (Girl Scouts of the U.S.A., 1969), the *Handbook for Recreation* (1960), and *Handbook of Recreational Games* (Boyd, 1973). The problem is usually not so much the finding of activities but the process of selecting them together with group members. Their interests are not always compatible with the attainment of treatment goals.

Selecting Activities

In general, major decisions regarding which program activities to use are based on members' behavior change goals and interests, and group conditions at the moment (for example, the level of group cohesion). Initially, potential activities are reviewed in terms of the criteria discussed earlier in this chapter. Decisions are then made by the group leader in consultation with the members. In later phases of group development, the members themselves may perform all of these functions.

Throughout this chapter we have made a distinction between the "work" of the meeting and the "play." In fact the distinction is arbitrary since both are aimed at facilitating the achievement of treatment goals. "Work" refers primarily to reviewing homework assignments and developing new ones, modeling or rehearsing responses to problematic or stressful situations, practicing various behaviors in which group members are deficient, and discussing and solving problems that occur in the group. "Play" consists of the activities listed in the previous sections. Initially, most meetings consist of so-called work activities for two-thirds of the meeting and play activities for the remaining third. Depending on the creativity of the group leader, the boundary between the two becomes increasingly blurred.

During a typical meeting, group members review the homework done since the previous meeting; introduce new problem situations; propose, evaluate, model, and rehearse potential solutions; and receive feedback from each other on their respective performances. In addition, an exercise based on a common problem is practiced and new assignments are designed. Then the group plays a game or performs some other activity. During special meetings, such as when preparing for a field trip, most of the meeting is devoted to planning the excursion and discussing the group problems that might ensue.

Ultimately, the group leader searches for various ways of integrating work and play activities. This permits extending treatment time for all members without increasing group time. Ideally, work and play become integrated through such activities as dramatics and social-skill board games. Integration can also occur by working in a playful fashion. Rehearsals can be done in costumes, problem solving can be carried out in game format, and homework can be reviewed like the game of Twenty Questions.

Initially, the major responsibility for choosing activities

belongs to the group leader. At the pregroup interview, group members are asked about games they are interested in and familiar with. The group leader builds up a catalogue of the group's common and individual interests, from which activities are selected.

Making decisions about program activities may be an excellent way for members to try out newly learned decision-making skills. But if decision-making skills are generally deficient or weakly developed in the group, planning may be so chaotic that members will have an aversive experience without ever deciding on an activity. Therefore, until the point that rudimentary decision-making skills are developed, program activity decisions remain largely in the hands of the group leader. At the same time, however, the leader gradually shapes decision-making skills. For example, the children might first choose between two possible activities described by the group leader, such as volleyball or kickball, or between two types of field trips. Successful decision making by the group at this level may lead to more open choices at subsequent meetings. When children and adolescents make choices, they too must take into consideration treatment goals just as the group leader did. Let us examine how the group leader and later the members themselves relate program to treatment goals.

Relating Activities to Treatment Goals. Priority is initially given to activities that the children are likely to enjoy and participate in. Gradually the group leader becomes concerned with the issue of treatment-goal orientation. Ultimately the leader's task is to help members increase goal-oriented activities. In the following example, the leader adjusts the structure of a commonly played and attractive game to shape greater treatment-goal orientation.

> In planning for a meeting of sixth-grade girls, the group leader recommended Concentration, a card game in which members try to guess or remember the location of pairs of cards by turning them over two at a time. If they choose correctly, they keep the pair. If not, they are returned face

down to their original location. When all the pairs are removed, the game is over. The winner is the one with the most pairs. The game is useful because (1) it is attractive and usually enthusiastically received, (2) it has a high reward potential (although one person wins, there are many opportunities throughout the game to have small successes, for example, when each pair is discovered), (3) it provides practice in concentration, a much needed skill for many children, as well as turn-taking and good loser behavior, (4) the game itself can be used as a reinforcer for work activities, and (5) it has relatively high peer-group status for preadolescent children. After playing the game several times according to standard rules, the game was adjusted to be more goal oriented. A new deck was introduced that consisted of pairs of cards, each containing instructions to roleplay a specified problem situation. Whenever someone picked a pair of identical cards, she was required to carry out the roleplay. In this way, additional rehearsals and modeling for individualized problem situations were integrated into the program.

The group must be continually reminded that the activity is a vehicle to change behavior, perception, or value. As incidents arise that lend themselves to therapeutic analysis and/or behavioral change, they are usually brought to the group for consideration, as in the following example:

In the group of three boys and four girls, the members decided to put on a play. One day Jerry failed to get his lines straight and the others teased him every time he made a mistake. He found this so upsetting he decided to quit the play. Gale, the group leader, stopped the activity and wondered if any of them (other than Jerry) saw the teasing or the way in which Jerry responded to it as a problem. This

led to a brief discussion of giving and receiving
teasing and the decision to spend an entire work
session on the subject, since giving or receiving
teases was a problem for everyone.

In the above example, the discussion was brought about
by Jerry's sudden withdrawal from the play. If it were not a
crisis, the group leader may not have stopped the activity but
would have brought up the issue in a subsequent "work" portion of the meeting. In the above example, confrontation and
group discussion are the major means of group intervention. In
the following example, program planning is used in conjunction
with group discussion and operant and modeling procedures to
modify a common behavioral deficit in all the children in a
group—how to appropriately respond to losing a game.

In one group of six children, aged ten to twelve,
the usual response to losing a game was to get angry, cry, pout, or leave the group. Program planning involved organizing a series of competitive
games over several group meetings. They included
Fish, Capture the Handkerchief, volleyball, Detective, and a checkers tournament. In these games
there were frequent opportunities for losing and
winning.
        In the first game the group leader arranged
to lose a game of Chinese checkers. He then began
to pout, cry, get angry, and threatened not to play
any more. The members laughed and he asked
them what he did that caused them to laugh. They
pointed out his "poor loser" behaviors. He then
asked what he might do. They recommended
thanking the others for a good game or congratu-
lating the others on winning. Both behaviors were
then modeled by the group leader. He then had
each member, one at a time, pretend he lost a game
and respond with the "good loser" behavior noted
above. In subsequent games, when "good losing"

occurred, the leader and members reinforced it with praise and with tokens. Eventually, the tokens were faded out and the frequency of praise reduced. Children were encouraged to observe similar situations on the playground. They were given the assignment of reporting on both their successes and failures at the next group meeting.

Stimulating New Interests. Although a vast array of activities for groups have been suggested, most clients have an extremely limited repertoire of sociorecreational skills and interests. The history of failure in attempting new activities tends to have discouraged many to explore new possibilities. For this reason, it is often necessary for the group leader not only to incorporate activities into the program but also to stimulate interest in new ones. One major procedure for stimulating interest is the use of tokens.

Tokens may be distributed for every new activity in which a member participates. If all members participate, a bonus might be added. Members are also reinforced for suggesting new activities that are both accepted by the group and meet established standards. Another procedure is the use of a "program table." The materials needed for group activities are placed on the table along with books, articles, or pictures illustrating the activity in more detail. The group leader is responsible for keeping the table full at first, but as members gain skill and interest, they are encouraged to add materials and pictures of their own. Similar to this approach is planned observation of an activity on videotape or television.

Modeling procedures are also used to stimulate interest in and reduce anxiety about new programs. A novel way of stimulating interest has been for group members to observe slightly older peers participating in a new activity. If other groups are readily available, observing the entire group at opportune moments may provide excellent program models. If groups are not available, having slightly older children teach a new activity to the group will also make the activity more palatable than if taught by the adult group leader. For example, one leader arranged for her group of ten-year-olds to observe a group of twelve- and thirteen-year-olds rehearse a skit. Another group leader and one member of the group who had the necessary skills modeled how to play Scrabble while the group was waiting for the meeting to begin.

Adolescents may be provided with recreation books or game books. Their group leader might ask a pair to learn and practice teaching a new activity as a homework assignment to be done by a subsequent group meeting. Using a pair rather than individuals increases opportunities for cooperative planning. In addition, activities introduced by peers tend to be more acceptable than activities introduced by the group leader.

Another way of stimulating new program activities is "by doing it" (Whittaker, 1976). The group leader merely begins some small handicraft or game and, if possible, pulls in one or two others. As other children inquire what they are doing, the group leader asks the active members to explain.

Rejuvenating old standard games or other activities is still another way of stimulating new interests. The game of tag can be spruced up by requiring members to play it in pairs with the inside legs tied together, as in a three-legged race, or complicating it by turning it into the game of Blob (described earlier). Whitaker (1974) suggests changing the name of familiar games to make them more contemporary-sounding, such as changing the game of Ghost to Rocketship. Common games may be further enhanced by playing them in costumes, blindfolded, or as comic-book superheroes.

With so much to choose from, group leaders need not attempt to implement or stimulate activities with which they do not feel sufficiently comfortable or skilled. Generally speaking, the children respond best to those activities the group leader is most enthusiastic about. Of course, if the leader has highly limited program skills, they should be expanded before running a group alone. Using one program that provides many different types of activities reduces the constant need to stimulate new programs.

Multicomponent Programming. Initially, program activities are viewed as isolated events tacked onto the end of the meeting as reinforcement for doing the work of treatment.

Ideally, activities should create the stimulus condition for working on behaviors in the group. Programming with many components provides opportunities for extending the program into many more sessions. For example, in one adolescent group the children expressed the desire to put on a skit. Their first brief try, a one-act play written for young adolescents, was provided by the group leader. Their initial success stimulated them to do another play that they themselves wrote, directed, created props and costumes for, publicized, sold tickets for, and performed twice for the public. This provided rewards for all members, regardless of their interest. But more important, it provided conditions for conflict, cooperation, and the manifestation of all the problem behavior and constructive behavior in the repertoire of the adolescents. During the last fifteen minutes of every meeting, each individual's behavior was observed (based on monitoring by the group leader) and, where necessary, treatment was planned for further modifying a given behavior.

In the above example, program planning was relatively simple for the five-session period of the multicomponent program. Integration of activities and therapeutic process was, to a large degree, effectively achieved. Following the play, the focus of the group was primarily on behavior and strategies of transferring what they had learned to home and school.

Another example of multicomponent programming involved an adolescent group of five girls in a middle school. One of the girls had a camera and the members decided to monitor each other's behavior with the camera and the teacher's permission. They first photographed each other "being good." This had to be specifically defined for each person.

The group later decided to give a photography exhibition. They wrote brief stories about each photograph, learned to type their descriptions on a word processor, and then matted the stories with the photographs. As with the previous group, a portion of each meeting was used to look at individual behavioral achievements and interpersonal difficulties in carrying out the complex project, in addition to problem solving or negotiating conflicted interests.

Other multicomponent activities that have been used in

treatment groups include a job-hunting project in which older adolescents invited a number of people in different jobs to speak with them. This was followed by a series of field trips to their guests' places of employment and to an employment office. They later roleplayed employment interviews and filled out employment forms. A group of younger children who were particularly interested in outdoor activities organized their entire group program around planning for a canoe trip. This involved intense sharing behaviors, planning, decision making, examining their roles and behavior during inevitable conflicts, resolving group conflicts and interpersonal differences, and carrying out behavioral homework assignments (the completion of which added points to the group thermometer). When filled, the group thermometer indicated that the group had won the canoe trip. Multicomponent programming is useful only if there is sufficient group time to permit its completion. When there are fewer than six sessions it is often difficult to get a complex program started before the group ends. More sessions are usually required. From the above discussion it should be clear that the multicomponent program is merely a vehicle for increasing enthusiasm for the group activity without losing the treatment focus. One of the problems occasionally encountered with such continuing programs is that the program becomes more important than the treatment to the children. Keeping the treatment focus is a relevant issue for all types of programs, but it is not the only remaining issue.

Some Remaining Issues. There are several still unmentioned issues with which the group leader should be concerned in planning for and implementing program activities. The first issue emphasizes the need for adequate preparation by the leader when introducing new activities. Occasional failures due to inadequate familiarity with an activity have led to the conclusion that new activities should be tried out before being used with a group for the first time. One needs to know whether the space and materials are adequate, whether the instructions are clear, whether the level of member competence is sufficiently high to play the game, whether the activity provides sufficient reinforcement for the participants, and, finally, whether the activity is fun.

At least a part of the activity can be tried out on one's family, classmates, colleagues, or friends, even though they are not the same age as the client group. Major problems arise if the group activity collapses as a result of inadequate preparation. The whole meeting is often viewed as a failure, or at least a great disappointment, by the group members after such an event. The work, too, becomes less attractive. In most meetings time to do what is necessary is so limited that both the activity and the work must move efficiently if everything is to be completed in the allotted time.

Another often-raised issue is how one justifies "fun and games" for a treatment group. We always indicate to the children that the group is primarily designed to help them with their problems, but we see no reason why learning to deal with problems cannot be fun. To the parents and teachers we repeat what was said above, but emphasize that fun and games are essential for facilitating learning of prosocial behavior. They provide an opportunity for practicing such behavior in a less-structured setting. We also explain that recreational skills are, in themselves, tools for building better relationships and better lives.

Summary

In this chapter we presented a theory consisting of six dimensions that facilitate the analysis of sociorecreational program activities for groups. We presented examples of the various types of activities and analyzed them in terms of the above dimensions. We also illustrated how these activities might be used to increase cohesion and facilitate the achievement of treatment goals. We examined strategies for expanding the program interests of clients. We discussed a number of examples of long-term multicomponent programs and their advantages as a programming strategy. The most important aspect of this chapter has been its demonstration that treatment need not be painful when goal-oriented sociorecreational activities are included.

If the program activity is well prepared and meets the interests of group members, the members are usually highly satis-

fied with the meeting as a whole. This alone does not imply that
program activities are sufficient to correct specific behavioral
problems. It is an important and necessary tool—along with
social-skill training strategies, cognitive restructuring, and general problem-solving strategies—to ameliorate complex behavioral patterns. Activities take place in the group environment.
They serve the interests of the group and are served by them. In
the next chapter the nature of this relationship is detailed further.

Chapter Ten

Influencing Group Structure and Resolving Group Problems

The group is not only the context of treatment; as we have pointed out throughout this book, it is also a source of intervention strategies. Changes in group attributes can mediate changes in individual behavior, cognitions, and affect. Application of group intervention strategies is possible only if one is aware of patterns of group phenomena and the laws governing how these phenomena impinge on individual behavior, cognition, affect, and other group phenomena.

The concepts of *group structure* and *group process* have been proposed as a means of systematically analyzing group phenomena. Group structure refers to the various patterns of group interaction at a given point in time. Group process refers to these patterns of structural change over time. Group structures include: group norms (formal or informal sets of agreements) that govern interaction; role structure in which specified behaviors are attributed to certain positions or categories of persons in the group; patterns of interpersonal liking or group cohesion; and patterns of interpersonal communication. All of these structural concepts have been used extensively to analyze the group and its relation to member satisfaction and group productivity (see Cartwright and Zander, 1968; Nixon, 1979; and Shaw, 1976, for a review of the research literature).

Group processes include the patterns of change of norms, roles, cohesion, and other group structures. Other examples of group process might include changes in the intensity of anger or other affective responses over time, changes in the intensity and relevance of mutual self-disclosure, and changes in the degree of task orientation of interaction. Only limited research is available for linking structure and process to behavior change (Rose, 1981). The principles concerned with the interrelationship of group structural concepts are lumped together under the heading of group dynamics. However, these abstract notions, rather than representing a coherent theory, can be better viewed as analogues to physical principles. Many of the concepts overlap and are inadequately defined. Nevertheless, since many of these structural attributes are manipulable, indirectly or directly observable, and apparently related to the achievement of individual and group goals, they are useful to the group leader and the group and are included in this book. Let us briefly look at a number of principles used to guide group leaders in their goal-oriented practice.

The first principle is: the broader the participation, the more satisfied and the better motivated are the group members. (Rose, 1981, has demonstrated a high correlation [$r = .81$] between satisfaction and participation in adult groups.) This implies that the group leader should structure the program so as to assure the broad involvement of all members.

Another principle suggests that a high level of interpersonal attraction or cohesion in the early phase of group development will also yield high productivity provided the norms of the group are protherapeutic. This complex relationship of cohesion to productivity is reviewed by Nixon (1979, pp. 300–306). A third principle commonly adhered to by group leaders is that broad self-disclosure is a prerequisite to accurate assessment and treatment planning; that is, clients should be able to talk about themselves, their feelings, their insights, and their cognitions in the group setting (Bednar and Kaul, 1978). A fourth principle is that failure to deal with problematic structures and processes reduces the effectiveness of group treatment. For example, a structure characterized by a high intensity and frequency of interpersonal conflicts, dominance of one or more members and inadequate participation by many, or by norms that suggest that play is more relevant than work may pose barriers to goal attainment. A group process in which the intensity of anger toward the sponsoring agency and/or the group leader has been gradually increasing might prevent working on specific problems. Such group structures and processes interfere with treatment progress and group work, a fact noted by authors of many theoretical persuasions (Bion, 1959; Lieberman, Yalom, and Miles, 1973; Rose, 1977). Each of these authors labels these interfering group structures and processes in a different way.

We call group structures and processes that interfere with goal attainment *group problems,* but instead of viewing them as significant limitations to group treatment we consider them therapeutic opportunities. In identifying a problem, in planning for and carrying out problem resolution, and in evaluating the outcome of the entire process, the group leader models and provides many occasions for the group to practice a systematic problem-solving approach around a significant common issue.

With group problems, although no group member (or leader) can escape partial responsibility, none need take sole responsibility, either. Group members must interact in a new way to solve shared problems. Learning to deal with shared problems is an important task in itself. Thus, we can define a group problem as an intragroup interactive situation or the product of an interactive situation that interferes with effective task performance or goal attainment. The responsibility for amelioration of that problem cannot be attributed to a behavioral change in any one member or group leader but to interactive changes among all persons in the group.

Determining Group Structures and Problems

One of the major characteristics of a multimethod approach is its reliance on data as well as hunches in defining group structures and processes and in determining whether a problem exists. The data, of course, must be interpreted by the group leader and group members, who may or may not agree that a given group pattern is a problem.

Questionnaire Data-Collection Procedures. In order to describe most structures and processes, data are collected on a regular basis. Because these data-collection procedures are used

primarily by group leaders and not by researchers, only procedures that are minimally intrusive and relatively inexpensive to
administer are selected. These data-collection procedures include a questionnaire rating the children's satisfaction with the
meeting, given at the end of every meeting or at the end of
every hour (or half hour) of meeting time. Usually a scale of 1
to 6 is used with "1" signifying low satisfaction and "6," high
satisfaction. With children under the age of eight, a three-point
scale is used, indicated by smiling or unsmiling faces as in Exhibit 5.

Exhibit 5. Meeting-Satisfaction Rating Questionnaire.

I liked today's   I liked today's   I didn't like
meeting a lot.   meeting a little.   today's meeting
                                                  at all.

---------------   ---------------   ---------------

Although satisfaction ratings are relatively easy to administer and to code, as all subjective rating scales, they are subject
to a number of rating errors. For example, some individuals
tend to prefer center items and some tend to rate more positively or negatively. In addition, there is no fixed zero point on
the scale. Nevertheless, a dramatic drop in the average member
satisfaction appears to indicate that some problem may be interfering with the group work. Similarly, a sizable increase may indicate that a problem is resolved.

Observational Tools. A second set of data is collected
through direct observation. These data include the distribution
and frequency of participation. In general, data regarding who is
speaking are collected every ten seconds and are recorded as in

Table 4. The letters are the initials of the person who is speaking at the end of a given ten-second interval. The "X" is used to indicate silence. Other letters may be added for special categories, such as when two people are talking at the same time or the members are in subgroups or the given participant is role-playing.

Table 4. Typical Observation Results.

1- SL	11- TD	21- SC	31- BR
2- MA	12- MA	22- TD	32- BR
3- NA	13- MA	23- MA	33- BR
4- TR	14- RN	24- TR	34- NA
5- SL	15- MA	25- TR	35- NA
6- TD	16- RN	26- MA	36- BR
7- TD	17- RN	27- RN	37- NA
8- TD	18- MA	28- RN	38- BR
9- SL	19- RN	29- RN	39- NA
10- X	20- MA	30- RN	40- NA

Such a listing provides the group with each person's total and percentage of participation and permits an estimate of the ratio of individual to total group participation.

Noting who speaks every time the speaker changes is another simple method of recording participation. This is usually done on a pie chart with a segment for each person. The observer merely places a tally in the segment of the pie assigned to the person who is speaking. No consideration is given to the length of time, although some observers will give an additional check every twenty seconds that a given person is still speaking.

The first method (Table 4) gives an estimate of the length of time each person in the group is speaking. The second provides the group leader with a better estimate of the speaking frequency of low-frequency or short-response speakers since every response is recorded, regardless of length. Both methods are easy to learn and one can use former members, present members, visitors, or students as the observers. Because the method is simple, observers can be reliably trained in either method in about ten minutes.

In the first method discussed above (Table 4), if the observer is also asked to indicate who is being addressed (with the group as the default category), a whole new dimension of relationships is added, in terms of who speaks to whom. However, even this simple addition requires considerably more training before reliable observations can be made.

The observer can collect additional data on roleplaying, off-task behavior, positive reinforcement or praise, criticism, or other categories, depending on the leader's preassessment of the problem. If, for example, the leader has noted informally that there is too much off-task behavior, it becomes necessary to systematically observe on-task and off-task behavior for several meetings. Another commonly observed behavior has been interruptions of others, especially in groups where aggressive and shy children are mixed.

Other more sophisticated (and hence more costly) observational methods can also classify the content of the interaction. The reader is referred to Mash and Terdal (1976, pp. 261–352) for a critical review and a detailed presentation of various observation systems. Since these are usually too costly for the practitioner to use to train observers, carry out, and interpret in the typical clinical group program, they are not included here.

Rate of Assignment Completion. The percentage of completed homework assignments has been shown to correlate highly and significantly with behavioral change ($r = .62, p < .05$). A roleplay test with adults in assertiveness training groups has been used as an index of ongoing session-by-session productivity (Rose, 1981). Low session productivity, as evidenced by a low rate of homework completion, is a major group problem and usually requires group consideration as soon as it is detected. One way it can be assessed is to collect data on all assignments as if they were of the same importance or relevance to outcome. A problem with this index is that all assignments are assumed to be equal. A task such as "talking to a new person" might be far more important and more difficult than "writing down a stressful situation that you recently experienced." Some group leaders give more weight to behavioral tasks in ascertaining weekly productivity than to reading or self-observation because of their greater relevance to behavioral change. Most leaders consider the completion of all tasks alike in ascertaining productivity because of the difficulties involved in weighting.

Attendance and Promptness. In the Rose (1981) study already cited, attendance was also highly (though not significantly) correlated with outcome. Although promptness had not been considered, the same explanatory principle applies: The more time spent in the treatment situation, presumably, the greater the opportunity for learning. The statistic used is either the percent of members attending a given meeting and/or the percent of total minutes attended. For example, if a meeting of four persons is sixty minutes long and one person is ten minutes late, another leaves five minutes early, and a third is absent, then the ratio would be

$$(240 - 5 - 10 - 60)/240 = .69$$

The general formula is

$$(MT - t - AT)/MT = R$$

where R is the percentage of minutes all members are present in the group, M is the number of members in the group, T is time or length in minutes of a meeting, t is the total number of minutes missed (arriving late or leaving early) for all members, and A is the number of persons absent.

Evaluating the Data. After collecting data, the group leader reviews them and shows them to the group members, often in graphic form, as in Figure 8, which depicts a seventh-grade social-skills group at the beginning of the sixth session.

In Figure 8, the data reveal a serious group problem. Since the charts indicated that productivity and satisfaction were lower than at the previous meetings the group leader asked the members whether they believed these data indicated a group problem. After some hesitation they indicated that they were a little "sick of the group." The leader interviewed them about the specific causes of their "sickness." The members indicated that the games were not as much fun as they used to be and

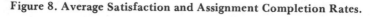

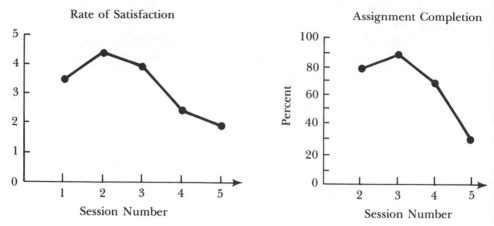

Figure 8. Average Satisfaction and Assignment Completion Rates.

they did not like the homework assignments as much as they used to. One child said she was sorry that they had stopped giving out tokens as they did in the first three meetings and the others agreed. It appeared that the group leader had prematurely faded the token system without involving the group. As a result of this discussion, she and the members designed a new system with a more gradual fading of tokens and with the children controlling the speed of fading. She also increased the children's involvement in planning extra-group assignments. When the problem is this obvious an experienced group leader may not need the data to suggest that something is going on. In our experience, however, where the problem is subtler, the data may reveal the problem long before it is revealed to the intuition of the leader.

If the leader and members agree a problem exists, they discuss whether or not it is relevant to the group's work. If they think a problem is not relevant or does not really exist, then the leader usually postpones dealing with it until new data arrive that, once again, suggest a group problem.

In a family-change group of seven- and eight-year-olds whose parents all had recently divorced, three of the eight children said very little at the first few sessions. The satisfaction was low, though gradually increasing, and the attendance was perfect. When the group leader noted that several people did not seem to be using the group as well as others, the members who had not participated as much suggested they needed more time. Besides, one said, she liked to listen to the others, and found that very helpful. The other two agreed. The group leader concurred that there were differences in how people used the group and dropped the subject. Participation of two of the three low participants increased noticeably at the following session, with no further intervention, and the satisfaction continued its gradual upward trend.

Intervening in the Group Structure and Process

Once the group leader and members decide that a structure or process requires changing, some form of intervention is required. In early sessions the group leader may suggest several alternatives, which the members may add to or embellish. Later, brainstorming may be more appropriate, since it permits greater involvement of members.

Table 5 lists a number of group problems, the measurements by which they were identified, and a brief description of how they might be dealt with. As with all summary descriptions, this table simplifies the process of group problem identification and resolution. Many of these problems and the strategies employed by the group leader are detailed below.

Group Cohesion. One of the primary jobs of a group leader in the early phase of treatment is to increase group cohesion, which refers to the degree and intensity to which members are attracted to one another, the program or group task, and the group leader (Lott and Lott, 1965). Cohesion is regarded as an essential attribute of groups because it appears to correlate, under certain conditions, to productivity, participation in and out of the group, self-disclosure, risk taking, attendance, and other vital group concerns (Stokes, 1983).

When the group begins, cohesion is usually too low for effective learning to take place. One exception is a previously established group, such as a family or peer neighborhood group. In order to get and keep the group as attractive as possible,

Table 5. Group Problems.

Problem	Evidence	Examples of Strategies*
Low cohesion	Drop in satisfaction, attendance-promptness rate; low ratio of critical statements to positive statements.	Increase attraction of group: serve food at meeting, use audiovisual aids and roleplaying.
One or two members dominate interaction	One or two members speak more than twice the average amount available to each member of the group.	Prepare low-frequency members prior to meeting; prompt them in meetings; reinforce low participants.
Member withdrawal from interaction	Usually goes together with above problem. Withdrawn members speak less than half of their allotted time.	Set limits on high participators. Play Five Minute game.
Too much off-task behavior	Off-task behavior more than 10% of total observed interaction.	Help group to define "off task," then have group set limits on off-task behavior.
Too little self-disclosure	Participants talk about self, own problems less than 10%.	Discuss similarities to cases. Gradually increase demand for self-disclosure.
Low rate of assignment completion	Percentage of homework assignment completion less than 75%.	Examine skills of members in carrying out assignment. If deficient in training skills, discuss with group. If pressure too much, reduce demand. Develop contingency reinforcement systems for assignment completion. Involve members in decision making as to what homework.
Excessive sub-grouping	Members of one sub-group tease, fight with, or argue with others. Drop in average satisfaction of 1/2 point or more.	Brainstorm, then roleplay alternative ways of increasing prosocial behaviors with others. Set up contingency contracts for prosocial behavior with others.

*In addition to presenting data and discussing the problem with group.

most group leaders make extensive use of activities that are highly attractive to the members. In addition, the groups are usually composed of persons with overlapping interests, so a program is created in which each member is likely to be interested and participate. Group leaders use their own observations and the results of the postsession questionnaire to determine the level of cohesion. Under these conditions, it has been rare to find a group with low cohesion. One such experience, however, is described below and demonstrates what additional measures can be taken to increase the cohesiveness of a group.

Ted (group leader): (pointing to the graphs on the wall) We've had two meetings so far and the satisfaction ratings went down at the second meeting. Some of you described the experience as boring and some of you felt unhappy, although others of you thought it was "fun." This sometimes happens in groups. I wonder what you don't seem to like about the group or would like to change.

Jerry: Aw, all we do in this group is talk about problems. It ain't that much fun. I'd like to quit. Pete, too. (Pete nods in agreement.)

Ted: What about the rest of you?

(In the discussion that followed, the group members felt that they would rather be playing during recess than sitting in the room talking. They did not like some of the games that the group leader had introduced.)

Ted: I wonder what we could do to make this group more fun? Anybody have any ideas?

Al: Yeah, I really like what we did the first week when we did that acting business. I thought that was fun.

Sid: Couldn't we play more games like Concentration?

Mort: Could we go on a trip sometime? We did that in the other group I was in, and the guys thought that that was really neat.

(The members went on to discuss a number of programmatic ideas.)

Ted: Wow, you guys have a lot of good ideas. I guess I just wasn't asking or listening. I think we can do a lot of these things. (He summarizes the ideas.) But remember, we are also here to work on our skills in making friends and keeping them, and in getting along with our parents better. We can play but we need to work, too. With that in mind let's plan what we can do next week.

(The group members then decided on several games they wanted to play and a system to earn a field trip by doing the homework. The work, they decided, would be helping each other do the homework.)

There was an increase in satisfaction at the end of this meeting and at the following meeting all the members had completed the assignments they had developed. The lack of cohesion seemed to be related to the group leader's failure to involve the members in program planning. Without losing the treatment focus of the group, the leader helped to increase cohesion by encouraging the members to talk about their complaints and to design, within specified limits, their own sociorecreational component of the program. Program revision, attentive listening, and involvement are often important ingredients in any group intervention strategy.

Other strategies have been used to increase cohesion. In a group in which all the members were quite shy and were low-status members of their class, the group leader introduced models who had slightly higher status than the original group members. As a result the original members no longer regarded themselves as what one child labeled "the weirdo group." In still another group in which cohesion was low, the group leader arranged for the group to meet during the school day at McDonald's. Since other children commented how lucky they were, many of the other threats to cohesion seemed to quickly fade away. In a group of early adolescent juvenile offenders, the group leader increased the group attraction by incorporating basketball lessons from a volunteer and a star basketball player and driving lessons into the program. The activities were contingent on specific task performances in the group. As we pointed out earlier, the vast majority of groups we have worked with are able to quickly achieve a high level of cohesion.

There is a common condition when the group can be too cohesive. As the group moves toward termination, other groups and individuals in the lives of the clients should grow in importance. It is not uncommon for maladaptive behavior to return as the highly attractive group terminates if there are no equally attractive alternatives.

To avoid this situation, members are encouraged to bring guests to the last few group meetings and to join new nontherapeutic interest or friendship groups (see Chapter Twelve for more details). The group leader becomes far less reinforcing and helps the clients to seek their reinforcement elsewhere. The leader may work in the environment with the family or schools to increase the likelihood that reinforcement will occur.

Communication Structure. The communication structure refers to the pattern of communication in the group. Who communicates with whom? What is the distribution of participation in the group? What are prevailing themes of communication or content in the group?

A common problem in discussion groups is the dominance of one or two people and the withdrawal of others in the interaction pattern. To attain individual treatment goals, it is frequently desirable to obtain a broad distribution of communication and participation in discussion and other activities. If some people are describing their problems, giving help and support to others, and generating ideas while others do this rarely, the former profit more from the group than the latter. Often the high participators become concerned about how the low participators are judging their disclosures. Furthermore, where the discrepancies are large, group cohesion and reported satisfaction tend to be low.

The usual way of modifying interaction distribution is to present the data or the leader's observations to the group. If they also perceive it as a problem, the group problem-solving process is invoked. In groups with little experience, the group leader must serve as the major source of ideas about what can be done. Some of these ideas are discussed below.

Using a cognitive approach, the leader would ask all members to examine what they say to themselves when they want to say something in the group. The persons whose negative self-talk prevents them from speaking are assisted, through cognitive restructuring, to change their self-talk. In the following example, thirteen- and fourteen-year-olds were asked to report what they thought.

Sal (the group leader):   It seems that Karen and Lauren rarely speak in the group. I wonder if what they are saying to themselves occasionally prevents them from speaking.

Karen: I usually say that what I have to say isn't so important. Sometimes I say they probably will think what I have to say is dumb.

Lauren: Yeah, me, too! I just don't think it's all that important. And sometimes I think the others will find it weird.

Sal: And then what do you do or say?

Lauren: I just get so scared I sometimes can't speak.

Karen: Oh, I just don't say anything—that's all.

Sal: Do the rest of you think that's true? What they are saying now or what they usually say is dumb?

(The others all indicate their disagreement. Several point to specific statements they thought were very clever.)

Angela: Gosh, what you just said is brave, because I say that to myself sometimes, but I was afraid to tell the group about it.

Sal: I wonder if that's a problem outside the group for several of you, too. I bet you'd be more active group members here and in other groups if you could learn to tell yourselves some more accurate things about your ideas. What could they tell themselves to help them to speak up in groups when they have something to say? And remember it has to be true.

Andy: They could tell themselves, "My ideas are as good as anybody's."

Sarah: They could say, "Everybody makes mistakes sometimes. I don't have to worry about it."

Angela: They could say that the group members think they are smart and their ideas are smart and we want to hear them, and that's true, too.

The group is guided through the problem-solving process. Group members eventually choose self-statements that would support increasing their participation or, in the case of two children who were speaking too much, of decreasing their statements. Each child wrote the statements on a cue card, and just before each spoke in subsequent discussions, they were instructed to look at their cards. The cards were gradually faded later.

Another way of modifying communication distribution was demonstrated by a group leader who provided all members with a stopwatch and taught them how to use it. After all members demonstrated competence in the use of the watches, they were instructed to measure the amount of time the neighbor on their right spoke. At the end of fifteen minutes, the group leader wrote down the names and the times on the blackboard, as in the first two columns of Table 6.

Table 6. Group Speaking Time.

Person	Time 1	Ideal	Time 2
MaryAnn	2:30	3	3:25
EmmyLou	4:10	3	3:00
Alice	0	3	2:35
Louise	7:10	3	2:47
Helen (g.l.)	1:20	3	3:03

The group then had the task of equalizing the time spoken by dividing the fifteen-minute period among five people. The low participants were given some help on how to participate. What could be talked about was briefly discussed, and members were encouraged to take notes. (With young children the group leader puts the notes or hints on the board.) A brief practice session then took place, and members again timed the neighbor on their right. Prompts were given to individuals when the three-minute limit was reached. If no member went thirty seconds above or below the allotted amount, the group was reinforced with points on the group thermometer.

There are a number of variations on this technique. One is to use counters instead of timers to record the number of times each person on the right speaks. The data are handled in the same way as timers. The advantage is that counters are cheaper than timers, although a record of the time spent participating is exchanged for the frequency. Counters have also been used to tally the number of times a member perceives that another person is rewarding or punishing him. This technique is especially effective in groups where interaction is primarily of a punishing nature, for example, where members are continually putting each other down. The definitions of reward and punishment are based on the interpretation of each individual. Once a baseline is established, a group goal may be set in which, for example, the total number of rewarding statements might be doubled and punishing statements halved. Later, goals may be set to eliminate punishing statements entirely, and a plan may be developed to achieve that goal. One such plan involves reinforcement and criticism exercises in which the members practice giving and receiving criticism following a specified criteria.

Another technique for modifying the group structure involves the use of subgroup competition. The group is divided into two or more subgroups, and a baseline is established for each subgroup in terms of either the distribution of communication or the reinforcement-punishment ratio (see above). After a group discussion on a given topic, outcomes are compared. The winning subgroup is the one that most nearly approximates the desired distribution or ratio. Both (or all) subgroups may win since each is competing against its own baseline. In another variation only certain content is timed. For example, in one group only problem-oriented talk in which the member blamed no one but himself for his problems was timed. In another group (of depressed adolescents in a mental institution) only positive self-references were counted. The general impression of group leaders who have used any of these procedures is that they must be employed intermittently in order to maintain the newly achieved structure.

In the recapitulation technique a participant must summarize aloud what the preceding speaker has said before being permitted to add something new to the conversation. This is another useful device for redistributing the degree of participation in a group. It is especially effective in curbing dominating individuals who do not listen but respond only to cue words. This form of confrontation is less aversive than more direct forms because most individuals discover for themselves their nonlistening behavior patterns as they attempt in vain to recapitulate their predecessor's remarks. On occasion, the group leader profits most from this procedure.

Normally, this procedure has to be applied for only a short period to get the necessary effect. However, to give members practice in listening and monitoring their listening, repeated trials at various intervals are recommended. If continued for too long a period (more than fifteen minutes), the conversation can become stilted, non-task oriented, and aversive. The procedure is more effective if used as a novelty or sporadically, as the situation calls for it, rather than regularly. With younger children we refer to the technique as the *repeating game.* Taping the meeting and replaying the tape is also an excellent exercise for confronting members with their particular patterns of communication.

Many of the above techniques were developed by group members and group leaders in response to a given problem. The techniques seem to be effective to the degree that the members themselves are involved in planning them or at least in deciding whether or not to carry one out. The number of variations are unlimited and depend on the creativity of the group and the leader as to their usefulness and enjoyment value.

Subgroup Structure. In most groups communication is not equally distributed in direction or quantity. That is, members tend to communicate more frequently with some than with others. They tend to choose to play or work in teams more with some than with others. These mutual preferences for work, play, or communication lead to subgrouping or the formation of small groups within the larger treatment groups.

Such subgrouping is an inevitable part of any group. In

the beginning, especially, members have difficulty interacting evenly with everyone else. Some children are comfortable only within very small groups in attempting to make initial social contacts with others. As a result, in the early phase of treatment, leaders usually encourage subgroup activities to get children to participate at all. More often than not the subgroup activity (for example, games carried out in pairs or triads) enhances rather than detracts from the attainment of most group goals. For example, we have found that the cohesion level is higher for sessions in which subgroup activities are used than those in which they are not used at all. However, on occasion the subgroup may be valued by the members so much more than the whole group that their relationships tend to disrupt the ongoing group process. At this point the group leader would increase group activities and reduce or entirely eliminate subgroup activities. The group leader is also able to change the makeup of subgroups in subgroup activities. This is especially advisable when one subgroup has a higher status than another and the higher-status group is beginning to reject or avoid the lower-status group. Rearrangement of subgroups with adolescents has proven to be more difficult than with younger children since adolescents experience this as an encroachment on their rights. In the following example, a particularly effective use of the subgrouping technique is demonstrated.

> Jay was referred to the group by his mother, who said he had no friends and he often cried. In the group he seldom talked to anyone except occasionally to Larry, who was also somewhat shy. During the course of the meeting, the group leader put Jay and Larry, who had demonstrated skills in throwing a softball accurately, together in a team for the sandbag throw. (He chose an activity that was likely to result in some success.) Later, at cleanup, the group leader asked them both to help him (which for these group members was reinforcing). At the next meeting, he noticed that the two

boys were sitting together, so he assigned them each the task of monitoring the other's behavioral assignment to be performed in the classroom that week. After the session it was no longer necessary to encourage the two boys to be together. In fact, it became necessary for the group leader to increase group activities as a means of broadening the contacts of each of the two boys.

In using this procedure the group leader must be careful to avoid putting together people who tend to punish one another or who trigger off maladaptive behaviors for each other. There must be some basis for positive interaction, as in the above example. Subgroups need not be limited to two members. However, we have found that on occasion triads seem to have more difficulty in making decisions. Furthermore, they occasionally form a pair with the extra person being somewhat excluded.

Group Norms. Group norms refer to implicit standards that govern group behavior (see Nixon, 1979, pp. 109–112, and Argyle, 1981, pp. 162–163, for a review of the theory and experimental literature on group norms). When anyone deviates from the norm, group pressure in the form of criticism, teasing, or expression of annoyance by other members quite frequently occurs. As seen in the following examples, some norms work against effective treatment. Other norms that might work against effective goal attainment would be implicit agreements that it is all right if one does not do one's homework; that missing a meeting now and then does not make any difference; and that roleplaying is unsophisticated or childish.

There appeared to be an unwritten law in the group that if any member complained about anything, the others would tease him. After a while, nobody complained about anything anymore.

In another group of older adolescents everyone was

expected to come ten to fifteen minutes late. If
someone did come on time, the others told him he
was being compulsive or a "ratebuster."

Many norms appear to further the achievement of group
or individual goals, such as an agreement that everyone be encouraged by everyone else to participate in the group, or the
standard that when giving feedback, one should always use an "I
statement." Some norms may both enhance and hinder goal attainment. For example, in one group the norm was that members should tell exactly how they felt on all issues. Openness
was important at all costs. On the one hand, this led to useful
self-disclosure. On the other, it prevented action-oriented
change plans from being rationally evaluated and caused people
to be hurt because of the harsh way in which feedback was
often delivered.

In order to assume the existence of group norms, it is
usually necessary to draw on behavioral evidence and repeated
statements made by different members of the group. For example, the group leader assumed that a norm existed because 75
percent of the members continued, over several sessions, to
come late. In another group, the leader assumed that a norm
against self-disclosure existed because, on the rare occasions
when it occurred, the members would tease or put down the
self-disclosing individual.

The disadvantage of norms, as previously mentioned, is
that they may work against the achievement of behavioral
change. The advantage of group norms when they are protherapeutic is that control of behavior is governed by a nonpersonal
standard rather than by the group leader. Such norms reduce
the likelihood of power struggles with and dependency on the
group leader.

In general, norms develop out of the previous experience
of the group members and out of the structure provided by the
group leader. Norms can be made explicit and can be examined
when they do not appear to serve the therapeutic interests of
the group members. Rules may be developed by the group that
go against the previously implicit norms.

Even if a rule is set by the group leader and/or the members, it may not necessarily become a group norm (see Nixon, 1979, pp. 112–115). For example, a rule was established in one group that everyone must come on time. In practice, few people did. Such a discrepancy between rule and norm represented a group problem, which the group discussed. What does the group leader do when a norm is established that works against treatment effectiveness? In the case below, one possible set of strategies is outlined.

In a group of highly anxious, somewhat angry, and often sarcastic adolescents of both genders, aged sixteen to eighteen, a norm seemed to be that the major form of communication was angry criticism and put-downs of each other. The following example is taken from the fourth meeting of the group. In this example the group leader used a wide variety of strategies to resolve not only the norm that encouraged excessive mutual criticism but also some other group problems that seemed to exist at the same time (such as lateness, low productivity, and low satisfaction).

> The group leader noted that the members spoke quite curtly with one another. Group interaction seemed to be characterized by a rather unfriendly tone. Several feeble attempts to be pleasant were immediately repudiated by others. Data at the end of the third meeting revealed that satisfaction continued to be low. Assignment completion rate was also low (45 percent to 60 percent). Participation was relatively even. At the beginning of the fourth session only one person showed up on time; two others arrived five minutes late, two more about twenty minutes late, and the last person, Marie, an hour late. (She said her headache had made it impossible to get out of bed until then.) In previous meetings everyone had come on time.
>
> At the last meeting, Pete and Tony had been subject to considerable criticism by other members of the group for still failing to bring a relevant

problematic situation to the group. As a result, both were the only persons who had not roleplayed or disclosed anything about themselves at a meeting. They both also had the lowest assignment completion rate. In response to the criticism, Pete became quite taciturn, and Tony became openly angry.

The first persons to arrive—Tom, Anne, and Edna—began to criticize the others for coming so late. The group leader interrupted them and proposed, for their consideration, that the lateness and low satisfaction might in fact be due to the style and high frequency of criticism they were all receiving.

Most members agreed that they were indeed annoyed by the arbitrary way in which criticism was delivered, and two members stated they were almost ready to quit the group. Several were also concerned about the unevenness in self-disclosure among the members, which caused them to feel guilty about telling too much about themselves. In general there was agreement that the group was not as effective as it could be at this point.

The group leader suggested that this appeared to be a problem belonging to the group, which included the group leader, rather than belonging to any one member. He suggested that it be handled as any problem, through brainstorming and problem solving. The members hesitantly agreed. The group leader pointed out that most groups have group problems at some point in their history and that resolution of them can be a learning experience. The first step proposed was to write down as many ideas as possible, what the members thought they could each do to increase the effectiveness and comfortableness of the group. They were told to aim at quantity, not quality, and to concern themselves with what they thought were possibilities. They were instructed to write down any general rules that might improve the quality of the program as well.

The suggestions were listed on a flip chart. After they were completed, suggestions rejected outright by the group included stopping the group, more lecture by the group leader, no interference from the group leader, skipping a meeting, going out to dinner, and overwhelming each person with as much criticism as possible until he or she hopefully would become immune to it or be moved by it to better behavior. The strategy ultimately decided on was training in effective group feedback by means of exercises and group leader modeling, with special emphasis on giving and receiving criticism. Cognitive analysis of each person's thoughts when criticized by others was to be applied in order to determine whether the pattern was self-defeating or anxiety producing. If such patterns existed, training in more effective covert and overt coping statements would be included. Finally, group reinforcement would be provided for all their hard work in the form of a cake baked by a group member.

The regular agenda for the meeting was set aside and the feedback and cognitive analysis exercises were rehearsed for the rest of the meeting.

At the end of the meeting, the satisfaction average was 5.3 on a 6-point scale. Comments on the questionnaire included such statements as "best meeting so far," "I really learned a lot—how to respond to group pressure and what I can do about it," "why didn't we do this sooner," and "that was a big load off my mind, I was ready to quit, but not now, for sure."

As is often the case, group problem solving increased the attraction of the group as well as provided a set of behavioral and cognitive alternatives for dealing with the problem. Yet it might have been difficult to come up with ideas of any merit if the members did not have any experience with groups or had not heard about some of these sophisticated strategies before. Cognitive analysis and feedback exercises had been briefly discussed in an earlier session so that members could propose these ideas as their own.

Working on this group problem clearly mediated specific individual behavioral and cognitive change. The major change was in giving feedback more competently and, for several members, in learning new internal coping statements for dealing with criticism. These skills were necessary to deal with the other problems members presented to the group so that, in spite of the necessity to scrap the agenda, no treatment time was lost because of the leader's having to deal with a group problem. To the contrary, the real treatment process did not appear to begin until the group problem was made explicit.

It should be noted that this group problem arose in the first place partially because the group leader permitted free flow of criticism among the members before they had been trained in effective feedback. Although in some groups this is not a problem, in most groups it appears to be necessary to first provide some preliminary training in receiving and giving feedback or to restrict members to only positive feedback in the first few meetings.

Role Structure. Small-group structure can often be analyzed in terms of regularly occurring or expected patterns of behavior from different individuals in the group. Each set of expected behaviors is referred to as a role. These roles may be of relative levels of importance or status and, as such, may be more or less desirable. They may be formally designated by the sponsoring organization or may develop informally, based on observed or expected characteristics of group members or staff. (For a further discussion of role theory see Biddle and Thomas, 1966.)

In most treatment groups, usually two formal roles are assumed: the group leader and the client. The former is the helper and therefore is of high status. The latter is the person to be helped and changed and is clearly of lower status in the group. Since most of our clients are usually in low-status and low-power situations, they must often rely on deviant behaviors to have some semblance of control over their situations. This is a major reason why an important principle in group work is to facilitate the members' increased status through their gradually assuming many of the functions of the higher-status roles.

Occasionally a discussion leader, an observer, a recorder, or a secretary will be designated by the group leader or selected by the members themselves. These roles usually have a set of clearly defined behaviors attributed to them, some of which were originally attributed to the group leader's role. Success is determined by the roleplayer's effectiveness in performing that role's prescribed behaviors. Usually formal training, through modeling and rehearsal in the prescribed role behaviors, is sufficient to ensure effective role performance. Multiple formal roles provide a vehicle by which more influential behaviors can be distributed to group members. To be most effective, this distribution should be negotiated with the members of the group.

Informal roles also seem to arise in treatment groups. These roles appear to be characterized by a person's identifiable patterns of behavior and others' behavioral expectations for that person. Examples of informal roles are the child who plays the clown, the person who usually seems to be annoying others, the adolescent who seems to assume most of the important decision-making functions, and the child who seems to act as a mother to all the other children in a variety of situations. An analysis of the specific behaviors of each role with a focus on how they are maintained by the behaviors and roles of others generally leads to a useful set of interventions. For example, in a group of young adolescents, Jerry was considered, by himself and others, to be the clown. In a group discussion of the in-group behavior of each member, Jerry, with the help of the group, defined his behavior as: making jokes when others were serious; teasing others when teasing was not appropriate; and acting silly, much of the time to the annoyance as well as the laughter of the others. The group leader pointed out that any person's behavior is in part dependent on the behavior of others. When the members complained about Jerry's clowning, the leader asked what the members could do to help Jerry become less the clown and more the contributing member that he was. The treatment plan involved increasing prosocial behaviors (which several group members were also working on) such as leading the group, asking serious questions, helping others, and performing cooperative behaviors. The members, including Jerry, agreed that they would not pay as much attention to Jerry when he got silly or made jokes at the wrong time but they would give him a great deal of attention when he gave suggestions or asked for help.

One form of role therapy (which focuses on changing the role as a whole) is a cross-age tutoring program in which the client is placed in the role of tutor for a younger child. This takes the individual out of the accustomed role of "client," and treatment becomes teacher training rather than therapy (see Chapter Two). Even in this form of therapy the child must learn how to work with others in highly specific ways for the cross-age tutoring to become successful. Another procedure for raising a child's status in roles played outside the group is to teach specific behaviors that are highly valued by the peer group (such as how to swing a baseball bat or how to break dance).

When the status of a given role within the treatment group is low, as evidenced by scapegoating, a high frequency of criticism of the individual, exclusion from certain activities, and/or rejection on sociometric tests, the problem belongs both to the children who are putting the scapegoat down as well as to the child with low status. In situations where children have difficulty dealing directly with group problems, an indirect approach is to present the group with a hypothetical situation. In this case, a fictional child who is scapegoated in a school situation is described. The case is first discussed by identifying the thoughts and behaviors of all interacting parties in the example. Second, the group is asked to design a plan in which all the interacting parties have to change something they are doing to improve the general group climate. The members might then discuss how each is similar to or different from the characters in the case study. This may lead to a discussion of their own situation and to a plan for group members' behavior modification to remedy the group problem. Case studies need to be not too similar to the group problem.

A more direct approach is presenting the problem as the group leader perceives it and asking the members how they perceive the situation. However, if the group leader identifies too closely with the victim or puts the responsibility solely on the others, the group may become unwilling to deal with the problem. As previously mentioned, problems involving more than one member must be viewed as a common responsibility rather than any one person's responsibility.

Leadership Structure. One particular role structure that warrants consideration by itself is the leadership structure of the group. (See Fiedler [1971] for an empirically based theory of small-group leadership.) Although usually associated with individuals or roles, leadership can be more usefully described as a set of behaviors that facilitates group and individual goal attainment and group maintenance (Cartwright and Zander, 1968). Often these behaviors may be attached primarily to one person, the group leader, as that person strives to give the group a focus. Later these leadership behaviors may also be associated with one or two group members. As we pointed out earlier, since high status and power are often associated with the leadership role, the major function of the group leader is to facilitate the distribution of leadership behaviors so that the rewards and control of leadership accrue to all members. Thus, the main function of the leader is to gradually eliminate the centralized leadership role. As a result, behavioral groups, though initially highly managed and structured by the group leader, are gradually run by the members themselves.

What is the value of members' performing their own leadership behaviors? First, practice in performing leadership functions that facilitate the attainment of treatment goals extends the member's area of competence to other social groups where leadership is usually highly valued. (And, as a result, leadership skills learned in the treatment group have the opportunity of being reinforced in other groups.) Second, the more the members provide their own leadership, the more likely that they will work on behaviors that concern them, using methods that are acceptable to them. Third, as we suggested above, treatment group members are more likely to be in low-status situations throughout their social world. They experience powerlessness in a wide variety of social situations. The performance of leadership activities enhances their power or feeling of efficacy in the group. This does not imply that all members become leaders but that they achieve incremental control over their own program and, hopefully to an increasing degree, over their own lives.

For the above reasons the group leader is constantly concerned with training all members in leadership behaviors and transferring his responsibilities to them. In fact, by the end of treatment, members should be helping to clarify problems, suggesting treatment plans, developing contracts for each other, choosing their own tasks, and organizing roleplays. The group leader shifts his or her functions from leading to prompting. Training in leadership behaviors occurs in the same way as all other behaviors that a group leader attempts to increase. The group discusses what the group leader specifically does as leader. The leader then asks the members to observe which of these behaviors are performed at a given meeting. The members are then encouraged to perform these behaviors whenever possible. Approximations of leadership behavior are reinforced in the group. In subsequent meetings members are provided with practice as leaders of the group, with the group leader acting either as coach or coleader. Some group leaders set up leadership seminars for adolescents in the later phases of treatment in order to directly focus on extending their leadership skills. In these seminars, discussion-leading skills as well as discussion-participating skills are taught and strategies for getting one's ideas across in a group meeting are presented and practiced. After treatment has terminated some members may be trained as group aides in an in-service program that further reinforces their leadership ability.

Group Contagion. Occasionally, a series of aggressive behaviors—"horseplay," giggling, or other disruptive behavior—can be triggered by one or two children in the group. Redl and Wineman (1956) refer to this child not as a leader but as a central person in the emotional life of the group. Group contagion may also result from a general state of fatigue, boredom, a recent stressful situation, or a sexually suggestive word. Quite often, however, it is the same one or two persons who seem to initiate or trigger the contagion.

Although in structured groups, the structure of the program often mitigates frequent contagion, it is not a rare phenomenon, especially with beginning group leaders. Normal handling procedures, such as extinction, sometimes do not work because the members are laughing at the initiator or in other ways mutually reinforcing one another. Giving time-out to one child occasionally settles the group down but often the "unfairness" of the punishment increases the intensity of the contagious behavior. The group leader's walking out of the room leaves the group to its own devices, which could be destructive and reinforce the contagion.

Occasionally "stopping the world"—that is, all organized activities come to an end—is effective, but only if highly valued activities are yet to come (such as an attractive game or refreshments) and insufficient time will be available to carry them out if the group does not settle down. However, contagious behavior may be more self-reinforcing than most alternatives.

Most often, using a firm and well-articulated tone of voice with intense eye contact is sufficient to gain control. The group leader looks from person to person and physically moves toward the most disruptive member. As the disruptive behavior begins to subside, immediate reinforcement should follow: "That's beginning to get better!" As the group calms down, the leader makes an appointment to discuss what happened, either at that point or at a later meeting. The discussion becomes a problem-solving session that relates the incident to similar incidents in school, including how the children handle themselves in school and the risks of such behavior there. Such a discussion maximizes the learning inherent in the situation. During the discussion children should also examine their role in response to the triggering stimuli and develop a plan for dealing with them. Obviously some silly disruptive behavior is not only tolerable, it is desirable. If the group is excessively serious and rigidly task oriented, cohesion is usually low and learning suffers. Only in a situation such as above, where contagion occurs with a high frequency or where it seriously imposes on the learning opportunities and rights of others, is it dealt with.

It should be noted that group contagion appears in excessive proportions primarily when program activities are unattractive to the members. Therefore the best prophylaxis for contagion is careful program planning and frequent evaluation.

Productivity. One way the group can ascertain whether it is moving toward the achievement of individual treatment goals is to measure the amount of work being performed by the members, or estimating the group's productivity. Estimates of productivity have been shown to significantly correlate (at least, in adult assertive-training groups) with outcome (Rose, 1981). As mentioned earlier in this chapter, group productivity for each session is measured at the beginning of the next session by the number of completed homework assignments. Other indices of session productivity could be participation and time spent in goal-oriented activity, such as assessment and intervention. Thus, at any point in time we have a picture of the individual's as well as the group's productivity record (which is usually the average for all the members). Since the performance of extra-group assignments is so essential to this approach and because of the high correlation of assignment completion with outcome ($r = .92$ [Rose, 1981]), the level of productivity is dealt with at every meeting. Low productivity is one of the more common group problems. In many of the previous examples, low productivity was at least a side effect of other problems, such as poor communications, nontherapeutic norms, and differential status of roles, to name a few. Sometimes low productivity is the major target of change.

Let us look at how one group leader dealt with low productivity as well as with several interrelated problems in a children's group.

Seven children, eleven to twelve years of age, had been referred to a group because of their difficulty in making friends in the classroom. At the end of

the third meeting, the group leader, Harry, noted
that the homework assignment—to talk to one person in their class whom they had never talked to
before—was completed by only one person and
that the average satisfaction had dropped from 5
on a 6-point scale to 3.4.

"Wow! We seem to be in trouble," he said
to the group. "We're certainly not getting the work
done we agreed to do. What do you all think?" The
children agreed that they were not doing the work,
but they also stated that the group was not as
much fun as it had been; some said there was too
much work. One said that a couple of guys did all
the talking. And several mentioned that only half
of the members got to roleplay the previous week.

Harry said he was impressed with the things
they felt were wrong with the group and that maybe they could do something about it. "I'll tell you
what, why don't each of you write down one thing
we as a *group* could do differently and one thing
you as an individual could do differently to make
this group more fun and a better place to learn
how to make friends. And remember, be specific—
a word we talked about last week."

Harry gave several examples. He could make
sure everyone got to roleplay and he could talk a
little less himself. After a few minutes, everyone
seemed to be finished writing. Harry asked for
their ideas. He was careful not to permit any evaluation until all the ideas were written on the board.
The list is reproduced in Table 7. As the group
evaluated the ideas, they decided they would call
their partners to remind them or even to help them
do their homework. Finally, they decided to have a
reward (an extra fifteen minutes of game time) if
they all did their homework. Each member then
decided with a partner the individual behaviors
each would try to perform during the meeting to

Table 7. Ideas for Improving Group Productivity.

Ideas for Group	Ideas for Me
Easier homework assignments.	I should talk less.
Everyone roleplay.	I could talk more.
We should use tokens for low talkers.	I will tell more nice things to others.
We should get up and move about more.	I will praise those who do their homework.
We should give better rewards for those who do their homework.	I will disagree aloud with Harry whenever I disagree with him.
We should play Concentration and Fish.	I won't argue so much, well, just a little.
We should have more homework.	I should do my homework.
We should play more, work less.	
We could call our buddies to help with homework.	

resolve the problem. In most cases it was the initial idea they had suggested for themselves.

At the end of the meeting, the satisfaction rate had gone up to 5.5 and the distribution of participation had evened out. The next week's assignment (which they agreed would be the same as last week's assignment) was completed by all but one person who was sick the entire week.

It should be noted that in this group, as in most groups, not one but several problems were detected in addition to low productivity. A drop in participation or increase in one person's dominance often accompanies a drop in the rate of assignment completion or another productivity index. The group leader focused his interventions on the program and the members' participation as well as on the group's low productivity.

When a Problem Is Not a Problem. Data are often convincing, especially when there are multiple indicators, such as low attendance, low satisfaction, and an uneven distribution of participation. Occasionally, however, for various reasons the data are regarded as nonproblematic by the group. There may not be enough evidence to convince the group of its problem, or it may be solely the group leader's problem. In either case it is usually advisable to leave the problem until more data become available and for leaders to examine their own stake in the problem. Sometimes the data point directly to the leader as the target person for intervention. Leaders are then obliged to work on their own behavior, such as when the leader's interaction is greater than all the other members collectively or when two leaders continually correct each other.

How to Prevent Group Problems. If resolving group problems is such an educationally valid experience, why would any group leader attempt to prevent them? The resolution of group problems, though valuable, requires a lot of time. If group problems abound, the group may not get to its other work of learning unique social and cognitive skills for which the clients originally may have been referred to the group. Certainly in a short-term group, preventive practices are necessary to preserve any possibility of treatment goal attainment. In long-term groups this may be less necessary. Certainly, in psychodynamically oriented groups, prevention may be undesirable, since dealing with group problems may be the major work of the group. Thus, prevention, though not universally desirable, may represent sound treatment practice in short-duration groups with a narrow skill-training focus.

Basically, prevention strategies are good intervention approaches. The attraction of the group should be kept high through a balance of effective work and attractive programming with adequate variation and challenge. Group leaders should make sure at every meeting that all persons talk and that those who talk excessively are limited in speaking as soon as possible. Meetings should be well-planned, with reasonable and achievable agendas. Group leaders should make judicious use of humor. If these conditions are met, it is unlikely that many group problems will arise. Fortunately, none of us is perfect and in the absence of perfection something is always overlooked or someone is slighted. Group leaders, too, vary in mood, experience, and ability to handle complex group stimuli. So problems are inevitable and an approach to group problem-solving is necessary.

Summary

It should be clear from the content of this chapter that the purpose of group-structure modification is individual behavior modification. However, the likelihood of success is dramatically reduced if one attempts to modify the behavior of an individual without regard to the level of group cohesion, group norms, the individual's status, and the group's communication pattern. Individual behavior in a group is largely dependent on others' behavior in the group. As we have noted throughout this chapter, changes in group structures and processes, for the most part, have involved the children in modifying the larger system, the group, of which they are a part. This has the added advantage of preparing them to deal with other systems, such as the family or the peer group at school. Other strategies for transferring what the child or adolescent has learned in the group to the world beyond the group are discussed in Chapter Twelve. Homework or outside behavioral assignments are so important in these transferring processes that the following chapter is devoted solely to this topic.

Chapter Eleven

Assignments for Practicing New Behavior Outside the Group

Next week, I will ask one kid in my class to play with me. That kid will either be Gary or Art because I see them all the time. I'll ask 'em to play catch.

Eileen and me are gonna go to the Y and ask about classes in Karate and Judo and we're gonna write down what they say and bring the info back to the group next week.

I'm going to ask my mom to help me with my homework just like we practiced in the group, loud like and looking right at her. If I do she'll sign my card, and I'll show it to the guys at the next meeting.

When I apply for the job next week, I'm going to take a deep breath, and remind myself to speak slowly and clearly. As soon as I have the interview, I'll call Orrin and tell him just what I said and what I thought.

I'm going to practice that roleplay we did in the group five times, the one where I tell my mom what happened at school when she asks. I'll be roleplaying with my buddy, Anita.

It is possible to view the entire treatment process as preparation for carrying out such assignments. Subsequent meetings may be used to evaluate the effectiveness with which the assignments were performed. In fact, a portion of almost every session is devoted to the monitoring of earlier assignments and the design of new ones.

All of the above are examples of extra-group assignments designed in various treatment groups by adolescents and children to be implemented at home, at school, in the employment office, on the playground, or in some other outside setting. The assignments are characterized by their specificity as to what, where, when, and with whom certain behaviors or cognitions will occur within a given time period. In most cases the children will report back to the group the results of their experiences.

Once children have been prepared to deal with the problem in the real world through roleplaying, reinforcement, and other previously mentioned group procedures, they design a plan to implement these newly learned behaviors or cognitions in the real world. The carrying out of this plan may be regarded as the implementation phase of the problem-solving process. Reporting back to the group or a buddy is the verification phase of the process.

Many authors have noted the importance of assignments in treatment (Kanfer and Phillips, 1970; Stokes and Baer, 1977; Goldstein and Kanfer, 1979), and several books on the theory and principles of behavioral assignments have already been written (Maultsby, 1971; Shelton and Levy, 1981; Shelton and Ackerman, 1974). Shelton and Levy (1981) found the homework component of treatment central to the therapeutic process. The following purposes have been mentioned by most of the above authors.

Purposes of Homework Assignments

One major purpose of homework in the treatment process is to encourage the children to try out in the real world what they have learned in the group. To a considerable extent, behavior appears to be specific to the situation in which it is learned. It is, therefore, necessary to create real-life situations in which new behaviors may be practiced. Thus, assignments are a major vehicle for the transfer of learning from the clinical to a real-world setting. Also, homework may be viewed as an opportunity to extend the training into the other waking hours of the week. Members may practice some of the techniques learned in the group as a means of integrating them into their own repertoire.

A second purpose is to provide members with the opportunity to try out new behaviors in the absence of both the group leader and the pressure of the group's immediate feedback. It is also a method of helping the children to become the principal agent of their own change and to decrease their dependence on the group as the major source of help. The absence of any supervisor when the assignment is being performed reduces control over a client. Fortunately, strategies have been developed to increase the probability of compliance with assignments, even in the absence of the group leader or adult monitor. These strategies will be discussed later in this chapter.

A third purpose is that homework permits treatment access to private behaviors, such as sleeping disorders, sexual disturbances, or private thoughts that would not be available in the group context. A fourth purpose in the absence of group and leader support is that the child is often forced to develop self-control strategies to comply with the homework requirements. A study by Bandura (1975) showed that self-control behaviors decreased when clients thought that treatment gains were due to group support rather than their own resources.

Finally, an important goal of assignments is to provide an opportunity for multiple trials beyond the limits of the group. Often in the group, because of the limited time available in a session, only a few roleplays can be carried out by each person. Homework provides an opportunity for continued and repeated practice.

Types of Assignments

Different kinds of assignments, each of which deserves separate examination, are interactive tasks; cognitive restructuring tasks; observational tasks; and noninteractive tasks, including observation of self and others, and reading assignments.

Interactive Tasks. Interactive tasks are assignments in which the child talks with (or in other ways interacts with), others outside the group in highly specific ways. In general, these tasks are observable social phenomena with limited boundaries in terms of time, place, and action.

The examples presented at the beginning of this chapter of one child asking two others to play with him and then playing with them, of the two girls asking for information at the Y, and of the child asking his mother for help represent interactive tasks. Since these are readily observable, their successful completion is readily monitored and reinforced. As a result, they are the most common type of assignment. Most of the generalizations we make on compliance later in this chapter are applicable to this category of assignment. Preparation for interactive assignments is most often done through group modeling and behavioral rehearsal, described in Chapter Seven.

Cognitive Restructuring Tasks. Cognitive restructuring tasks involve examining and changing self-talk associated with stressful or problematic situations. In an earlier example we described an adolescent who was about to have a job interview. His task was to covertly instruct himself to relax, to take one step at a time, and to remind himself that he really knew the job for which he was applying. Cognitive restructuring tasks may also involve shifting from self-put-downs or negative self-talk to more positive expressions of attitudes. For example, Juan constantly points out to family and friends that he is too dumb to do anything and that he is sure to fail if he tries. After training in recognizing when he makes these statements and rehearsing alternative statements in the group, he decides that his assignment will be that whenever he is presented with a difficult task, he will state only that he thinks it will be difficult, but if he is well prepared he will certainly give it his best effort and he has a good chance of succeeding. Finally, cognitive restructuring tasks may involve self-reinforcement after the completion of an interactive task or another cognitive restructuring task. After Juan has described his success in carrying out the above assignment, he will be taught to reinforce himself for his success. His assignment will be not only to carry out the above assignment, but to reinforce himself every time he succeeds in using non-put-down statements. These procedures are explained in more detail in Chapter Eight.

Often cognitive restructuring and interactive tasks are combined. One example where this might occur was described earlier, when the adolescent was preparing for a job interview by using self-enhancing self-talk. He also had to perform the actual verbal task of carrying out the interview. In fact, it would have been possible to combine most of the interactive tasks described earlier with a cognitive restructuring task.

Since cognitive assignments are difficult to monitor, only self-report at subsequent meetings or contacts with buddies is used to monitor whether the assignment was completed. With children, we have found that concrete reinforcement of cognitive or other nonmonitorable assignments is unadvisable. Since the material objects are often so highly valued by the children, we often end up reinforcing lying behavior. Praise alone, in our experience, seems to have this result less often.

Simulated Tasks. These are special cases of interactive tasks. They differ in that the behavior performed in the real world is a roleplayed interaction rather than an actual interaction with a significant other. An example of this was given at the beginning of the chapter: the child roleplayed a situation with her mother five times with another group member. These roleplays occurred between group sessions. Often there is not enough time to permit repeated practice in the group. Such simulated assignments are often given to provide this practice and to extend training time into the rest of the week. As pointed out earlier, such multiple trials also increase the probability of transfer to the real world.

Simulated assignments are only useful if situations to be roleplayed are clearly spelled out. To assure this, an abbreviated script is often developed in the group and given to the protagonist, who also acts as director of the roleplay. Usually this type of assignment is used in middle sessions and with individuals who have previously demonstrated roleplay skills. It is especially useful with adolescents who require a lot of preparation before trying out something new.

Noninteractive Tasks. Noninteractive tasks are assignments that do not directly involve the client in interaction with other persons, such as keeping a budget, writing down one's ideas for treatment goals, keeping an exercise program, learning a game to teach to the other group members, practicing relaxation, or reading a chapter in a book or an article.

The major intervention procedures for preparing for this type of assignment are self-control strategies. These assignments often have concrete products. When shown to the group, these products may be evaluated by the group members or leader. Examples of such products include budgets and data to support how each budget item was met, a written statement of treatment goals, a game taught to other group members, and a report on a book or an article that was read. Of the noninteractive tasks, reading assignments have been the most common among literate children and adolescents. For example, having the adolescents read the first chapter of Alberti and Emmons (1975) saves a lot of leader time in the adolescents social-skills group.

Observational Assignments. In self-observational assignments, clients observe their own behavior, cognitions, or feelings in specific situations and record them. In the early phase of treatment, this is a common assignment to further the assessment process. Common examples of such assignments are monitoring one's own level of anxiety in given situations on a scale of one to ten, counting the number of arguments with a sibling, keeping track of the amount of time spent in chore behavior, recording one's thoughts in stressful situations, and keeping a diary.

Observation of others involves noting observable behavior of potential models in the community, when insufficient models exist in the group. In a group of teenagers who were interested in improving their dating skills, they were assigned the task of identifying one person in their class who seemed to have these skills and noting those physical and verbal behaviors that the members of the opposite sex seemed to respond to. The group members were then to report back their observations, which were discussed in the group.

Compliance with Assignments

It is not sufficient to merely give assignments. The clients must comply with the assignment if the desired effects are to be achieved. A number of strategies have been established to maximize the probability of compliance. These strategies and their empirical foundation have been described by Shelton and Levy (1981) as they apply in individual, primarily adult, therapy. Below we describe and elaborate on most of these strategies as they apply to child and adolescent groups.

Specificity. Clients should be well versed in specific details of the assignment if they are to complete it. That is, each group member should know when the assignment is to be carried out, with whom, under what conditions, what behaviors or cognitions are to be implemented, and if and how the results are to be monitored and reported back to the group. The group leader should be sure that the conditions necessary for the assignments to be carried out have a high probability of occurring.

For example, Arnie's assignment was to explain to his mother that he took the car without permission and to offer to pay for the car damages that were incurred while he had it by working around the house. He also agreed to promise that he would not take the car again without permission. He agreed to listen to whatever his mother had to say about the car incident without making excuses and without arguing with her. The assignment had to be carried out at the next opportunity, namely, at dinner immediately following the group meeting. As soon as the conversation took place Arnie was to call his partner and describe what happened in detail. He was also to report to the other group members at the following meeting. If Arnie perceived that he could not carry out the assignment, the above description provided the script for further practice in the group.

Likely Stimulus Conditions. It should also be noted that the likelihood of the stimulus conditions for Arnie's desired behavior—that his mother would be home—was very high. In some cases the stimulus conditions may be less likely. For example, Jerry, who rarely was confronted with angry peers or fights, felt obliged to defend himself verbally on the playground the previous week. He had failed to do this. He worked on his response to this provocation in the group. However, since the likelihood that someone would try to "push him around" again was low, he was given the assignment to roleplay the situation with two of the group members who would act as playground bullies.

Adequate Preparation. If the client is unsure how to carry out the assignment, preparation in the group through behavioral or cognitive rehearsal may be necessary. In the above example, Arnie was prepared for the conversation with his mother by observing modeling by one of the members and by rehearsing the conversation in the group. Since there was insufficient time in the group, Arnie also rehearsed the situation several times in the period between the group meeting and dinner.

In general, even if the problem is interactive in nature—for example, when a child consistently says to himself, "I can't do anything right"—then some form of cognitive restructuring is called for—in this case, disputation by the group. Cognitive modeling and rehearsal of the new cognitions might be appropriate.

In some preliminary sessions, preparation for an assignment might merely consist of first getting information necessary to carry it out. For example, Ronnie's assignment was to join the Y. Preparation involved finding out how to get there on public transportation as well as calling to find out about costs and times of available programs. Ronnie had no difficulty in asking for information on the phone. If he did have difficulty, preparation would also consist of roleplaying the phone call. The group members were used to help Ronnie prepare by generating ideas of what he would have to know in order to carry out the assignment and how and where he would get the necessary information.

To be certain that each group member is well prepared, at the end of each meeting the group leader or the buddy reviews with each child exactly what assignment will be done prior to the next session and whether each member feels comfortable in performing the necessary activities.

Reinforcement. If the assignment is successfully completed the individual should be reinforced by either someone in the environment when the assignment is performed or by the group at a subsequent meeting when the client reports on the success. In addition, clients should covertly reinforce themselves for performance of the assignment at the time of the performance. Going back to a previous example, ideally Arnie's mother would reinforce him for the discussion he held with her. Unless the group leader had arranged this in advance with the mother, the reinforcement might not be forthcoming. For this reason, a buddy might be instructed to reinforce Arnie with enthusiastic praise for each instance of compliance with each of the instructions. Similarly, when Arnie told his experience to the group, the members enthusiastically endorsed his successes. With younger children tokens might have been awarded either for purchasing something in the group store or for adding to their group thermometer. Through peer reinforcement, self-reinforcement, and, if possible, concrete reinforcement for the same or similar behaviors on frequent occasions, it is possible to establish assignment compliance in the repertoire of a child.

Contingency Contracts. In most groups, assignments are put into writing at the end of the meeting and signed by both the group member and the group leader or buddy. Written assignments, if calling for explicit rewards or contingencies following successful completion, are called *contingency contracts.* The following are two examples of contingency contracts for two girls in a group of eleven-year-olds.

> When Naomi brings back her slip signed by her mother to indicate that she completed it, she will receive the right to choose the first group activity of the meeting. She will also receive five points for purchasing something from the group store, and ten points for the group thermometer.

> When Elizabeth brings her signed note indicating that she has argued with her sister the previous week two or fewer times, she will receive ten points to put on the group thermometer and five points for her personal purchase from the group store.

It should once again be noted in the above examples that considerable diversity and frequency of reinforcement is possible. Individual purchases from the group store and the opportunity to be the one who selects a group activity are highly individualized reinforcers, which increase their potency. In the above two examples, Naomi and Elizabeth received approval and the signature of the mother as immediate reinforcement. Wherever possible, immediate reinforcement should be built into a contract. When it is not possible to obtain quick reinforcement from others, immediate self-reinforcement for compliance should be built into the contract.

In summary, an effective contingency contract should have the following features: first, a clear and detailed description of the behaviors to be performed in the assignment; second, a specification of the immediate reinforcement to be received as well as the group reinforcement; and, finally, a description of the means by which the assignment is observed, measured, and recorded.

Cueing. Initially, it is difficult for children to remember what they must do in a given assignment and when it is to occur even if heavy reinforcement is used. To this end, the group leader uses a variety of cueing strategies to remind the client when and what is to happen. For example, Larry was called by his buddy every day at six to remind him to ask his mother to help him with his English homework. Hank had a timer watch that was set for every hour. When the timer went off, Hank wrote down what he was doing and thinking at that very moment. Martina put a large calendar on her bathroom mirror. The instructions for each day were written in the appropriate box. In the evening she circled it if instructions were completed.

All of these techniques—phone calls, timers, and calendars—serve as cues or reminders to perform an assignment at that moment or for that day. Although frequently used in the initial phase of treatment, cues, like other devices, are rapidly faded as the clients show competence in remembering to carry out assignments. If cues seem to be insufficient, it is possible that some other principle is being ignored.

Gradually Increased Demand. Initial assignments should

be relatively easy to perform, but subsequent assignments should gradually increase in difficulty and complexity as they gradually approximate the treatment goal. Even though assignments must usually increase in difficulty if they are to be relevant to the client, if they become difficult too suddenly, the likelihood of completion is reduced. Let us explain this by the following example.

> In a group of highly disorganized ten-year-olds, the children could not even get their initial assignments home to their parents without losing them or crumbling them into nothing.
>
> The first assignment after this discovery was merely to take the note home and have it signed and bring it back without losing it. It took three weeks before the members achieved this, in spite of heavy reinforcement. The second step was to have the children do one simple home chore, such as taking out the garbage, then bring back a signed note indicating that the assignment was completed. The subsequent assignments were to carry out the given chore—first two, then three, and eventually more times a week—and then bring a note signed by a parent each time.

Multiple Monitoring Sources. The group leader should initially help each client to develop as many external monitoring sources as possible. Later such monitoring sources should be phased out and only self-report should be used. For children the major monitoring sources are buddies from the group, teachers, parents or other relatives, and friends not in the group. It is our experience that the more public a person goes with the assignment, the more likely it is to be completed. Also, the more monitoring sources, the greater likelihood of assignment completion. The responsibility and identity of the monitor are, as we mentioned earlier, always written into the contingency contract or made highly explicit in the unwritten contract. As previously mentioned, the most reliable monitors are those with the greatest interest in behavioral change on the part of the given client. However, since these persons also have a history of nagging or other inefficient ways of cueing, they also need the most detailed instructions as to their monitoring activities.

Usually, with teachers and parents, the simplest instruction is to sign a note that during a morning a given behavior did or did not occur. It is often better to use the population that the group leader has ready access to—the other group members. On those occasions when a parent group is running parallel with the children's group, a great deal of attention can be paid to monitoring the completion of the children's assignments. Occasionally the group leader provides one meeting for the parents to tell them about the group and to instruct them in the various assignment-monitoring procedures. If this is not possible, phone contacts are also often used.

Maximum Involvement. Maximum involvement in the selection and planning for an assignment is another way of increasing the client's private commitment to the effective performance of that assignment. Initially children and adolescents do not have the basic skills to design their own assignments. Thus, the group leader plays a major role in planning assignments in the first few sessions of treatment, carefully taking into consideration the child's interests, which the leader will have determined in pregroup interviews and in prior group discussions.

As assignments are given, group leaders also point out the principles that guide them in developing the assignment. These criteria, which have already been discussed, are (1) specificity, (2) frequent monitoring, (3) relation to treatment goal, (4) gradual increased demand, and (5) opportunity for reinforcement if successfully completed (Shelton and Levy, 1981). As the members learn these principles, they take increasing responsibility for designing assignments until they assume total responsibility for their design and execution. Soon pairs of children design their own assignments for a given week. Each gives feedback to the other on whether the criteria mentioned above are being met. In very small groups (of four or five members) there is usually sufficient time to do this in the group.

In a previous example, Arnie was able to choose his own assignment by the third session. First, he told his buddy the assignment was related to his general problem of getting along better with his mom. Second, it was much harder than the previous assignment, when all he had to do was talk to his mother about the group. Third, it was sufficiently specific that he knew what he had to do and when, and, finally, it would be reinforced by the group. The buddy asked Arnie how the assignment would be monitored and Arnie replied that his mom could monitor it or he could do it himself and report back to the group. In the above example, the group leader served as consultant to the subgroup and, had it been necessary, he would have raised questions or issues the pair had overlooked.

Another exercise commonly used to prepare group members in assignment formulation is as follows. One of the members assumes a hypothetical assignment only for purposes of the exercise. The group leader then asks that member and the rest of the group to evaluate the assignment. In the following example, the leader has just put the criteria for an effective homework assignment on the board.

Karen (the group leader):   Okay Evie, you have selected the assignment to talk to two new people next week. (pause) What's good about this assignment?

Evie: I guess it's related to why I'm in the group, to meet other people and be comfortable with them.

Angie: You gave the time limits for the assignment: "sometime during the week."

Karen: Well, what might I have done differently?

Jean: For one thing you assigned it; Evie didn't agree to it. I don't think that's such a good idea.

Karen: Right on. What else?

Linda: You were way too general. She doesn't know how it is to be monitored or hardly anything.

Evie: Besides, it's too easy. I could have done that two weeks ago.

Karen: It looks like you are putting me out of a job. It was a great evaluation. You understand these principles well.

As observed in the above example, the adolescents are fully involved in the assignment development process. By using a hypothetical example, the exercise permitted the group to discuss the principles nondefensively. Of course, after the exercise, the group members are usually sufficiently familiar with the principles to apply them to their own assignments or at least to the assignments of their partners.

Private Commitment. As noted above, maximum involvement increases private commitment to completion of the contract. There are a number of other strategies for increasing private commitment, according to Shelton and Levy (1981). In early sessions, one way to increase children's private commitment to completing assignments is to discuss with them what they have already done to help themselves with problems.

Previous group experiences or individual treatment is discussed in terms of what was tried and what seemed to be helpful. The group leader discusses how some of the successful attributes might be incorporated into the present group activities and how some of the less successful activities might be changed or improved on to make them more successful.

Whenever an assignment is given, it behooves the group leader to explain how the assignment is related to the problem for which the child was referred to the group. This is an excellent opportunity to use the group discussion to talk about members' beliefs and fears about performing a given assignment. To achieve this, questions from the members are encouraged. This is also an opportunity to incorporate into the group a model who testifies how the various assignments were helpful to him or her. If a live model is not possible, audio or video cassettes can be used. Cognitive rehearsal may be used to practice private commitment statements that evolve out of the discussions. Shelton and Levy (1981, pp. 62–63) review research supporting the efficacy of this approach to compliance enhancement.

Public Commitment. The client should be encouraged to make a public commitment to the group and eventually to the immediate social circle on which the assignment impinges. When the client has described the assignment to the group, the group leader usually asks why the assignment is important. If the given child does not know the answer, the group leader might ask the group. In our experience, a statement that one believes an assignment is important and one intends to carry it out increases the likelihood of completion. The fact that almost everyone else in the group is making a similar public commitment increases the pressure on each individual to make such a statement as well. The research of Levy and her associates lends support to this assumption (Levy, 1977; Levy and Carter, 1976; Levy, Yamashita, and Pow, 1979; Levy and Clark, 1980).

Correct Cognitive Distortions. In situations where a client's cognitive distortions seem to be preventing the client from completing the assignment, cognitive restructuring strategies should be used. For example, when Cindy claimed that she could not ask her teacher for help because she would think Cindy was a nuisance, the group suggested that other children often asked for help and none of these were considered nuisances. When she agreed, they suggested that she replace this self-defeating statement with the statement that it was the teacher's job to help the kids with their math problems and that Ms. Kale seemed to actually like it when kids asked questions. After considerable rehearsal of these statements, Cindy was ready to carry out the behavioral assignment of asking Ms. Kale for help with math when she got stuck.

Summary

Not all the work of the group can and should occur within the group session. In this chapter we have spelled out the purposes and characteristics of the various kinds of extra-group assignments commonly used in group treatment. Equally important, we have described and illustrated various principles for the correct formulation of effective homework. Assignments are useful only if they are completed. For these reasons we have reviewed the major strategies for enhancing compliance to the mutually agreed-upon assignments. These guidelines are not only useful when compliance is low, but should be integrated into the group plan to prevent the problem of low rates of assignment completion from occurring.

As we review the problem-solving process discussed in Chapter One, we note that the implementation phase (extragroup assignments) and the validation phase (monitoring extragroup assignments) complete the first cycle of the process. Thus treatment without extra-group assignments, though possible, appears to reduce the power of the entire treatment process. Extra-group assignments draw on all of the procedures we have thus far discussed, such as modeling, reinforcement, and cognitive restructuring, and are the major strategy in implementing transfer of change to the real world. In Chapter Twelve, we shall discuss the remaining strategies for enhancing the generalization of learning in the group.

Chapter Twelve

Principles and Strategies
for Maintaining New Behavior

At the beginning of our group, Greg, the group leader, suggested a lot of the things we did. After the first couple of meetings we started to get to suggest and choose the games we would play and what kinds of situations we'd act out. Each of us even got a chance to be the discussion leader for a while, with the help of a little card with hints on it. And later we didn't even use the cards.

And now, by the end, we almost don't need Greg anymore. We decide who is going to take turns being the group leader, what problems we work on, what games we are going to play and what assignments we are going to do before the next meeting. We even decided not to have points anymore. Sometimes a couple of us even meet on our own.

Next week we're each bringing a friend from school to the meeting. We are going to explain to them what we've learned in the group and how the group works. Most of us belong to other groups now where they don't work on problems, but just have fun or learn something.

This preadolescent group member has just described the process by which members are helped to generalize what they have learned to nontherapeutic settings (transfer of change) and to a time when the group is no longer meeting (maintenance of change). Preparation for generalization occurs throughout treatment with increasingly greater emphasis as the group approaches termination. The termination process traditionally involves the final meetings of a group and dealing with such feelings as guilt, denial, ambivalence, and loss among group members (see Toseland and Rivas, 1984). In our experience, such feelings appear to be less pronounced and traumas fail to materialize if the children are gradually prepared to return to and perform newly learned behaviors in the real world as the group progresses. This chapter deals with that preparation and the principles that guide it.

In the multimethod approach to group work, termination is not merely discussed with the members. Instead, a gradual and systematic program for the generalization of change from the group to the natural environment is planned for and conducted. The most fundamental observation about generalization is that it rarely happens if nothing is done about it (Stokes and Baer, 1977). Generalization requires a plan in order to occur. Once changes begin to be performed on a regular basis in the group, the focus of planning and treatment activities shifts to maintaining these desired changes in the members' lives outside the group. As we discussed in Chapter Eleven, extra-group assignments are one of the major strategies of generalization since most extra-group assignments require practice of new behaviors in the "real world" outside the group. In the following sections we discuss many other guiding principles of change generalization for planning group interventions and between-session assignments.

Principles of Generalization

In the past twenty years, surprisingly little has been written about generalization when compared to the volumes devoted to intervention procedures. Over these years, however, a number of authors have offered a general set of principles for implementing generalization of changes achieved in the group (Goldstein, Heller, and Sechrest, 1966; Goldstein and Kanfer,

1979; Stokes and Baer, 1977; Walker and Buckley, 1972). A few research projects with individual treatment programs have tested some of these principles as well (Stokes, Baer, and Jackson, 1974; Walker and Buckley, 1972; Walker, Hops, and Johnson, 1975).

These principles pertain to actions by the group leader to increase the probability of generalization. These include those actions (1) that take place within the group setting and (2) that take place primarily in the child's natural environment or after the group has terminated.

Leader Actions Within the Group Setting

Transferring changes from the group setting to the natural environment begins with agendas that incorporate the following principles: increasing members' responsibility for their own treatment; providing multiple and varied situations for members to practice with; simulating the real world in the training context; preparing for the unexpected, for a hostile environment, and for potential setbacks; overtraining members in the desired target behavior and cognitions; training in conceptualizing specific experiences and in mediating generalization; and directly instructing members in practicing generalization. Many of these principles overlap and some incorporate subprinciples. Each principle is discussed in more detail below.

Increasing Member Responsibility. The transfer of group leadership behaviors and intervention skills from the group leader to the members increases member responsibility. The group leader begins to train and delegate treatment planning activities, modeling, feedback, problem solving, discussion leading, and decision making as early as possible in the treatment process—increasing members' responsibilities at each successive session. Underlying this principle is the belief that as members become increasingly responsible for leading and planning group sessions they will more readily conceptualize the steps necessary for change and will be more able to apply them independent of the group leader and the treatment setting. The process of delegating control is linked to the process of training the members in these group functions: the group leader is highly directive in early sessions and the members progressively more self-directing in later sessions.

This principle was well illustrated in the example at the beginning of this chapter. The members initially were given responsibility for selecting games played during breaks. Later they served as discussion leaders of the group for short periods with and later without the help of cue cards. As the group continued to meet, the members made decisions regarding rewards and points and the content of homework assignments; eventually they met on their own outside of the group. In anticipation of termination, most of the members had joined nontherapeutic groups that would continue after the group had terminated.

If one assumes that group leadership functions are behaviors, just like any other, then they can be taught through the modeling sequence, problem solving, or the cognitive change sequence. The specific components of leadership skills, such as keeping people on task and involving everyone in the discussion, are modeled, rehearsed, and corrected through feedback and further practice. The group leader demonstrates or models leadership skills from the first meeting on. To make sure that the members have observed the behavior, they are asked to write down specifically what the group leader did to make the group work; these observations are then discussed. Soon thereafter, the members are provided with the opportunity to lead the group for five to ten minutes. They are either coached by the group leader in their role as group discussion leader or they are provided with a cue card with tips about the leader's role. Later both the cue card and the coaching are faded. After each member leads the group, the group leader requests the members to provide both group reinforcement and constructive feedback to the individual member.

Cue cards have been especially helpful with elementary and middle school children. A commonly used cue card for reviewing homework gives the following pointers.

Ask member to show his homework card to group.
Ask member to tell what he did.

Praise him if he did even a part of the assignment.

Ask others in group what they thought he did well.

Ask others in group what they might have done differently.

If group discussion was helpful, let members know.

Go on to next member.

Good luck!

After several sessions in which all members rotate as discussion leader of the homework assignment review, with the help of the cue card, each member is asked to direct the assignment review without the cue card. If assistance is needed, the member can peek at the card. Eventually, the cue card is no longer needed as the "routine" of assignment review becomes common knowledge.

Discussion leading, though important, is not the only leadership activity in which group members are trained and for which they assume responsibility. As was pointed out earlier, members are trained in the skills required to plan their own group program, to help other members to design their own assignments, to deliver reinforcement to each other, to model appropriate behaviors to each other, to provide information for each other (about such resources as special school programs and community resources), and so forth. Once these and other leadership skills are learned, the group leader creates opportunities for and encourages the members to carry out these behaviors themselves. Successful performance of leadership behaviors is initially followed by verbal reinforcement.

Using Multiple and Varied Examples. To prepare the child to handle the unpredictable problem situations that may occur in the real world, numerous, varied, and unpredictable examples eventually must be dealt with. Classical and operant conditioning research has repeatedly demonstrated that cues, regularly correlated with reinforcement, eventually gain control over the associated behaviors. Variation tends to expand the behavior-reinforcing cues (Goldstein, Heller, and Sechrest, 1966). This, in turn, increases the likelihood that a variety of cues, rather than just those associated with the group and the group leader, will elicit the desired behaviors.

It is therefore more likely that when a variety of cues elicits a behavior, it will generalize to the natural environment and be maintained over time. Since the natural environment is often very unpredictable, it becomes necessary to structure increased unpredictability of practice situations in the group setting as well. Additionally, it is important that the examples used in group sessions vary in a manner similar to the outside world to ensure that the members are prepared for the range of situations likely to arise.

Problem situations in the real world vary a great deal. Significant others change, the content of the interactions change, and the environments in which these situations take place change. For this reason, the group leader must encourage such variation to occur in group exemplars also.

Situations used in the group vary in a number of ways. In early sessions group leaders usually act as significant others in most roleplays. As members' roleplaying skill increases, they are increasingly included in the modeling roleplays. In some cases nongroup members are invited to a session just to perform the significant others' roles in the roleplays. These same nonmembers may also be employed to discuss problematic situations from another perspective. Not only roleplaying and discussion, but board games, dramatics, and group exercises may recreate common problem situations that members might deal with.

Content of problem situations should also vary. The group leader may build in variety of content in a number of ways. One way is to generate real-life situations through situational analyses, as described in Chapter Three. Situational analysis generates a pool of relevant and difficult situations likely to arise in a child's life. Other situations may be obtained from the children's weekly diaries or logs. These situations can also be used as the theme of a group exercise or as the content of group roleplays, problem-solving sessions, or cards in a board game.

Variation of the practice problem situations should simulate as nearly as possible the real world if it is not possible to actually go out into the real world. Transferring from the sterile office to the classroom is a far greater leap than transferring from the classroom (after school) to the classroom during the day, when most of the problems occur.

To prepare for uncertainty, members may be asked to describe a relevant surprise situation to be roleplayed or problem solved by another member. This is usually done after the group members have become familiar with each other's difficulties. These situations are then performed or dealt with spontaneously, with little prior planning time available, unlike previous situations, when members have had several days to think about their likely response.

When varying the content of exemplar problem situations, the group leader may also vary the environment in which the roleplays, discussions, exercises, or games occur. This can be done by adding other group members and props to the roleplays in order to better simulate realistic environments. Moreover, roleplays need not be confined to the room where the group meets. The group might meet in different environments to emphasize particular variations, such as in the cafeteria, the gym, a nearby restaurant, or the middle of a department store. Later in this chapter we will discuss conducting group sessions in the natural environment in greater detail.

Including Significant Others in Group Sessions. Essentially, including significant others in group sessions is an extension of using varied examples. Props and settings may be changed to increase the similarity between group and environment. The real-life actors may be included in the group process to increase its similarity to the outside world. Friends from the neighborhood, parents and siblings, or teachers and classmates may be included in group meetings from time to time.

In work with schools and families we have found this principle especially useful as a guide to group planning. With a group of adolescents working on communication with their parents, we first spent a number of sessions identifying problem situations and working on new overt and covert responses. After the members felt confident in their abilities to use new skills, parents were contacted by the group leader. The parents were invited to two specially arranged group meetings. During the first meeting, the leader met with the parents to orient them to the purposes and procedures of the group. With the prior approval of group members, a videotape of part of a group meeting was also shown to the parents.

The adolescents and their parents attended the second special meeting together. During this session specific problem situations were discussed and the members attempted to work out mutually acceptable solutions with their parents. At the end of this meeting, specific behavioral assignments were given to the parent-child dyads to be completed before the next regular group meeting.

Including parents in group sessions not only helps to simulate the real world; hopefully, it also develops the beginnings of a natural support system that reinforces the use of new behaviors by the members. This model has been taken one step further by creating parallel parent and child groups with the two memberships merging during the last several group meetings. This principle can be extended one step further by treating in the natural environment.

Treating in the Natural Environment. It is far easier to transfer learning from the therapeutic setting to the real world if the treatment actually occurs in the real world. For practical reasons, this is not always possible. In some rare cases the group goes to a member's home, or observes members' classrooms and treats their fellow classmates. Treatment may also be incorporated into the ongoing school program (see Hepler and Rose, 1986). Often however, a compromise can be developed. Certainly the use of homework, at least sometimes, extends the program into the real world. Preparation for the most part remains in the group.

Occasionally sessions are held in restaurants, classrooms, gymnasiums, storefronts, the back of station wagons, in a park, or at a teenage hangout. Sometimes the leader is present only for a part of the meeting or, if for the entire meeting, only as a consultant. This provides practice for the members in handling their own problems when the group has terminated. As a group nears the end of its treatment, more variations in natural-environment settings are encouraged.

Of course, group work in these settings with limited supervision is not without problems: the unsupervised meeting may result in the development of antitherapeutic norms; group members may not have the leadership skills to be helpful to one another; and many diversions in the outside world may keep the members off task. Nevertheless, these conditions are similar to those encountered by members after treatment has terminated. If adequately prepared, children may be able to make better use of these informal sources of help and to avoid those who would interrupt their progress.

Preparing for Setbacks. Another possible problem variation is the situation in which a setback takes place. For example, a child who learned to use the telephone successfully, both with his peers and adults, one day found that he could do neither. He dropped out of the group claiming he was even too "weird" for the treatment group. To prevent such dramatic responses to setbacks, they become one of the regular topics of group discussion. Often older children are brought in to discuss setbacks they had experienced and how they handled them. Case studies in which a child has had a setback are also presented, and the group brainstorms what they might do about it. In this way preparation for setbacks becomes a natural part of treatment, with all children developing a set of strategies they might employ in the event of a setback.

In summary, problem situations in the beginning are quite brief and simple to handle, as a means of ensuring early success. As part of the generalization process, they are extended in length, in degree of difficulty for the person with the problem, in the number of interacting persons, and in the level of complication. The way situations are dealt with are varied and may include roleplaying (both overt and covert), systematic problem solving, games, group exercises, and homework. Furthermore, roleplays, exercises, and other forms of member interaction are carried out in a variety of different locations including the natural environment. Performing these activities under varied conditions increases the frequency of trying out and finding new solutions, both by the children's own experience and by their observation of others. This frequency of varied trials

in practicing solutions may result in overtraining, the next principle of generalization.

Overtraining in Target Behaviors. The old proverb "practice makes perfect" is the historical predecessor to overtraining
members in target behaviors and conditions. Olympic athletes,
concert musicians, and skilled orators all repeatedly practice
their particular exertise in advance of an important event. The
more they practice the skill the easier it becomes to perform
and the more likely they are to perform it without mistakes.
In the same sense, the more one practices a new cognitive or
overt behavioral response to a problem situation the more likely
that one will be able to use it effectively in the "real event."
Thus, overlearning a new skill will, in most instances, increase
both its probability of use and the degree to which it is applied
effectively.

As previously described, when new skills are taught they
are rehearsed repeatedly in order to improve skill performance.
Play situations are created so that the same situations will be
practiced during a game. In addition, behavioral assignments are
given in order to give the members initial practice in the natural
environment. Reports about the success or failure of an assignment will often lead to further practice in group sessions.

The implication of this principle is that it is usually more
effective to focus on a few important cognitions or overt skills
than to attempt to treat too many problem situations, especially if only a limited time (for example, six to eight hourly sessions) is available.

Conceptualizing the Specific Experiences. It is not possible to train children in every conceivable problem situation that
may occur. At some point they will have to make a leap from
the specifics that they have learned to the application of a general principle. For example, a child may have learned that when
teased by a brother, if ignored, the teasing will eventually stop;
when teased by a neighbor, the child may observe, often with
the group's help, that it can be ignored with the same result.
After the child has learned to handle several such concrete situations, the group leader will help the child to conceptualize
the general principles that might be applied to a novel situation;

for example, that teasing by others, when unpleasant, can usually be ignored and it will stop. How this generalization might be handled in a group is demonstrated in the following example.

Group leader: Well, Juanita, could you summarize for the group the situations you have worked on so far?

Juanita: (after a moment) My mom got real mad at me and I didn't have the foggiest idea why. I started to get mad and then I remembered to tell myself to take it easy and ask. So I asked my mom what I did wrong instead of screaming back at her like I usually do. That seemed to help. And a couple of times when I disagreed with kids at school, I relaxed and just told them in a quiet voice that I disagree. Were they surprised! There was something like that with the teacher, too. I started to yell but I saw Meg and then I asked the teacher exactly what I did wrong.

Group leader: Does anybody see any pattern that Juanita has learned? (pause) Yeah, Dale?

Dale: Yeah, well Juanita yells a lot—I mean used to yell a lot. And that got everybody mad. Now she tells herself to cool it when she gets upset and just tells people how she feels or asks them what's wrong in a quiet voice. Well, most of the time. (group members laugh)

Group leader: Does that sound right, Juanita?

Juanita: I'll say! I guess I still need to remember to tell myself to stay calm and talk softly, and then really talk softly.

Group leader: I guess that's Juanita's general principle. I wonder what the rest of you see as your general pattern? First, review the specific situation you learned to handle.

Mediating Generalization. The group leader may train the members to use self-instruction to mediate performance of the target behavior in the real world. In the above example, whenever anyone became angry with Juanita or she began to become angry with them, she instructed herself to relax and remain calm and to ask why the other person was so angry. (Self-instructional training is detailed in Chapter Eight.) One can also train clients to take cues into the real world in order to remember the content of the desired behavior and/or the conditions under which it should occur.

Clients have also used acronyms to remind themselves to apply self-instructions in the real world, such as stopping to think before acting. One client of ours invented the acronym "STOTH," which he wrote on his hand to cue him to "STOp and THink" before acting.

Stokes and Baer (1977) recommend that clients be instructed to try out generalized behaviors in the real world and when they provide evidence that they have succeeded, they should be reinforced. For example, in the group the children are taught to problem solve around a number of specific situations, such as, how to get a job, how to deal with a teacher who makes unfair requests, and how to handle the sexual hassling of boy classmates. Solutions to these problems go beyond but may include simple interactive responses. The group members are instructed to use the principles of systematic problem solving learned in the group on the next problem that occurs in the real world and report the results back to the group. Knowledge of the general principles mediates performance of the generalized behaviors in an unforeseen situation. In this way, the children can be prepared for novel as well as familiar problem situations.

In all of the above principles, the group leader is guided to work directly with the members within the group setting to facilitate generalization of change. Often, however, the leader must go outside of the physical and time boundaries of the group, as detailed below.

Leader Activities Beyond the Group Boundaries

It was noted in the first chapter that in the multimethod group approach, one of the methods of change is the extra-group method. What the group leader does outside of group sessions to facilitate desired changes has not yet been discussed. Effective generalization, however, can occur only with difficulty unless the group leader is intimately aware of events occurring in the natural environment. The leader may even become involved in environmental change, if necessary, for the success of the group intervention.

If parents and teachers are not involved in the process, if children associate after group sessions with delinquent peers, if relatives and friends pressure and reinforce children for anti-therapeutic behaviors or for no behavior at all, the effect of a one-hour-a-week session is mostly mitigated. Although the external environment cannot be controlled, the group leader can contribute to establishing a protherapeutic environment or can help the child to establish that environment. To increase naturally occurring incentives and to create protected situations for the members to practice newly learned behaviors, the group leader will work with parents, teachers, classmates, and others who interact with the children. To maintain changes after the group has terminated, the group leader will set up booster sessions (monthly or semiannual sessions for reviewing achievements). The leader will also encourage members to become active in maintenance groups or other groups in which reinforcement for newly learned behavior is likely to continue, but with less frequent reinforcements. Let us examine some strategies of working with parents and teachers.

Working with Parents and Teachers. Parents and teachers are two of the major sources of reinforcement and are excellent resources for structuring situations that are conducive to the performance of target behaviors. When we work with parents individually, we can ask permission for their children to be in the group. This often leads to questions about problems their children are having. In this way, opportunities are created for establishing a joint effort on behalf of the children. In addition, some group leaders have continued the contact, usually at the request of the parents, by telephone throughout the treatment period. Another commonly used procedure is parallel parent groups. At the very least, one parent group meeting permits parent training in appropriate reinforcement and monitoring procedures for behaviors worked on in the group. Additional meetings provide greater support for the parents and ongoing information about the process. Furthermore, parent meetings permit more effective selection of their children's appropriate target behaviors and problem situations.

We have also worked intensively with teachers, individually and in groups, encouraging positive incentives for the children's behavioral and cognitive achievements in the classroom. This may occur with the group leader's participation in inservice training programs or with the introduction of our programs into the schools. When school counselors or school social workers are consulting about other classroom problems, they can also encourage the teachers to reinforce the group members for the targeted behaviors.

It is also important that whatever sequential changes we attempt to generate in the natural environment are supported by regularly occurring incentives in that environment. Parents' and teachers' perceptions of what needs to be done might be another helpful source of what will probably be reinforced at home or at school. Similarly, the peer culture will also indicate what is likely to be reinforced. Furthermore, not all problem situations occur in the classroom or at home. Much occurs on the playground and in other places out of sight of adults. For this reason auxiliary contacts with peers is a step to seriously consider.

Working with Classroom Peers. Even when the targeted behavior also concerns people in the environment, it is often necessary to train, or at least encourage, significant others to reinforce the desired behaviors and ignore the undesirable ones. Furthermore, it would be helpful if the peers who are rejecting clients would begin to accept them. A number of strategies have been employed to achieve this. In several projects, we divided entire classes or grades of children into small groups and gave all children the same program, without identifying targeted individuals (see LeCroy and Rose, 1986; Hepler and Rose, 1986). In the latter study we trained the high-status children in ways of accepting the low-status children into their activities. We also trained the low-status children to involve themselves. Furthermore, we trained all members to reinforce one another and to give and receive criticism appropriately. Too often the entire burden of change is placed on the target child, which reduces the probability of success.

Still another incentive strategy in the child's natural environment is the development of a buddy system, which was discussed previously. In addition to improving assignment completion, the buddy system is useful in developing a new support network in the natural environment—be it school, home, neighborhood, or institution—which is capable of creating incentives for change. Before buddies meet, they are trained in how to give reinforcement for achievements and how to give and receive criticism. It has become common practice to gradually increase the days between group sessions and build in greater reliance on buddies in resolving difficult issues. At their best, buddy systems become self-help networks that function long after the group has terminated. Children are also encouraged to form relationships with people outside the group who can also serve as buddies. They may even be brought to the group, where they are trained and reinforced for their helping behavior.

Working with Community Resource People. One example of increasing external incentives as a means of ensuring success is to meet with the job counselor in advance of the adolescent's interview and to ask the counselor to reinforce the interviewing behaviors that the group member manifests. Group leaders have also contacted the leaders of YMCA, YWCA, or school groups to pave the way for members interested in joining, when the children did not yet have sufficient faith in their own skills.

Another area of extra-group contacts involves contacting social service agency personnel when it is necessary to address needs that are not behavioral or cognitive. In one group a child was thought to be abused. The problem was referred to the local social service agency. In another group a child seemed undernourished and her clothes were in disrepair. Her single mother was contacted and introduced to a local church organization that offered to help her while she was paying off some bills. The group leader's role sometimes extends to that of client advocate and service broker (Toseland and Rivas, 1984). Though not detailed in this book, this area is important. In school and agency practice, these functions may often be called on.

Training Beyond Termination. If a group lasts eight hourly sessions and ends abruptly, it is unlikely that changes will be maintained after treatment has terminated. Two sources of support for group members can be developed in order to maintain what the children have learned in the group. One strategy for increasing the likelihood that members will maintain what they have learned in the group is the use of occasional supplemental sessions, often referred to as *booster sessions.* These sessions create an opportunity for reviewing learned behaviors, updating the group on successes and failures, and keeping members accountable for changes or lack of them. New problems may be dealt with as well. A booster session is often held two months after group termination and again four to six months later. Occasional phone calls may replace the booster session. Although research on booster sessions with adults has not been encouraging (Ashby and Wilson, 1977, with obese women, and Maletzky, 1977), a children's study by Kazdin (1982) demonstrated the efficacy of booster sessions in maintaining and even increasing gains from the group. Thus, booster sessions, as a strategy for promoting member-mediated transfer or change, are finding modest but growing support in the research literature. We shall have to wait for future studies with children and adolescents to shed more light upon their impact among this population.

Another variation of the booster session is the use of existing groups that do not have a therapeutic focus. For example, overweight teenage members decided at termination to join Weight Watchers. The first few sessions of Weight Watchers and the last few of the treatment group overlapped so that the adolescents could deal with the new philosophy and any other problems that membership in the new organization entailed. Similarly, we have encouraged children in social-skills groups to join Girl Scouts, Boy Scouts, 4-H clubs, musical groups, school interest groups (dramatic clubs in particular), and so forth. In fact, few children in any of our intensive treatment groups terminated treatment prior to joining some type of nontherapeutic group.

Summary

In this chapter we have reviewed the major principles that guide group planning of generalization. These principles are central to the design of group interventions and are omnipresent in all phases of the group history. Group success is measured by its members' success in altering their behavior and effectively handling problem situations in the natural environment. It is therefore likely that careful planning to incorporate most of these principles will increase the likelihood of maintaining behavioral changes achieved in the group.

In the next and final chapter we present a detailed excerpt from a group session that demonstrates many of the principles espoused throughout this book. For a systematic review of these principles the reader may return to Chapter One, which provides an overview of the major issues and principles that practitioners of a multimethod group approach must consider.

Chapter Thirteen

Applying the Multimethod Approach: A Case Example

Most of the examples in this book have been brief excerpts to demonstrate one or two principles at a time. To provide the reader with a picture of a complete session and to demonstrate many of the concepts discussed in the previous chapters, the following excerpts are presented. They were taken from the fourth of fourteen weekly hour-long meetings of the Friends, six boys and girls, aged eleven and twelve. These excerpts represent most of an entire meeting. The group members have just told in detail what their homework was and what they accomplished.

Paul (group leader):   Well it's great. You all seem to have done your homework and got your cards signed. Who'll summarize what we achieved as a group this week? Okay, Joelle, why don't you give it a try?

Joelle: To begin with, I invited a friend over to play. Dinah was in only one fight this week, which is better than last week. Jeff described how he lost at checkers and told his brothers, "Thanks for a good game." Toby asked his teacher (Whispering to Paul, "What was it again? Oh, yeah!") . . . if there was anything he could do to show he could listen really well. That's all I remember.

Paul: Well, Ronnie you seem to be signaling that you want a turn.

Ronnie: I said I went to the "Y" and asked about groups I could join next semester, and then I asked the man behind the counter a whole lot of questions about the gymnastic group. And Bobbie didn't get angry when his mom asked him to clean his room. He said, "Sure, Mom," and his mother wrote he did a good job.

Paul: That seems to be everybody. Let's give ourselves a big hurrah. (claps hands)

Group: (cheers loudly and claps hands)

Dinah: And you brought the stickers?

Paul: So I did. Let me give 'em out. (Children laughingly put stickers on arms and foreheads.) Now put the points on the thermometer. I think we're almost to the top. (Members put points on large thermometer for completing assignment.) What's going to happen when we reach the top?

Bobby, Joelle: (at same time) We're going to the zoo!

Paul: What's next on the program?

Toby: It's diary time.

Paul: Okay, then, who's going to help the others to review their diaries?

Joelle: It's my turn, I only done it once.

Paul: Okay, Joelle, and as is my custom, I'll sit behind you in case you need me. And of course, you get the leader's card with the helpful hints. Who wants to be first?

Joelle: Ronnie, what did you write in your diary?

Ronnie: I was visiting my aunt, the old one I told you about last week with the cat, and the one I was afraid to talk to. She asked me about the club.

Joelle: What did you say?

Ronnie: I sort of muttered, "Okay." I really wanted to answer her but I still couldn't say nothin'.

Joelle: That's a good diary example. (pauses)

Paul: (whispering) We can work on it later, on to the next.

Joelle: And, if you like, we can work on it later and see if we can help you to figure out what to do. Okay, who's next?

(Joelle goes around the room asking each person for diary reports that describe stressful situations. The previous two weeks had been spent training the members on the criteria for selection of a good situation.)

Joelle: Okay, everyone except Dinah brought in something from their diary. So that gives us twenty-five points. I'll just put that on the thermometer.

Paul: Joelle, thank you for doing my job. What do you all think she did well?

Toby: She kept us on track. And she didn't have to look at the cue card much.

Dinah: She wasn't mean when I said I didn't do a diary.

Paul: Anything else?

Jeff: She spoke clear. I could understand her.

Bobby: She looked at us when she talked.

Paul: Those are all important things. Would you have done anything differently?

Joelle: I coulda told 'em to shut up, when Dinah was talking to Toby.

Paul: That's something to consider.

Ronnie: Yeah, and she could of talked a little louder. I couldn't always hear 'er.

Paul: That's another possibility. I think someone else mentioned that in the roleplay last week. (pause) Okay, Joelle, you did a great job and got a couple of good tips for next time. Okay, what's next?

Bobby/Jeff: Roleplay time.

Paul: How about a new leader for the roleplays?

Bobby: How about me?

Paul: Okay, Bobby, you're it. And I'll be your right-hand man. Here's a card to help you remember the order.

Bobby: Okay, Ronnie, you went first before. You want to be the first again?

Ronnie: Oh sure. You remember, I have trouble talking to grown-ups even when they're nice. Just last week I told you about how I couldn't talk to my aunt. (reviews situation)

Paul: (whispering) Ask about the "tough point." (This is the point at which the client finds the situation difficult to handle.)

Bobby: What was "the tough point"?

Ronnie: When my aunt asked me to tell her about the club.

Bobby: (looking at leader) I forgot what else I can ask.

Paul: (whispering) "What were you thinking? Feeling?"

Bobby: (assertively) Ronnie, what were you thinking at that moment? How did you feel?

Ronnie: Well, I thought I might say something wrong, or funny or talk like a little kid, and then I'd be embarrassed. And I felt scared, real scared, cause she seems like a witch—especially with that cat. But she really is a nice old lady, but she's real strict.

Bobby: (pause, looks at card) Oh yeah, you guys got questions?

Dinah: What did you want to do in that situation?

Ronnie: I wanted to talk to her, and to tell her that it's a great group and tell her about all the neat things we do here.

Bobby: That sounds pretty good. (looking at card) Oh yeah, listen, anybody got any ideas what he could say to himself to keep from being so scared and getting himself not to worry about making a mistake?

Dinah: He could say to himself, "She may look like a witch, but she ain't one. She's just a nice old aunt" and "everybody makes mistakes."

Toby: He could also take a deep breath and let it out slowly, and then relax like we learned last week, and then maybe think what you said.

Jeff: You can think, "What's the worst that can happen? Nothing. She might laugh, that's all, since she ain't really a witch and laughin' never hurt nobody."

Bobby: You could make the worst mistakes here you can think of and let us laugh at you like in the game we played last week. We sure have a lot of ideas. Any more? (pause) Okay guys, what's next?

Joelle: Someone show him how to do it.

Bobby: How about you, Jeff?

Paul: Slow down just a bit, let Ronnie decide which of the ideas he likes best.

Ronnie: Oh, I like reminding myself to relax and then saying she really does mean well. Everybody makes mistakes. Besides, the worst that will happen is she might laugh.

Bobby: Okay, and then what would you say aloud?

Ronnie: Oh, I'd tell her that this is a great group. We roleplay hard things to do. We play games and we help each other.

Bobby: Does that sound pretty good?

Others: That sounds good.

Bobby: I guess you don't need no more help. (Whispers to leader, "Okay?" Leader nods yes.) Who will be the model? How about you, Jeff? You had a good suggestion.

Jeff: Okay, let me think a minute.

(Leader reviews suggestions decided on by Ronnie, then Jeff goes through the entire process of imagining he was in the situation, talking to himself, then talking aloud.)

Bobby: Okay, Ronnie, are you satisfied with what he did and said?

Ronnie: (nods yes) Yeah, that was great.

Bobby: Are you ready to try it out?

Ronnie: I guess I am ready as I'll ever be (turns to leader) but do I gotta?

Paul: No, of course not. Only if you think it will be useful to you and it won't be too embarrassing.

Group members: C'mon, Ronnie. Try it, Ronnie.

Paul: Not if he doesn't feel ready.

Ronnie: Okay, I'll try it. I always get a little scared when I role-play.

Paul: Nothing wrong with that and I'll be behind you and give you help if you need it.

Ronnie: (practices the situation with little difficulty)

Bobby: Hey, that was great. (looks at cue card) Okay, what did he do good? What do you guys like?

Joelle: He didn't sound scared at all.

Dinah: He sure looked relaxed.

Toby: He spoke up loud and clear.

(pause)

Bobby: He seemed to follow our instructions pretty well, I thought. Okay, what would you guys do differently? (turns attention to Joelle, who is talking to Dinah) Hey, Joelle, when you were leader, I paid attention; so knock it off. Okay, Ronnie, what would you do differently?

Ronnie: I guess it was okay.

Paul: Guess?

Ronnie: No, I really liked it. It felt right.

Bobby: Since no one else has comments, let's do it one more time. This time Ronnie will whisper the thinking part and then say aloud what he wants to say to his aunt. (Ronnie repeats the statement whispering, and then makes the final statement to his aunt.)

Bobby: What's next, guys (looks at Dinah and Joelle) and girls?

Paul: (nods and smiles approval)

Joelle: He says it completely to himself, the thinking part. Is that right?

Paul: Right. Okay, Ronnie.

(Ronnie repeats the roleplay, silently going through the part he is supposed to think and then he makes the final verbal statement aloud to his "aunt.")

Bobby: How did he do?

Joelle: Even better than the first time.

Paul: Anything more specific?

Dinah: He really looked like he was relaxed. I wish I could do it like that.

(Evaluation continues, generally positive.)

Paul: Okay, how did Bobby do as leader? What did he do that you thought was good?

Ronnie: I like the way when Toby was talking, he told him to keep quiet. Just like you do it sometimes, Paul, only he was a little meaner.

(Others agree. Evaluation continues for a few minutes.)

Paul: Okay, who else has a situation you would like to present to the group? (pauses, sees Toby trying to get his attention) Okay, Toby, I guess you're next. And Dinah, you said last week you'd like to be a discussion leader this week. How about now?

At this point the process is repeated. At this session, a total of four children were able to present situations that were dealt with. Only Ronnie did not bring a situation. Dinah brought one in which she was satisfied with her response. The group leader merely reinforced her for her success.

Paul: You guys have really worked hard. One more job before game time. Let's break up into pairs to plan our homework for next week. Most of you have a few notes you jotted down to remind you what you thought you could do this week. What are some of the things you have to remember for a good assignment?

Bobby: Well, you have to be pacific, I mean specific.

Group: (laughter)

Paul: Anything else?

Dinah: It's best if you can try out something you roleplayed in the group.

Toby: And it's a situation that's likely to occur during the week.

Paul: You have those ideas down pat. Okay, now into groups. I'll float around and see if I can help any.

The assignments are then reported back to the larger group, adjusted where necessary, and written down.

Paul: That was a great crop of assignments. You didn't need me at all. I'll bet you all will be able to do them even though they are really tough. I think each one of you has a real challenge. And now . . . and NOWWWW, it's . . . ?

Everyone: It's game time. (Laughter)

Paul: I made the paper money.

Jeff: Me and Ronnie made the board.

Bobby: And I, the king, made roleplay cards with the help of Joelle, my assistant.

Joelle: Assistant, my eyeball. I did most of it because he was sick.

Bobby: Only kidding. But I did bring the dice, so let's start. I'll roll 'em first. Oh boy, pick a roleplay card.

The members play the board game for five minutes, after which they have a snack of milk and cookies. Then Paul asks them to fill out the evaluation forms. After these are filled in, he walks back with them to their respective classrooms.

Comments

The above case illustrates many of the principles and procedures discussed throughout this book. In the beginning we observed the group leader monitoring the homework of all the children from the previous week. One item of homework was to come up with a problematic situation. The leader used both individual and group contingencies to reinforce the members for their completion of assignments. He also distributed ample verbal reinforcement throughout the rest of the meeting. He summarized or encouraged the group to summarize. He set limits when they got off the task.

It should also be noted that the group leader continued to delegate leadership functions to the group members. He had two of the members summarize the assignments. Since the members were inexperienced in leading the group, he both provided them with a cue card and prompted them himself.

The group began to work on one problem with systematic problem solving. After the group brainstormed solutions, the given member evaluated and selected what he wanted to do. The group prepared him to carry out the assignment through modeling, behavioral and covert rehearsal, and group feedback. Following the practice the member developed an assignment to carry out during the week.

The session ended with a game that the group members had earned. Thus, even in this brief example, we see the intermixture of operant strategies, systematic problem solving, social-skill training, cognitive restructuring, sociorecreational activities, and group strategies.

Even as early as the fourth session, the group leader was already concerned with generalization of change. Homework, delegation of responsibilities, members' planning for homework, and working more or less unsupervised in pairs are all the first steps in the preparation for generalization process.

Although we have attempted to be as thorough as possible in presenting the multimethod approach for the treatment of children in groups, no book such as this is ever truly complete. Only the readers can fill the necessary gaps through selected trips into the reference list and through their own experience. If readers require an overview of the entire process, they are advised to return to Chapter One where the principles and procedures are outlined in summary fashion. It is fitting that one return to the beginning, because the process of group treatment is a cycle in which teaching and learning are repeated in diverse ways to reach a set of unique and common goals.

References

Achenbach, R. M. "The Child Behavior Profile: I. Boys Aged 6 through 11." *Journal of Consulting and Clinical Psychology,* 1978, *46,* 478–488.

Alberti, R. E., and Emmons, M. L. *Stand Up, Speak Out, Talk Back!* New York: Pocket Books, 1975.

Alden, S. E., Pettigrew, L. E., and Skiba, E. A. "The Effect of Individual-Contingent Group Reinforcement on Popularity." *Child Development,* 1970, *41,* 1191–1196.

Archable, C. "Social Problem-Solving with Children." Unpublished master's thesis, University of Maryland, 1977.

Argyle, M. "Methods of Social Skills Training." In M. Argyle (ed.), *Social Skills and Health.* New York: Methuen, 1981.

Aronson, E. "The Jigsaw Route to Learning and Liking." *Psychology Today,* Feb. 1975, pp. 43–50.

Ashby, W. A., and Wilson, G. T. "Behavior Therapy for Obesity: Booster Sessions and Long-Term Maintenance of Weight Loss." *Behaviour Research and Therapy,* 1977, *15,* 451–463.

Asher, S. R., Oden, S. L., and Gottman, J. M. "Children's Friendships in School Settings." In L. G. Katz (ed.), *Current Topics in Early Childhood Education.* Vol. 1. Norwood, N.J.: Albex, 1976.

Ausubel, D. P. *The Psychology of Meaningful Verbal Learning.* New York: Grune & Stratton, 1963.

Ayllon, T., and Azrin, N. H. *The Token Economy: A Motivational System for Therapy and Rehabilitation.* East Norwalk, Conn.: Appleton-Century-Crofts, 1968.

Azrin, N. H., Flores, T., and Kaplan, S. J. "Job-Finding Club: A Group-Assisted Program for Obtaining Employment." *Behaviour Research and Therapy,* 1975, *13,* 17–27.

Bandura, A. *Principles of Behavior Modification.* New York: Holt, Rinehart & Winston, 1969.

Bandura, A. "Psychotherapy Based on Modeling Principles." In A. E. Bergin and S. L. Garfield (eds.), *Handbook of Psychotherapy and Behavior Change.* New York: Wiley, 1971.

Bandura, A. "Generalizing Change Through Participant Modeling with Self-Directed Mastery." *Behaviour Research and Therapy,* 1975, *13,* 141-152.

Bandura, A. "Self-Efficacy: Toward a Unifying Theory of Behavioral Change." *Psychological Review,* 1977a, *84,* 191-215.

Bandura, A. *Social Learning Theory.* Englewood Cliffs, N.J.: Prentice-Hall, 1977b.

Bandura, A., Blanchard, E. B., and Ritter, R. "The Relative Efficacy of Desensitization and Modeling Approaches for Inducing Behavioral, Affective, and Attitudinal Changes." *Journal of Personality and Social Psychology,* 1969, *13,* 173-199.

Barlow, D. H., and Hersen, M. *Single-Case Experimental Designs: Strategies for Studying Behavior Change.* Elmsford, N.Y.: Pergamon Press, 1982.

Barrios, B. A., and Shigetomi, C. C. "Coping-Skills Training for the Management of Anxiety: A Critical Review." *Behavioral Therapy,* 1979, *10,* 491-522.

Barton, E. J., and Osborne, J. G. "The Development of Classroom Sharing by a Teacher Using Positive Practice." *Behavior Modification,* 1978, *2* (2), 231-250.

Beck, A. T. *Cognitive Therapy and Emotional Disorders.* New York: International Universities Press, 1976.

Beck, A. T., Mendelson, M., Mock, J., and Erbaugh, J. "An Inventory for Measuring Depression." *Archives of General Psychiatry,* 1961, *4,* 561-571.

Beck, A. T., Rush, A. J., Shaw, B. F., and Emery, G. *Cognitive Therapy of Depression: A Treatment Manual.* New York: Guilford Press, 1979.

Becker, G. M., and McClintock, C. G. "Value: Behavioral Decision Theory." *Annual Review of Psychology,* 1967, *18,* 239-286.

Bednar, R. L., and Kaul, T. J. "Experiential Group Research: Current Perspectives." In S. Garfield and A. Bergin (eds.),

Handbook of Psychotherapy and Behavior Change. (2nd ed.) New York: Wiley, 1978.

Bellack, A. S., and Hersen, M. *Research and Practice in Social Skills Training.* New York: Plenum, 1979.

Bernstein, D. A., and Borkovec, T. D. *Progressive Relaxation Training: A Manual for the Helping Professions.* Champaign, Ill.: Research Press, 1973.

Bertcher, H. J., and Maple, F. F. *Group Composition: An Instructional Program.* Ann Arbor: University of Michigan School of Social Work, 1971. (Mimeographed.)

Biddle, B. J., and Thomas, E. J. *Role Theory: Concepts and Research.* New York: Wiley, 1966.

Bion, W. P. *Experiences in Groups.* New York: Basic Books, 1959.

Bloom, M., and Fischer, J. *Evaluating Practice: Guidelines for the Accountable Professional.* Englewood Cliffs, N.J.: Prentice-Hall, 1982.

Bootzin, R. "Treatment of Sleep Disorders." Paper presented at the annual meeting of the American Psychological Association, Montreal, Aug. 1973.

Borkovec, T. D., and Sides, J. K. "Critical Procedural Variables Related to the Physiological Effects of Progressive Relaxation: A Review." *Behavior Research Therapy,* 1979, *17,* 119–125.

Bornstein, M., Bellack, A., and Hersen, M. "Social Skills Training for Unassertive Children: A Multiple-Baseline Analysis." *Journal of Applied Behavior Analysis,* 1977, *10,* 183–195.

Boyd, N. L. *Handbook of Recreational Games.* New York: Dover Publications, 1973.

Brierton, D., Rose, S. D., and Flanagan, J. "A Behavioral Approach to Corrections Counseling." *Law in American Society,* 1975, *4,* 10–16.

Brillhart, J. K., and Jochem, L. M. "Effects of Different Patterns on Outcome of Problem-Solving Discussion." *Journal of Applied Psychology,* 1964, *48,* 175–179.

Buchanan, H. T., Blankenbaker, J., and Cotten, D. "Academic and Athletic Ability as Popularity Factors in Elementary School Children." *Research Quarterly,* 1976, *47,* 320–325.

Camp, B. W. "Verbal Mediation in Young Aggressive Boys." *Journal of Abnormal Psychology,* 1977, *86,* 145–153.

Camp, B. W., Bloom, G. E., Herbert, F., and Van Doorninck, W. J. "Think Aloud: A Program for Developing Self-Control in Young Aggressive Boys." *Journal of Abnormal Child Psychology*, 1977, *5*, 157-169.

Campbell, D. T., and Stanley, J. C. *Experimental and Quasi-Experimental Designs for Research*. Skokie, Ill.: Rand McNally, 1963.

Cantor, D. W. "School-Based Groups for Children of Divorce." *Journal of Divorce*, 1977, *1* (2), 183-187.

Cantwell, D. P., Russell, A., Mattison, R., and Will, I. A. "A Comparison of DSM-II and DSM-III in the Diagnosis of Childhood Psychiatric Disorders: I. Agreement with Expected Diagnosis." *Archives of General Psychiatry*, 1979a, *36*, 1208-1213.

Cantwell, D. P., Russell, A., Mattison, R., and Will, I. A. "A Comparison of DSM-II and DSM-III in the Diagnosis of Childhood Psychiatric Disorders: IV. Difficulties in Use, Global Comparison, and Conclusions." *Archives of General Psychiatry*, 1979b, *36*, 1227-1228.

Carkhuff, R. R. *The Art of Helping*. Amherst, Mass.: Human Resource Development Press, 1972.

Carrington, P. *Clinically Standardized Meditation (CSM). Instructor's Manual*. Kendall Park, N.J.: Pace Educational Systems, 1978a.

Carrington, P. *Learning to Meditate: Clinically Standardized Meditation (CSM). Course workbook*. Kendall Park, N.J.: Pace Educational Systems, 1978b.

Carter, D. C., DeTine, S. L., Spero, J., and Benson, F. W. "Peer Acceptance and School-Related Variables in an Integrated Junior High School." *Journal of Educational Psychology*, 1975, *67*, 267-273.

Cartledge, G., and Milburn, J. F. *Teaching Social Skills to Children*. Elmsford, N.Y.: Pergamon Press, 1981.

Cartwright, D., and Zander, A. (eds.). *Group Dynamics: Research and Theory*. New York: Harper & Row, 1968.

Cautela, J. R., and Groden, J. *Relaxation: A Comprehensive Manual for Adults, Children, and Children with Special Needs*. Champaign, Ill.: Research Press, 1978.

Chandler, M. "Egocentrism and Antisocial Behavior: The Assessment and Training of Social Perspective-Taking Skills." *Developmental Psychology,* 1973, *9,* 1-6.

Charlesworth, R., and Hartup, W. W. "Positive Social Reinforcement in the Nursery School Peer Group." *Child Development,* 1967, *38,* 993-1003.

Chennault, M. "Improving the Social Acceptance of Unpopular Educable Mentally Retarded Pupils in Special Classes." *American Journal of Mental Deficiency,* 1967, *72,* 455-458.

Churchman, C. W. *Prediction and Optimal Decision.* Englewood Cliffs, N.J.: Prentice-Hall, 1961.

Cobb, J. A., and Ray, R. S. "Manual for Coding Discrete Behaviors in the School Setting." In G. R. Patterson, J. B. Reid, R. R. Jones, and R. E. Conger (eds.), *A Social Learning Approach to Family Intervention.* Vol. 1. Eugene, Ore.: Castalia, 1975.

Conger, J. C., and Keane, S. P. "Social Skills in Intervention in the Treatment of Isolated or Withdrawn Children." *Psychological Bulletin,* 1981, *90,* 478-495.

Conners, C. K. "Rating Scales for Use in Drug Studies with Children." *Psychopharmacology Bulletin* (Special Issue, *Pharmacotherapy with Children*), 1973, pp. 24-84.

Cook, T. D., and Campbell, D. T. *Quasi-Experimental Design and Analysis Issues for Field Settings.* Skokie, Ill.: Rand McNally, 1979.

Cooke, T. P., and Apolloni, T. "Developing Positive Social-Emotional Behaviors: A Study of Training and Generalization Effects." *Journal of Applied Behavior Analysis,* 1976, *9,* 65-78.

Cormier, W. H., and Cormier, L. S. *Interviewing Strategies for Helpers: Fundamental Skills and Cognitive Behavioral Interventions.* (2nd ed.) Monterey, Calif.: Brooks/Cole, 1985.

Cowen, E. L., and others. "Long-term Follow-up of Early Detected Vulnerable Children." *Journal of Consulting and Clinical Psychology,* 1973, *41,* 438-446.

Cox, R. D., Gunn, W. B., and Cox, M. J. "A Filmed Assessment and Comparison of the Social Skillfulness of Behavior Problem and Non-problem Male Children." Paper presented at the

Association for the Advancement of Behavior Therapy, New York, 1976.

Creer, T. L., and Miklich, D. R. "The Application of a Self-Modeling Procedure to Modify Inappropriate Behavior: A Preliminary Report." *Behaviour Research and Therapy,* 1970, *8,* 91-92.

D'Alelio, W. A., and Murray, E. J. "Cognitive Therapy for Test Anxiety." *Cognitive Therapy and Research,* 1981, *5,* 299-307.

Daley, M. F. "The 'Reinforcement Menu': Finding Effective Reinforcers." In E. J. Mash and L. G. Terdal (eds.), *Behavior Therapy Assessment.* New York: Springer, 1976.

De Lange, J. M., Lanham, S. L., and Barton, J. A. "Social Skills Training for Juvenile Delinquents: Behavioral Skill Training and Cognitive Techniques." In D. Upper and S. M. Ross (eds.), *Behavior Group Therapy.* Champaign, Ill.: Research Press, 1981.

Deutsch, M. "An Experimental Study of the Effects of Cooperation and Competition on Group Process." *Human Relations,* 1949, *2,* 199-231.

Diagnostic and Statistical Manual of Mental Disorders. (3rd ed.) Washington, D.C.: American Psychiatric Association, 1980.

Dowrick, P. W. "Self-Modeling: Rapid Skill Training for Handicapped Children." Paper presented at the Association for the Advancement of Behavior Therapy, Los Angeles, Nov. 1982.

D'Zurilla, T. J., and Goldfried, M. R. "Problem Solving and Behavior Modification." *Journal of Abnormal Psychology,* 1971, *78,* 107-126.

Edleson, J. L. *Group Social Skills Training for Children: An Evaluative Study.* Madison: University of Wisconsin, 1979.

Edleson, J. L. "The Effect of Sex Differences on Sociometric Data Generated by a Roster-rating Scale Instrument." *Journal of Behavioral Assessment,* 1980, *2,* 249-254.

Edleson, J. L., Ordman, A., and Rose, S. D. "Assessing Children's Social Skills: The Development of and Failure to Validate a Behavioral Roleplay Test." *Journal of Social Service Research,* 1983, *6,* 47-61.

Edleson, J. L., and Rose, S. D. "Investigations into the Efficacy of Short-Term Group Social Skills Training for Socially Isolated Children." *Child Behavior Therapy*, 1981, *3*, 1-16.

Edwards, W., Lindman, H., and Phillips, L. D. "Emerging Techniques for Making Decisions." In T. M. Newcomb (ed.), *New Directions in Psychology*. Vol. 2. New York: Holt, Rinehart & Winston, 1965.

Elder, J. P., Edelstein, B. A., and Narick, M. M. "Adolescent Psychiatry Patients: Modifying Aggressive Behavior with Social Skills Training." *Behavior Modification*, 1979, *3*, 161-178.

Ellis, A. *Humanistic Psychotherapy*. New York: McGraw-Hill, 1974.

Everly, G., and Rosenfeld, R. *The Nature and Treatment of the Stress Response: A Practical Guide for Clinicians*. New York: Plenum Scientific and Medical Publications, 1981.

Eyberg, S. M. "Eyberg Child Behavior Inventory." *Journal of Clinical Child Psychology*, 1980, *9*, 29.

Ferster, C. B., and Skinner, B. F. *Schedules of Reinforcement*. East Norwalk, Conn.: Appleton-Century-Crofts, 1957.

Festinger, L. "A Theory of Social Comparison Processes." *Human Relations*, 1954, *7*, 117-140.

Fiedler, F. E. *Leadership*. Morristown, N.J.: General Learning Press, 1971.

Flaxman, J. "Quitting Smoking." In W. E. Craighead, A. E. Kazdin, and M. J. Mahoney (eds.), *Behavior Modification: Principles, Issues and Applications*. Boston: Houghton Mifflin, 1976.

Flowers, J. V. "Behavioral Analysis of Group Therapy and a Model for Behavioral Group Therapy." In D. Upper and S. M. Ross (eds.), *Behavioral Group Therapy*. Champaign, Ill.: Research Press, 1979.

Fluegelman, A. *The New Games Book*. Garden City, N.Y.: Dolphin Books/Doubleday, 1976.

Foster, S. L., and Ritchey, W. L. "Issues in the Assessment of Social Competence in Children." *Journal of Applied Behavior Analysis*, 1979, *12*, 625-638.

Freedman, B. J. "An Analysis of Social-behavioral Skill Deficits in Delinquent and Non-delinquent Adolescent Boys." Unpublished doctoral dissertation, University of Wisconsin, 1974.

Freedman, B. J., and others. "A Social-Behavioral Analysis of Skill Deficits in Delinquent and Nondelinquent Adolescent Boys." *Journal of Consulting and Clinical Psychology,* 1978, *46,* 1448–1462.

Galinsky, M. J., and Schopler, J. H. "Structuring Co-Leadership in Social Work Training." *Social Work with Groups,* Winter 1980, *3* (4), 51–64.

Gambrill, E. D. *Behavior Modification: Handbook of Assessment, Intervention, and Evaluation.* San Francisco: Jossey-Bass, 1977.

Gartner, A., Kohler, M., and Riessman, F. *Children Teach Children.* New York: Harper & Row, 1971.

Garvin, C. D. *Contemporary Group Work.* Englewood Cliffs, N.J.: Prentice-Hall, 1981.

Giannoni, J. *Card Games for Kids.* New York: Golden Press, 1974.

Girl Scouts of the U.S.A. *Games for Girl Scouts.* New York: Girl Scouts of the U.S.A., 1969.

Gittleman, M. "Behavior Rehearsal as a Technique in Child Treatment." *Journal of Child Psychology and Psychiatry,* 1965, *6,* 251–255.

Giuli, C. A., and Hudson, W. W. "Assessing Parent-Child Relationship Disorders in Clinical Practice: The Child's Point of View." *Journal of Social Service Research,* Fall 1977, *1,* 77–92.

Goldfried, M., Decenteceo, E., and Weinberg, L. "Systematic Rational Restructuring as a Self-Control Technique." *Behavior Therapy,* 1974, *5,* 247–254.

Goldfried, M. R., and D'Zurilla, R. J. "A Behavioral Analytic Model for Assessing Competence." In C. D. Spielberger (ed.), *Current Topics in Clinical and Community Psychology.* Vol. 1. New York: Academic Press, 1969.

Goldman, B. L., Domitor, P. J., and Murray, E. J. "Effects of Zen Meditation on Anxiety Reduction and Perceptual Functioning." *Journal of Consulting and Clinical Psychology,* 1979, *47,* 531–536.

Goldstein, A. P., Carr, E. G., Davidson, W. S., II, and Wehr, P. *In Response to Aggression.* Elmsford, N.Y.: Pergamon Press, 1981.

Goldstein, A. P., Heller, K., and Sechrest, L. B. *Psychotherapy and the Psychology of Behavior Change.* New York: Wiley, 1966.

Goldstein, A. P., and Kanfer, F. H. *Maximizing Treatment Gains: Transfer Enhancement in Psychotherapy.* New York: Academic Press, 1979.

Goleman, D. J., and Schwartz, G. E. "Meditation as an Intervention in Stress Reactivity." *Journal of Consulting and Clinical Psychology,* 1976, *44,* 456–466.

Gottman, J. M., and Leiblum, S. P. *How to Do Psychotherapy and How to Evaluate It.* New York: Holt, Rinehart & Winston, 1974.

Gottman, J., Gonso, J., and Rasmussen, B. "Social Interaction, Social Competence, and Friendship in Children." *Child Development,* 1975, *46,* 709–718.

Gottman, J., Gonso, J., and Schuler, P. "Teaching Social Skills to Isolated Children." *Journal of Abnormal Child Psychology,* 1976, *4,* 179–197.

Gronlund, N. E. "Generality of Sociometric Status over Criteria in the Measurement of Social Acceptability." *Elementary School Journal,* 1955, *56,* 173–176.

Groveman, A. M., Richards, C. S., and Caple, R. B. "Literature Review Treatment Manuals" and "Bibliography for Study Skills Counseling and Behavioral Self-Control Approaches to Improving Study Behavior." Journal Supplement Abstract Service, Ms. No. 1128. New York: American Psychological Association, 1975.

Gump, P., and Sutton-Smith, B. "Therapeutic Play Techniques." In P. Gump and B. Sutton-Smith (eds.), *Conflict in the Classroom.* Belmont, Calif.: Wadsworth, 1965.

Hand, I., Lamontagne, Y., and Marks, I. M. "Group Exposure (Flooding) in Vivo for Agoraphobics." *British Journal of Psychiatry,* 1974, *124,* 588–602.

Handbook for Recreation. Washington, D.C.: U.S. Government Printing Office, 1960.

Hansen, J. C., Warner, R. W., and Smith, E. J. *Group Counseling: Theory and Practice.* (2nd ed.) Skokie, Ill.: Rand McNally, 1980.

Hartup, W. W. "Peer Relations and the Growth of Social Competence." In M. W. Kent and I. E. Relf (eds.), *Primary Prevention of Psychopathology.* Vol. 3: *Social Competence in Children.* Hanover, N.H.: University Press of New England, 1979.

Hartup, W. W. "Peer Relations and Family Relations: Two Social Worlds." In M. Rutter (ed.), *Scientific Foundations of Developmental Psychiatry.* London: Heineman Medical, 1980.

Hazel, J. S., Schumaker, J. B., Sherman, J. A., and Sheldon-Wildon, J. *Asset: A Social Skills Program for Adolescents.* Champaign, Ill.: Research Press, 1981.

Heide, J. F., and Borkovec, T. D. "Relaxation-induced Anxiety: Paradoxical Anxiety Enhancement Due to Relaxation Training." *Journal of Consulting and Clinical Psychology,* 1983, *51,* 171-182.

Heitzmann, W. R. *Educational Games and Simulations.* Washington, D.C.: National Education Association, 1974.

Hepler, J., and Rose, S. D. "Social Skills Training in the Classroom: An Experimental Study." Unpublished manuscript, School of Social Work, University of Wisconsin, 1986.

Heppner, P. P. "A Review of the Problem-Solving Literature and Its Relationship to the Counseling Process." *Journal of Counseling Psychology,* 1978, *25,* 366-375.

Hersen, M., and Bellack, A. S. (eds.). *Behavioral Assessment.* (2nd ed.) Elmsford N.Y.: Pergamon Press, 1981.

Hillenberg, J. B., and Collins, F. L., Jr. "A Procedural Analysis and Review of Relaxation Training Research." *Behaviour Research and Therapy,* 1982, *20,* 251-260.

Hoehn-Saric, R., and others. "Systematic Preparation of Patients for Psychotherapy: I. Effects on Therapy Behavior and

Outcome." *Journal of Psychiatric Research,* 1964, *2,* 267–281.

Homme, L., and Tosti, D. *Behavior Technology: Motivation and Contingency Management.* San Rafael, Calif.: Individual Learning Systems, 1965.

Hops, H., Wills, T., Weiss, R., and Patterson, G. R. *Marital Interaction Coding System (MICS).* ASIS/NAPS Document no. 02077. New York: Microfiche Publications, 1972. Also in G. R. Patterson, "Some Procedures for Assessing Changes in Marital Interaction Patterns." *Research Bulletin* (Oregon Research Institute), 1976, *16* (7), 1–30.

Hudson, W. W. *The Clinical Measurement Package.* Homewood, Ill.: Dorsey Press, 1982.

Jacobsen, E. *You Must Relax.* New York: McGraw-Hill, 1978.

Jacobson, E. *Progressive Relaxation.* Chicago: University of Chicago Press, 1929.

Kanfer, F. H., and Phillips, J. S. *Learning Foundations of Behavior Therapy.* New York: Wiley, 1970.

Kazdin, A. E. *Single-Case Research Designs: Methods for Clinical and Applied Settings.* New York: Oxford University Press, 1982.

Keats, D. B. "Survey Schedule of Rewards for Children." *Psychological Reports,* 1974, *35,* 287–293.

Keller, M. F., and Carlson, P. M. "The Use of Symbolic Modeling to Promote Social Skills in Preschool Children with Low Levels of Social Responsiveness." *Child Development,* 1975, *45,* 912–919.

Kelly, G. A. *The Psychology of Personal Constructs.* New York: Norton, 1955.

Kelly, J. A., Wildman, B. G., and Berler, E. S. "Small Group Behavioral Training to Improve the Job Interview Skills Repertoire of Mildly Retarded Adolescents." *Journal of Applied Behavior Analysis,* 1980, *13,* 461–471.

Kendall, P. C. "On the Efficacious Use of Verbal Self-Instructional Procedures with Children." *Cognitive Therapy and Research,* 1977, *1,* 331–341.

Kendall, P. C., and Finch, A. J. "A Cognitive-Behavioral Treatment for Impulse Control: A Case Study." *Journal of Consulting and Clinical Psychology,* 1976, *44,* 852–857.

Kendall, P. C., and Finch, A. J. "A Cognitive-Behavioral Treatment for Impulsivity: A Group Comparison Study." *Journal of Consulting and Clinical Psychology,* 1978, *49,* 110–118.

Kendall, P. C., and Wilcox, L. E. "Self-Control in Children: Development of a Rating Scale." *Journal of Consulting and Clinical Psychology,* 1979, *47,* 1020–1030.

Kerlinger, F. N. *Foundations of Behavioral Research.* (2nd ed.) New York: Holt, Rinehart & Winston, 1964.

Klein, A. *Effective Group Work.* New York: Association Press, 1972.

Kohn, M., and Clausen, J. "Social Isolation and Schizophrenia." *American Sociological Review,* 1955, *20,* 265–273.

Kratochwill, T. R. *Single Subject Research.* Orlando, Fla.: Academic Press, 1978.

Kunkel, J. H. *Behavior, Social Problems, and Change: A Social Learning Approach.* Englewood Cliffs, N.J.: Prentice-Hall, 1975.

Kunzelman, H. D. (ed.). *Precision Teaching.* Seattle, Wash.: Special Child Publications, 1970.

La Greca, A. M., and Santogrossi, D. A. "Social Skills Training with Elementary School Students: A Behavioral Group Approach." *Journal of Consulting and Clinical Psychology,* 1980, *48,* 220–227.

LeCroy, C. W. "Social Skills Training with Adolescents: A Review." In C. W. LeCroy (ed.), *Social Skills Training with Children and Youth.* New York: Haworth Press, 1983.

LeCroy, C. W., and Rose, S. D. "Evaluation of Preventive Interventions for Enhancing Social Competence in Adolescents.'" *Social Work Research and Abstracts,* Summer 1986, *22* (2), 8–17.

Levitt, J. L., and Reid, W. J. "Rapid-Assessment Instruments." *Social Work Research and Abstracts,* 1981, *17* (1), 13–20.

Levy, R. L. "Relationship of an Overt Commitment to Task Compliance in Behavior Therapy." *Journal of Behavior Therapy and Experimental Psychiatry,* 1977, *8,* 25–29.

Levy, R. L., and Carter, R. D. "Compliance with Practitioner Instigations." *Social Work,* 1976, *21,* 188–196.

Levy, R. L., and Clark, H. "The Use of an Overt Commitment to Enhance Compliance: A Cautionary Note." *Journal of Behavior Therapy and Experimental Psychiatry*, 1980, *11*, 105–107.

Levy, R. L., Yamashita, D., and Pow, G. "Relationship of an Overt Commitment to the Frequency and Speed of Compliance with Decision Making." *Medical Care*, 1979, *17*, 281–284.

Lieberman, M., Yalom, I., and Miles, M. *Encounter Groups: First Facts*. New York: Basic Books, 1973.

Lilly, M. S. "Improving Social Acceptance of Low Sociometric Status, Low Achieving Students." *Exceptional Children*, 1971, *37*, 341–347.

Linehan, M. M., and others. "Group Versus Individual Assertion Training." *Journal of Consulting and Clinical Psychology*, 1979, *47*, 1000–1002.

Lippitt, P. "Children Can Teach Other Children." *The Instructor*, May 1969, *78*, 41–99.

Lott, A. J., and Lott, B. E. "Group Cohesiveness, Communication Level, and Conformity." *Journal of Abnormal and Social Psychology*, 1961, *62*, 408–412.

Lott, A. J., and Lott, B. E. "Group Cohesiveness as Interpersonal Attraction: A Review of Relationships with Antecedent and Consequent Variables." *Psychological Bulletin*, 1965, *64*, 259–309.

Lovaas, O. I. "A Behavior Therapy Approach to the Treatment of Childhood Schizophrenia." In J. P. Hill (ed.), *Minnesota Symposia on Child Psychology*. Vol. 1. Minneapolis: University of Minnesota Press, 1967.

Lyles, J. N., Burish, T. G., Korzely, M. G., and Oldham, R. K. "Efficacy of Relaxation Training and Guided Imagery in Reducing the Aversiveness of Cancer Chemotherapy." *Journal of Consulting and Clinical Psychology*, 1982, *50*, 509–524.

McCarty, T., Griffin, S., Apolloni, T., and Shores, R. E. "Increased Peer-Teaching with Group-Oriented Contingencies for Arithmetic Performance in Behavior-Disordered Adolescents." *Journal of Applied Behavior Analysis*, 1977, *10*, 313.

McClure, L. F., Chinsky, J. M., and Larcen, S. W. "Enhancing Social Problem-Solving Performance in an Elementary

School Setting." *Journal of Educational Psychology*, 1978, *70*, 504–513.

McFall, R. M. "Behavioral Training: A Skill Acquisition Approach to Clinical Problems." *University Programs Modular Studies*. Morristown, N.J.: General Learning Press, 1976.

McFall, R. M., and Lillesand, D. B. "Behavioral Rehearsal with Modeling and Coaching in Assertion Training." *Journal of Abnormal Psychology*, 1971, *77*, 313–323.

McFall, R. M., and Marston, A. R. "An Experimental Investigation of Behavioral Rehearsal in Assertion Training." *Journal of Abnormal Psychology*, 1970, *76*, 295–303.

McFall, R. M., and Twentyman, C. T. "Four Experiments on the Relative Contribution of Rehearsal, Modeling and Coaching to Assertion Training." *Journal of Abnormal Psychology*, 1973, *81*, 199–218.

McLaughlin, T. F. "The Effects of Individual and Group Contingencies on Reading Performance of Special Education Students." *Contemporary Educational Psychology*, 1981, *6*, 76–79.

McLaughlin, T. F. "A Comparison of Individual and Group Contingencies on Spelling Performance with Special Education Students." *Child and Family Behavior Therapy*, 1982, *4*, 1–10.

Mahoney, M. J. *Cognition and Behavior Modification*. Cambridge, Mass.: Ballinger, 1974.

Maletzky, B. M. " 'Booster' Sessions in Aversion Therapy: The Permanency of Treatment." *Behavior Therapy*, 1977, *8*, 460–463.

Mash, E. J., and Terdal, L. G. (eds.). *Behavior-Therapy Assessment: Diagnosis, Design, and Evaluation*. New York: Springer, 1976.

Mash, E. J., and Terdal, L. G. (eds.). *Behavioral Assessment of Childhood Disorders*. New York: Guilford Press, 1981.

Maultsby, M. "Systematic Written Homework in Psychotherapy." *Rational Living*, 1971, *6*, 17–23.

Meadow, A., Parnes, S. J., and Reese, H. "Influence of Instructions and Problem Sequence on a Creative Problem-Solving Test." *Journal of Applied Psychology*, 1959, *43*, 413–416.

Meichenbaum, D. "A Cognitive-Behavior Modification Approach to Assessment." In M. Hersen and A. S. Bellack (eds.), *Behavioral Assessment*. Elmsford, N.Y.: Pergamon Press, 1976.

Meichenbaum, D. *Cognitive-Behavior Modification*. New York: Plenum, 1977.

Meichenbaum, D., and Goodman, J. "Training Impulsive Children to Talk to Themselves: A Means of Developing Self-Control." *Journal of Abnormal Psychology*, 1971, *77*, 115–126.

Middleman, R. R. "Co-Leadership and Solo-Leadership in Education for Social Work with Groups." *Social Work with Groups*, Winter 1980, *3* (4), 39–50.

Miller, L. C. "School Behavior Checklist: An Inventory of Deviant Behavior for Elementary School Children." *Journal of Consulting and Clinical Psychology*, 1972, *38*, 134–144.

Mischel, W. "Toward a Cognitive Social Learning Reconceptualization of Personality." *Psychological Review*, 1973, *80*, 252–283.

Mungas, D. M., and Walters, H. A. "Pretesting Effects in the Evaluation of Social Skill Training." *Journal of Consulting and Clinical Psychology*, 1979, *47*, 216–218.

Nanjo, C., and Ornstein, R. E. *On the Psychology of Meditation*. New York: Viking Press, 1971.

Nelson, R. O., and Barlow, D. H. "Behavioral Assessment: Basic Strategies and Initial Procedures." In D. H. Barlow (ed.), *Behavioral Assessment of Adult Disorders*. New York: Guilford Press, 1981.

Nelson, W., and Birkimer, J. "Role of Self-Instruction and Self-Reinforcement in the Modification of Impulsivity." *Journal of Consulting and Clinical Psychology*, 1978, *46*, 183.

Nixon, H. L., II. *The Small Group*. Englewood Cliffs, N.J.: Prentice-Hall, 1979.

Oden, S., and Asher, S. "Coaching Children in Social Skills for Friendship Making." *Child Development*, 1977, *48*, 495–506.

O'Donnell, C. R., Lydgate, T., and Fo, W. S. O. "The Buddy System: Review and Follow-up." *Child Behavior Therapy*, 1979, *1*, 161–169.

Ollendick, T. H., and Hersen, M. *Child Behavioral Assessment: Principles and Procedures.* Elmsford, N.Y.: Pergamon Press, 1984.

Orlick, T. D. *The Cooperative Sports and Games Book.* New York: Pantheon Books, 1978.

Orlick, T. "Children's Games: Following the Path That Has Heart." *The Elementary School Guidance and Counseling Journal,* 1979, *14* (2), 156–161.

Osborne, J. G. *Applied Imagination: Principles and Procedures of Creative Problem Solving.* (3rd ed.) New York: Scribner's, 1963.

Patterson, G. R., Ray, R. S., Shaw, D. A., and Cobb, J. A. *Manual for Coding of Family Interactions.* ASIS/NAPS Document no. 01234. New York: Microfiche Publications, 1969.

Patterson, G. R., Reid, J. B., Jones, R. R., and Conger, R. E. *A Social Learning Approach to Family Intervention.* Vol. 1. Eugene, Ore.: Castalia, 1975.

Paul, G. L. *Insight Vs Desensitization in Psychology: An Experiment in Anxiety Reduction.* Stanford, Calif.: Stanford University Press, 1966.

Pekarik, E. G., and others. "The Pupil Evaluation Inventory: A Sociometric Technique for Assessing Children's Social Behavior." *Journal of Abnormal Child Psychology,* 1976, *4,* 83–97.

Phillips, E. L. "Achievement Place: Token Reinforcement Procedures in a Home Style Rehabilitation Setting for 'Pre-Delinquent' Boys." *Journal of Applied Behavior Analysis,* 1968, *1,* 213–223.

Pincus, A., and Minahan, A. *Social Work Practice: Model and Method.* Itasca, Ill.: F. E. Peacock, 1973.

Premack, D. "Toward Empirical Behavior Laws. Part 1: Positive Reinforcement." *Psychological Review,* 1959, *66,* 219–233.

Quay, H. C., and Peterson, D. R. *Manual for the Behavior Problem Checklist.* Published in 1979 by the authors at 59 Fifth St., Highland Park, N.J. 08904.

Quinsey, V. L., and Varney, G. W. "Social Skills Game: A General Method for the Modeling and Practice of Adaptive Behaviors." *Behavior Therapy,* 1977, *8,* 279–281.

Rapoport, I. J., and Ismond, D. R. *Training Guide for Child Psychiatry.* New York: Brunner/Mazel, 1984.

Redl, F. "Group Emotion and Leadership." In P. Hare, E. Borgotta, and R. Bales (eds.), *Small Groups: Studies in Social Interaction.* New York: Knopf, 1955.

Redl, F., and Wineman, D. *Controls from Within.* New York: Free Press, 1956.

Reese, E. P. *The Analysis of Human Operant Behavior.* Dubuque, Iowa: Brown, 1966.

Ritter, B. "The Group Treatment of Children Snake Phobias, Using Vicarious and Contact Desensitization Procedures." *Behavior Research and Therapy,* 1968, *6,* 1-6.

Robin, A. L. "Problem-Solving Communication Training: A Behavioral Approach to Treatment of Parent-Adolescent Conflict." *American Journal of Family Therapy,* 1979, *7,* 69-82.

Robin, A. L. "Parent-Adolescent Conflict: A Skill-Training Approach." In D. P. Rathism and I. P. Forest (eds.), *Social Competence: Interventions for Children and Adults.* Elmsford, N.Y.: Pergamon Press, 1980.

Robin, A. L. "A Controlled Evaluation of Problem-Solving Communication Training with Parent-Adolescent Conflict." *Behavior Therapy,* 1981, *12,* 593-609.

Robin, A. L., and others. "An Approach to Teaching Parents and Adolescents Problem-Solving Communication Skills: A Preliminary Report." *Behavior Therapy,* 1977, *8,* 639-643.

Roff, M. "Childhood Social Interaction and Young Adults' Bad Conduct." *Journal of Abnormal Social Psychology,* 1961, *63,* 333-337.

Roff, M., Sells, B., and Golden, M. *Social Adjustment and Personality Development in Children.* Minneapolis: University of Minnesota Press, 1972.

Roistacher, R. C. "A Microeconomic Model of Sociometric Choice." *Sociometry,* 1974, *37,* 219-238.

Rose, S. D. *Treating Children in Groups.* San Francisco: Jossey-Bass, 1972.

Rose, S. D. *Group Therapy: A Behavioral Approach.* Englewood Cliffs, N.J.: Prentice-Hall, 1977.

Rose, S. D. "How Group Attributes Relate to Outcome in Behavior Group Therapy." *Social Work Research and Abstracts,* 1981, *17,* 25-29.

Rose, S. D., Hanusa, D., Tolman, R. M., and Hall, J. A. *A Group*

Leader's Guide to Assertiveness Training. Crownsville, Md.: Crownsville Hospital Center, 1982.

Rose, S. D., Hepler, J., and Vinton, L. "Factors Influencing a Shift in Sociometric Status Following Social Skill Training." Unpublished manuscript, School of Social Work, University of Wisconsin, 1986.

Rose, S. D., and others. "The Hartwig Project: A Behavioral Approach to the Treatment of Juvenile Offenders." In R. Vlrich, T. Stachnic, and J. Mabry, *Control of Human Behavior.* Vol. 2. Glenview, Ill.: Scott, Foresman, 1971.

Rosenthal, L. "The Development and Evaluation of the Problem Inventory for Adolescent Girls." Unpublished doctoral dissertation, University of Wisconsin-Madison, 1978.

Ross, A. L., and Bernstein, N. B. "A Framework for the Therapeutic Use of Group Activities." *Child Welfare,* 1976, *56,* 776-786.

Ross, A. O., Lacey, H. M., and Parton, D. A. "The Development of a Behavior Checklist for Boys." *Child Development,* 1965, *36,* 1010-1027.

Rotter, J. B. "Generalized Expectancies for Internal Versus External Control of Reinforcement." *Psychological Monographs,* 1966, *80,* 69.

Sarason, I. G., and Ganzer, V. J. "Developing Appropriate Social Behaviors of Juvenile Delinquents." In J. D. Krumboltz and C. E. Thoresen (eds.), *Behavioral Counseling: Cases and Techniques.* New York: Holt, Rinehart & Winston, 1969.

Schopler, J. H., and Galinsky, M. J. "The Open-Ended Group." In M. Sundel and others (eds.), *Individual Change Through Small Groups.* (2nd ed.) New York: Free Press, 1985.

Selltiz, C., Wrightsman, L. S., and Cook, S. W. *Research Methods in Social Relations.* (3rd ed.) New York: Holt, Rinehart & Winston, 1976.

Shaw, M. E. *Group Dynamics: The Psychology of Small Group Behavior.* (2nd ed.) New York: McGraw-Hill, 1976.

Shelton, J. L. "Homework in AT (Assertive Training): Promoting the Transfer of Assertive Skills to the Natural Environment." In R. E. Alberti (ed.), *Assertiveness: Innovations, Applications, Issues.* San Luis Obispo, Calif.: Impact, 1977.

Shelton, J. L., and Ackerman, J. M. *Homework in Counseling and Psychotherapy*. Springfield, Ill.: Thomas, 1974.

Shelton, J. L., and Levy, R. L. *Behavioral Assignments and Treatment Compliance: A Handbook of Clinical Strategies*. Champaign, Ill.: Research Press, 1981.

Sherif, M. "Experiments in Group Conflict." *Scientific American*, 1956, *195* (32), 54-58.

Shure, M. B., and Spivack, G. "Means-Ends Thinking, Adjustment, and Social Class among Elementary-School-Aged Children." *Journal of Consulting and Clinical Psychology*, 1972, *38*, 348-353.

Singleton, L. C., and Asher, S. R. "Peer Preferences and Social Interaction Among Third-Grade Children in an Integrated School District." *Journal of Educational Psychology*, 1977, *69*, 330-336.

Skinner, B. F. "The Experimental Analysis of Behavior." *American Scientist*, 1957, *45*, 343-371.

Spector, S. I. "Climate and Social Acceptability." *Journal of Educational Sociology*, 1953, *27*, 108-114.

Spitzer, R. L., Skodol, A. E., Gibbon, M., and Williams, J. *DSM-III Case-Book*. Washington, D.C.: American Psychiatric Association, 1981.

Spivack, G., Platt, V. V., and Shure, M. B. *The Problem Solving Approach to Adjustment*. San Francisco: Jossey-Bass, 1976.

Spivack, G., and Shure, M. B. *Social Adjustment of Young Children: A Cognitive Approach to Activating Real-Life Problems*. San Francisco: Jossey-Bass, 1974.

Spivack, G., and Spotts, J. *Devereux Child Behavior Rating Scale*. Devon, Pa.: Devereux Foundation, 1966.

Stendler, C., Damrin, D., and Haines, A. "Studies in Cooperation and Competition: The Effects of Working for Group and Individual Rewards on the Social Climate of Children's Groups." *Journal of Genetic Psychology*, 1951, *79*, 173-179.

Stermac, L., and Josefowitz, N. *Social Skills Board Game: Enhancing Social Competence in Emotionally Disturbed Adolescents*. Los Angeles: Association for the Advancement of Behavior Therapy, 1982.

Stokes, J. P. "Components of Group Cohesion: Intermember

Attraction, Instrumental Value, and Risk Taking." *Small Group Behavior,* 1983, *14,* 163–173.

Stokes, T. F., and Baer, D. M. "An Implicit Technology of Generalization." *Journal of Applied Behavior Analysis,* 1977, *10,* 349–367.

Stokes, T. F., Baer, D. M., and Jackson, R. L. "Programming the Generalization of a Greeting Response in Four Retarded Children." *Journal of Applied Behavior Analysis,* 1974, *7,* 599–610.

Stovya, J. "Why Should Muscular Relaxation Be Useful?" In J. Beatty and H. Legewie (eds.), *Biofeedback and Behavior.* New York: Plenum, 1977.

Stovya, J. "Guidelines in the Training of General Relaxation." In J. Basmajian (ed.), *Biofeedback: Principles and Practices for Clinicians.* Baltimore, Md.: Williams & Wilkins, 1979.

Stuart, R. B. (ed.). *Behavioral Self-Management: Strategies, Techniques and Outcome.* New York: Brunner/Mazel, 1977.

Sundel, M., Glasser, P., Sarri, R., and Vinter, R. (eds.). *Individual Change Through Small Groups.* (2nd ed.) New York: Free Press, 1985.

Swetnam, L., Peterson, C. R., and Clark, H. B. "Social Skills Development in Young Children." In C. W. LeCroy (ed.), *Social Skills Training for Children and Youth.* New York: Haworth Press, 1983.

Taylor, C. B. "DSM-III and Behavioral Assessment." *Behavioral Assessment,* 1983, *5,* 5–14.

Teri, L., and Lewinsohn, P. M. "Group Intervention for Unipolar Depression." *Behavior Therapist,* 1985, *8* (6), 109–111.

Thoresen, C. E., and Mahoney, M. J. *Behavioral Self-Control.* New York: Holt, Rinehart & Winston, 1974.

Titkin, E. A., and Cobb, C. "Treating Post-Divorce Adjustment in Latency Age Children: A Focused Group Paradigm." *Social Work with Groups,* 1983, *6* (2), 53–66.

Toseland, R. W., and Rivas, R. F. *An Introduction to Group Work Practice.* New York: Macmillan, 1984.

Toseland, R. W., and Siporin, M. "When to Recommend Group Treatment: A Review of the Clinical and the Research Literature." *International Journal of Group Psychotherapy,* Apr. 1986.

Tyler, V. O., and Brown, G. D. "The Use of Swift, Brief Isolation as a Group Control Device for Institutionalized Delinquents." *Behaviour Research and Therapy,* 1967, *5,* 1-9.

Ullman, C. A. "Teachers, Peers, and Tests as Predictors of Adjustment." *Journal of Educational Psychology,* 1957, *48,* 257-267.

Van Hasselt, V. B., Hersen, M., and Bellack, A. S. "The Validity of Role Play Tests for Assessing Social Skills in Children." *Behavior Therapy,* 1981, *12,* 202-216.

Van Houten, R., Hill, S., and Parsons, M. "An Analysis of a Performance Feedback, Public Posting, and Praise upon Academic Performance and Peer Interaction." *Journal of Applied Behavior Analysis,* 1975, *8,* 449-457.

Vinter, R. (ed.). *Readings in Group Work Practice.* Ann Arbor, Mich.: Campus, 1967.

Vinter, R. "The Essential Components of Social Group Work Practice." In P. Glasser, R. Sarri, and R. Vinter (eds.), *Individual Change Through Small Groups.* New York: Free Press, 1974a.

Vinter, R. "Program Activities: An Analysis of Their Effects on Participant Behavior." In P. Glasser, R. Sarri, and R. Vinter (eds.), *Individual Change Through Small Groups.* New York: Free Press, 1974b.

Walker, H. M. *Walker Problem Behavior Checklist.* Los Angeles: Western Psychological Services, 1970.

Walker, H. M., and Buckley, N. K. "Programming Generalization and Maintenance of Treatment Effects Across Time and Across Settings." *Journal of Applied Behavior Analysis,* 1972, *5,* 209-224.

Walker, H. M., Hops, H., and Johnson, S. M. "Generalization and Maintenance of Classroom Treatment Effects." *Behavior Therapy,* 1975, *6,* 188-200.

Walls, R. T., Werner, T. J., Bacon, A., and Zane, T. "Behavior Checklists." In J. D. Cone and R. P. Hawkins (eds.), *Behavioral Assessments: New Directions in Clinical Psychology.* New York: Brunner/Mazel, 1977.

Weisskopf-Joelson, E., and Eliseo, S. "An Experimental Study of the Effectiveness of Brainstorming." *Journal of Applied Psychology,* 1961, *45,* 45-49.

Whitaker, J. K. "Program Activities: Their Selection and Use in a Therapeutic Milieu." In P. Glasser, R. Sarri, and R. Vinter (eds.), *Individual Change Through Small Groups.* New York: Free Press, 1974.

Whittaker, V. K. "Differential Use of Program Activities in Child Treatment Groups." *Child Welfare,* 1976, *55,* 450-468.

Wilkinson, G. S., and Bleck, R. T. "Children's Divorce Groups." *Elementary School Guidance and Counseling,* 1977, *11* (3), 205-212.

Wodarski, J. S., Hamblin, R. V., Buckholdt, R. R., and Ferritor, D. E. "Individual Contingencies Versus Different Shared Consequences Contingent on the Performance of Low Achieving Group Members." *Journal of Applied Social Psychology,* 1973, *2,* 276-290.

Wolpe, J. *The Practice of Behavior Therapy.* (2nd ed.) Elmsford, N.Y.: Pergamon, 1973.

Wood, R., and Michelson, L. "Children's Assertive Behavior Scales." Unpublished manuscript, Las Vegas Mental Health Center, Las Vegas, Nev., 1978.

Wood, R., Michelson, L., and Flynn, J. M. "Assessment of Assertive Behavior in Elementary School Children." Paper presented at the Association for Advancement of Behavior Therapy, Chicago, 1978.

Yalom, I. D. *The Theory and Practice of Group Psychotherapy.* New York: Basic Books, 1985.

Name Index

Subject Index

A

Absolutizing, 222-223
Active coping skills, 9
Activities, 15-16, 25, 239-274; analyzing, 241-243; competence required for, 246-247; controls and, 244-245; dimensions of, 243-248; interactiveness in, 245-246; medical clearance and, 82-83; multicomponent, 270-272; physical field and, 241-242; physical movement in, 246; planning, 270-273; prescriptiveness and, 243-244; purposes of, 240; as reinforcement, 184-185, 192-193; relating, to goals, 266-269; rewards and, 248; selecting, 264-272; teaching new, 269-270; types of, 248-264
Affective responses, 67-68
Agendas, 57-58, 139-140
American Guidance Service, 160
Antecedent conditions, 13-14, 65, 182. *See also* Situation
Arts and crafts, 258-259. *See also* Activities
Assessment: phase in multimethod approach, 23-24; purposes of, 61-64; roster-rating scales for, 111; situational, 63-87
ASSET videotape program, 158, 175
Audiotape, 101, 174-175, 227-228, 260

B

"Behavior Checklists," 114

Behavior Problem Checklist, 114
Behavior rehearsal, 161-170. *See also* Roleplaying
Behavior Role Play Test (BRT), 98-99
Behavioral: alternatives, 127-136; consequences, 13-14, 69-70, 80, 132-135; specificity, 76-81
Book Finder, 160
Booster sessions, 340
Brainstorming, 127-132
Buddy system, 17, 106, 339

C

Case study technique, 72-74
Catastrophization, 222
Child Assertive Behavior Scale, 107-108
Child Behavior Checklist, 114
Child's Attitude Towards Father (CAF) scale, 108-109
Child's Attitude Towards Mother (CAM) scale, 108-109
Coaching, 166-169
Coding systems, 96-97
Cognitions, 67, 77-79; self-defeating/enhancing, 218-219, 221-228
Cognitive change, 10, 14-15; goals of, 206. *See also* Cognitive restructuring, Self-instructional training
Cognitive coping skills, 8-9
Cognitive restructuring, 14, 207-208, 217-228; approaches to, 217-219; and homework completion, 323; homework tasks,